P9-DNW-037

Better Homes and Gardens®

CRAFTS
TO DECORATE YOUR
HOME

© Copyright 1986 by Meredith Corporation, Des Moines, Iowa.
All Rights Reserved. Printed in the United States of America.
First Edition. First Printing.
Library of Congress Catalog Number: 86-60268
ISBN: 0-696-01490-4

BETTER HOMES AND GARDENS® BOOKS

Editor: Gerald M. Knox
Art Director: Ernest Shelton
Managing Editor: David A. Kirchner
Copy and Production Editors: James D. Blume, Marsha Jahns,
    Rosanne Weber Mattson, Mary Helen Schiltz

Crafts Editor: Jean LemMon
Senior Crafts Books Editor: Joan Cravens
Associate Crafts Books Editors: Sara Jane Treinen,
    Beverly Rivers

Associate Art Directors: Linda Ford Vermie, Neoma Alt West,
    Randall Yontz
Assistant Art Directors: Lynda Haupert, Harijs Priekulis,
    Tom Wegner
Senior Graphic Designers: Jack Murphy, Stan Sams,
    Darla Whipple-Frain
Graphic Designers: Mike Burns, Sally Cooper, Blake Welch,
    Brian Wignall, Kimberly Zarley

Vice President, Editorial Director: Doris Eby
Executive Director, Editorial Services: Duane L. Gregg

President, Book Group: Fred Stines
Director of Publishing: Robert B. Nelson
Vice President, Retail Marketing: Jamie Martin
Vice President, Direct Marketing: Arthur Heydendael

Crafts to Decorate Your Home
Contributing Editors: Ciba Vaughan, Judith Veeder
Crafts Editor: Joan Cravens
Copy and Production Editor: James D. Blume
Graphic Designer: Tom Wegner
Electronic Text Processor: Penny Forest

W elcome to this exciting collection of Crafts to Decorate Your Home. *Whatever your favorite craft technique, your level of skill, or your decorating preference, you're sure to find just the right project to spark your imagination and set your fingers flying. You'll discover dozens of traditional designs to work in time-honored techniques, as well as an innovative selection of contemporary crafts. Whether you long to stitch a quilt from now till next Christmas, or just want to spruce up the family room over the weekend, we'll show you how!*

CONTENTS

WITH PLEASURE AND PRIDE

Whatever your favorite craft technique, whatever your level of skill, there's no more appropriate showcase for your efforts than your own home—the space you share with the people you love.

ESTABLISH AN AMBIENCE

Whether you're faced with a whole house to furnish, a room to redecorate, or just a couple of cushions to stitch for the den, look to the "feel" of a favorite handcrafted item for inspiration. Chances are that colors, patterns, and textures that please you in one incarnation will be equally appealing in different materials and new combinations.

Case in point: The crocheted afghan, appliquéd table runner, quilted magazine rack cover, and even the throw pillows, all in the family room *at left,* take subtle cues from the heirloom quilt, *above.*

Instructions for the quilt and crocheted afghan begin on page 97; instructions for the table runner and quilted rack cover are on page 101.

CHERISH
THE PAST

Antique needle-work—often seen in America's historic houses—provides a wonderfully rich and varied source of design motifs for stitchers. The hand towels, *near right* and *below,* are from Sagamore Hill in New York, once the home of President Theodore Roosevelt.

Mrs. Roosevelt had the towels stitched with the "R of S" monogram, for Roosevelts of Sagamore Hill, so the local laundry would not confuse the family linens with those of other Roosevelts in the area.

To add a comparable touch of distinction to your linens, compose your own monogram using the alphabet on page 79.

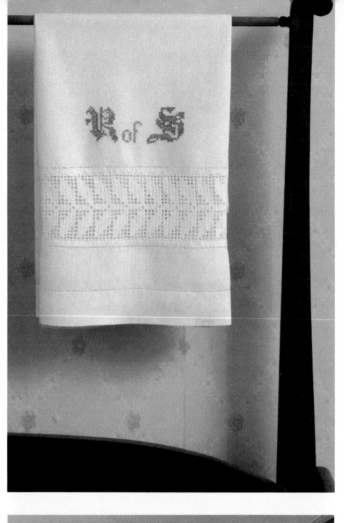

The lovely
cornucopia-
patterned rug,
above, is on display
at Woodlawn
Plantation near
Washington, D.C.
In 1799, George
Washington
presented this
Georgian-style

mansion and estate
to his adopted
daughter, Nelly
Lewis. Today
Woodlawn, like
Sagamore Hill, is
part of the National
Trust for Historic
Preservation.

Although both the
source of this rug
design and the
name of its maker
are long forgotten,
the pattern still has
a naive charm that
complements many
of today's
decorating styles.

With a crochet
hook or rug hooking
tool, work the
design into backing
fabric using narrow
strips of wool. For
pattern and
instructions, see
pages 130–131.

CREATE AN HEIRLOOM

Beautiful hand-crafted furnishings needn't require a major investment of time, money, or talent. In less than a week, and with just a few tools and modest skills, for example, you can create this intricately patterned chest, an heirloom-quality piece that will give pleasure for years to come.

The secret is to begin with a piece of unfinished furniture; then, with artist's oils and simple wood chisels, to transform the plain wooden chest into this one-of-a-kind keepsake for a special youngster.

To interpret this design for your child, follow the steps, *above* (from upper left). First, transfer the motifs to each drawer front and carve the recessed areas with a wood chisel.

Apply a coat of wood stain to drawer fronts. Then brush a mixture of artist's oil paints and linseed oil onto the carved areas. Finish with a coat of spray varnish.

Instructions for the chest are on page 199.

EXPLORE A NEW CRAFT

Whatever your favorite craft technique or level of expertise, you're sure to find projects in this book that you can start to work on right away. If you're looking for crafts materials or techniques that may be unfamiliar to you, check out the "Homework" chapters.

An old-fashioned craft with limitless and exciting possibilities, for example, is simple cut-and-paste paper collage. You don't need special skills or hard-to-find materials to create an imaginative— and amazingly sophisticated— work of art like this pleasing porch scene, *opposite*.

Just cut snippets of paper and paste them to a background to make wonderfully personal pictures, recapture favorite vacation sights, or create an abstract composition from paper souvenirs and family mementos.

Instructions begin on page 199.

INDULGE YOUR FANCY

Artist Mary Engelbreit's handcrafted touches enliven every room in her house. The result is a sprightly mix of function and fantasy that's an inspiration for every crafter.

Mary hunts for old furniture at flea markets and garage sales, then paints her finds with inventive, eye-catching designs. The high chair, *near right,* is typical of her artful reclamations. The cow-scape on the cabinet door, *below,* is clever camouflage for a damaged panel.

The whimsical cat-and-mouse chair, *left,* designed by Mary for her son Evan, makes a charming accessory for a child's room. (For project instructions, please turn to page 51.)

Evan is especially fond of the gaily painted chair and landscaped chest of drawers, *below left,* that his mother painted for him. You can easily turn an inexpensive, rush-seated chair into a colorful copy of this one with a flutter of hearts, checks, stripes, and polka dots painted in bright enamel colors. Simple designs like these are relatively easy to sketch freehand. Or, if you like, rely on simple stencil motifs and bright, bright colors to achieve the same effect.

A scene such as the landscape on the chest of drawers requires a bit more artistry. If you're feeling less than confident about your sketching abilities, try tracing suitable designs from coloring books, posters, or prints.

15

SHARE THE DELIGHT

Children love to be included in your crafts activities, and the results of such shared adventures are often delightful.

Children's drawings, for example, make wonderful designs for pillows and wall hangings. For a real "hands-on" experience in cooperative crafting, you and your child can create this charming heart and hand wall hanging together.

Each square is a machine-appliquéd rendition of the traditional Heart and Hand theme, incorporating a traced image of the child's hand holding a heart, or a heart-shaped butterfly or flower.

If you wish to include the hands of more than one child in the design, choose a different color of fabric for each child.

You might experiment with variations on this design to create a quilt that features the handprints of each member of the family.

Or design a friendship quilt that includes blocks with the handprints of all the children in your child's class at school, or all of the neighbors on your block.

Directions are on page 51.

CELEBRATE THE SEASONS

Creating holiday trims to harmonize with the seasons is one of the special joys of decorating your home.

The red-breasted robin is a traditional symbol of Christmas in Britain, but the little wooden bird, *above,* makes a graceful accent for a wreath or centerpiece in any season.

Wood-burned and painted on cut-to-shape pieces of pine, a flock of these colorful songsters are secured on dowels, ready to perch atop a fruit bowl or a simple vine wreath.

For an elaborate salute to the harvest season, wood-burn and paint a sumptuous Della Robbia-style wreath of fruits and vegetables around a plain pine tabletop, *right;* or transfer the design onto a plywood round to make a removable holiday table cover.

Instructions for the tabletop and bird are on page 97.

A Sampler of
Traditional Designs

Time-honored needlework techniques and designs inspired the patterns on this winsome collection of animals. You'll find these versatile patterns easy to interpret in your favorite craft.

The original models for this delightful menagerie include a knitted fair isle cat, a cross-stitch bear, a patchwork pig, a needlepoint cow, and a crewel sheep.

To make a set of pillows like those plumped on the sofa, *right,* just trace the designs of your choice onto muslin, then color in the stitchery patterns with fabric paints or acrylics.

If working with wood is more your style, translate one or more of the designs into charming folk art pull toys like the gaily painted pair *above.*

For more ways to adapt these designs to your favorite craft techniques, please turn the page. Instructions begin on page 26.

20

A SAMPLER OF TRADITIONAL DESIGNS

This small flock of fabric sheep depicts just three of the many different ways you might interpret these animal designs.

There's enough beautifully detailed embroidery—a veritable catalog of crewel motifs—on the shaped pillow, *above,* to delight the most ardent stitcher.

More modestly embellished, but equally charming, are the two framed designs *at right.* To re-create the miniature picture *near right,* trace and paint onto muslin just the outline of the sheep, as well as a sprig or two of flowers. Cut out the shape and mount it on a pretty print fabric before framing.

For a more elaborate rendition of the same design, *far right,* paint the complete pattern onto muslin. Embroider selected portions in bright cotton floss, as shown, and add a border of woven ribbons.

A SAMPLER OF TRADITIONAL DESIGNS

Even if you're a novice at needlepoint, you'll find this colorful cow, *left,* easy to work in basket-weave and continental stitches. A long-stitch border adds interesting texture to the finished pillow top.

If needlepoint is not your forte, you might consider the painted fabric and wooden versions of the cow, shown on pages 20 and 21. Or create your own hooked or appliquéd version of the design. With a bit of patience and imagination, you can adapt most line drawings to more than one craft technique.

Changing the scale of a design is another way to alter patterns to suit a variety of projects. The teddy bear and kitten sachets, *above right,* are charming examples of miniaturization.

A basketful of cats, *below right,* invites comparisons between knitted, painted, and embroidered versions of the same design.

INSTRUCTIONS FOR A SAMPLER OF TRADITIONAL DESIGNS

General Instructions

For small projects such as toys or sachets, trace patterns directly from the book, simplifying design details if desired. For larger projects, enlarge patterns and transfer them to wood, needlepoint canvas, or fabric. (The scale given with each pattern yields a 16x16-inch design.)

For additional hints on adapting patterns for specific projects and techniques, see directions following these general instructions and refer to tips below each animal design.

TO TRANSFER DESIGNS: For muslin or other lightweight or light-color fabrics, place each design under a square of fabric, allowing adequate margins for seams. Trace designs onto fabric using a brown fine-point *permanent* marker. (Test the marker first on scrap fabric to determine the pressure needed for sharp lines.) Iron the fabric on the wrong side to set the ink.

For heavier fabrics, place dressmaker's carbon paper between fabric and design; outline the design using a tracing wheel.

For wood, place graphite paper between design and wood surface and trace outlines with a pencil.

For needlepoint canvas, lay canvas atop the design and trace lines with a nonstaining, water-erasable needlework marking pen.

For counted-thread embroidery, use graph paper to adapt the design to desired size according to your choice of fabrics.

DECORATING ON FABRIC: Embellish designs with paint, embroidery, appliqué, or quilting. Decorate designs before assembly.

For painting on fabric: Use high-quality acrylic or fabric paints. Place a small amount of paint on a glass plate and thin it with a few drops of water until the paint is the consistency of light cream.

Place fabric atop newspapers or paper towels. Dip a small brush in paint; remove the excess paint by

dabbing the brush on a paper towel. Avoid overloading the brush.

Beginning with large design areas, paint *up to but not over* the design lines. Leave a sliver of unpainted fabric between painted areas. Allow painted areas to dry before working on adjacent areas.

When the fabric is dry, gently press the wrong side with a warm iron to heat-set the paint.

Note: Painted fabrics may shrink. Unless the size of a project is critical, this should not be a problem.

For colored pencils, crayons, and permanent fabric markers: Choose fine-tip marking pens that will not bleed on the fabric or cause the brown outlines to bleed. Test your pens on scrap fabric before beginning work on the designs. Use light colors because ink often looks darker when applied to fabric. Heat-set colors by pressing fabric on wrong side with a warm iron.

For hand or machine embroidery: Use these techniques alone or in combination with painted designs. Work motifs in simple embroidery stitches using a variety of cotton, silk, and metallic threads; or use decorative sewing machine stitches.

For appliqué: Motifs may be embellished with fabrics, laces, ribbons, or beads, as desired.

For quilting: Once decorated, the designs may be quilted. Place quilt batting or other filler between decorated fabric and backing fabric; machine- or hand-quilt along design lines as desired.

DECORATING ON WOOD: Transferred designs on wood may be wood-burned, painted, or both. To wood-burn, practice on scrap lumber before beginning the project. When painting on wood, use high-quality acrylic paints, enamels, or watercolors. (*Note:* Be sure the paint and varnish you plan to use for the project are compatible.)

Painted Pillows
Shown on pages 20–21.

MATERIALS
Painted animal squares
Beads; ribbon scraps; embroidery floss
Coordinating calico fabric (pillow backs) and piping
Polyester fiberfill for stuffing

INSTRUCTIONS
Embellish the pillow fronts by embroidering the outlines or filling in the painted shapes with satin stitches. Trim designs with beads, ribbons, or fabric appliqués if desired.

Finished pillows may be square, or shaped to follow an animal outline. Baste piping to the animal pillow fronts, matching raw edges. With right sides facing, sew pillow fronts and backs together, leaving openings for turning. Turn right side out and stuff; sew openings closed.

Wooden Toy Animals
Shown on page 20.

MATERIALS
2-inch-thick pine for animal cutouts
¾-inch pine for wheels and base
Two 5¼-inch-long (¼-inch-diameter) dowels; jigsaw; drill
Sandpaper; wood glue
Nails; carbon paper
Wood-burning tool
Artist's oil paints; oil
Turpentine; brushes
Paper towels; varnish

INSTRUCTIONS
Enlarge patterns and trace onto 2-inch pine; cut out shapes using a jigsaw. Sand all edges. From ¾-inch pine, for each animal, cut four 2½-inch-diameter wheels and a 3½-inch-wide base to match length of decorative stand. Sand all edges and transfer design motifs to the base and wheels.

Wood-burn the design motifs on the animals as desired.   *continued*

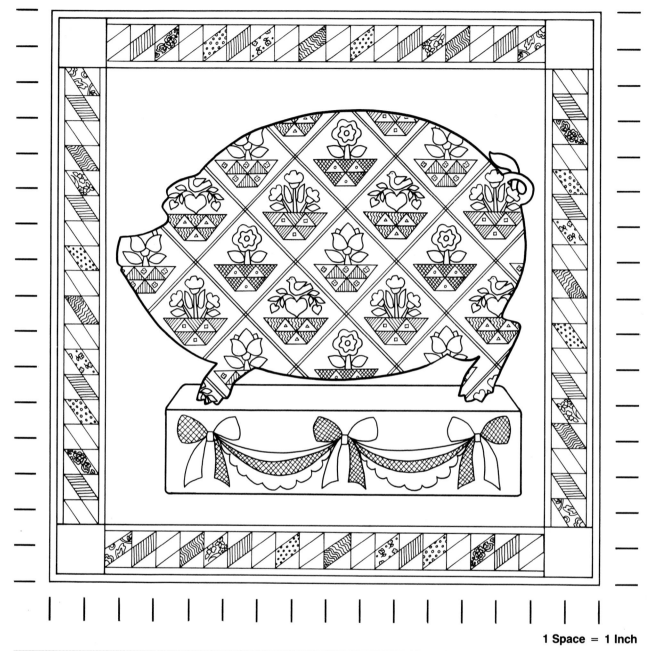

1 Space = 1 Inch

TIPS FOR CRAFTING THE PATCHWORK PIG

Sufficiently enlarged, this charming patterned pig can be reproduced in pieced and appliquéd patchwork (pieced baskets, appliquéd flowers). You might use it as the center of a child's quilt, or for a pillow. The border can be reproduced by using strip-piecing techniques.

For a simpler version, piece together small squares on the bias. Back the pieced fabric with lightweight interfacing, then cut out the pig shape. Hand- or machine-appliqué the pig to a background.

27

1 Space = 1 Inch

Tips for Crafting a Crewel Sheep

To make a framed picture, similar to the one shown in the blue chair on pages 22–23, enlarge the sheep *above* to the desired size and trace onto muslin. Back with lightweight, iron-on interfacing.

Embroider or appliqué some of the crewel motifs; paint or outline-stitch the others. Then cut out the sheep, just outside the traced outlines. Glue or machine-appliqué sheep to a rectangle of print fabric. Pad picture with a layer of batting and frame as desired.

1 Space = 1 Inch

TIPS FOR CRAFTING A NEEDLEPOINT COW

The cow design *above* is patterned after an old-fashioned floral motif and is wonderfully suited for embroidery or appliqué. To make the pillow shown on the sofa on pages 20–21, enlarge the pattern to the desired size, trace onto muslin with a permanent marker, and paint as desired; back with lightweight interfacing. Cut out the cow shape, just outside the outline. Glue or machine-appliqué cow to a rectangle of contrasting print fabric and stitch into a pillow.

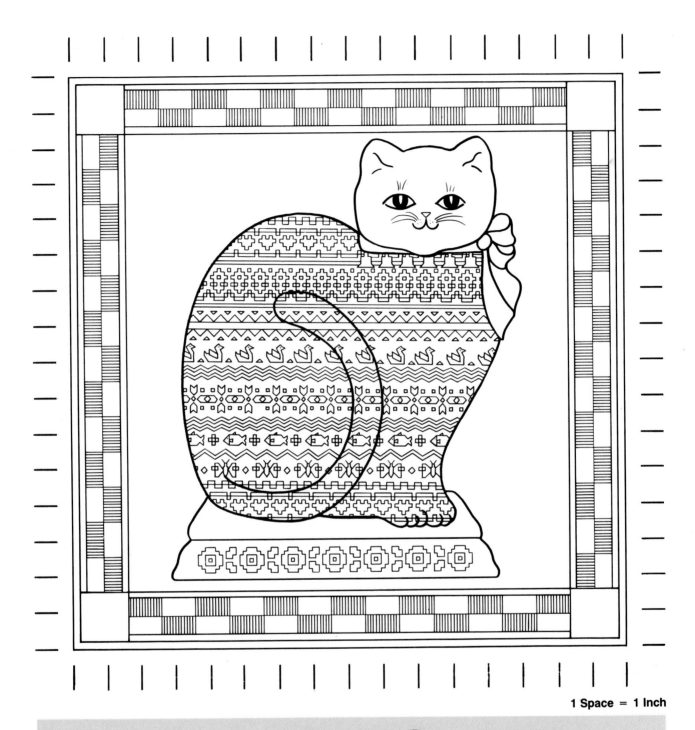

1 Space = 1 Inch

TIPS FOR CRAFTING A FAIR ISLE CAT

For the knitted versions of this cat, page 25, only selected patterns on the design *above* are reproduced. All rows of pattern, however, are reproduced on the square, painted pillow and cat-shaped pillow.

For the cat sachet, shown in the closeup photograph, outlines and facial features were traced from the pattern *above* onto a finely gridded cotton fabric. The duck and heart motifs were enlarged, transferred to graph paper, and painted on the fabric to resemble cross-stitches.

1 Space = 1 Inch

TIPS FOR CRAFTING A CROSS-STITCH BEAR

The tiny bear sachet pictured in the foreground on page 21, and again on page 25, is worked in cross-stitches on fine Aida cloth with double strands of cotton embroidery floss. The more complex details (chest and knee motifs) have been eliminated.

This pattern would make a handsome, oversize pillow, too. Enlarge the pattern to about 36 inches tall and transfer it to heavy, linenlike fabric, omitting the border. Transfer cross-stitches to the fabric and stitch the design using No. 3 pearl cotton.

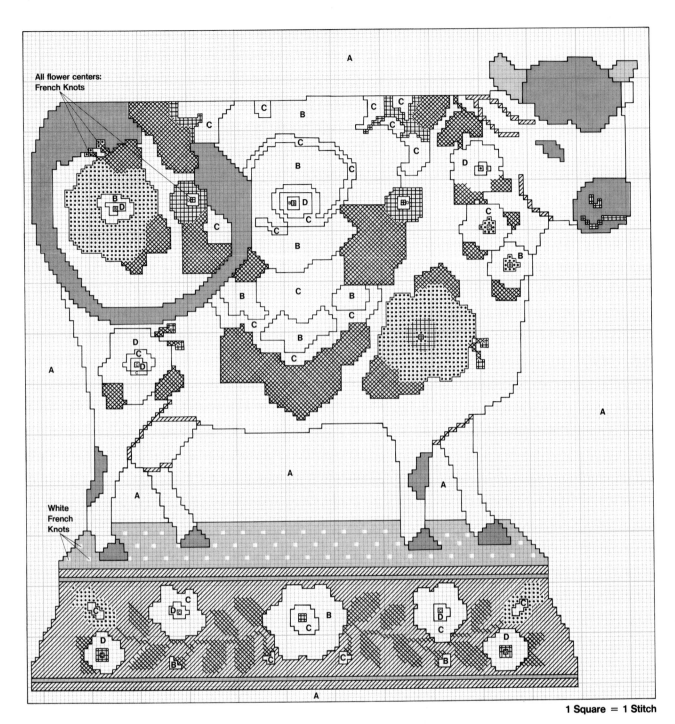

1 Square = 1 Stitch

continued from page 26
A Sampler of Traditional Designs

TO PAINT DESIGNS: Mix equal portions of oil paint and oil thoroughly. Thin to a watery consistency with turpentine. Brush paint onto design, applying the paint as you would wood stain; wipe away excess color with paper towels.

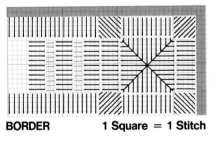

BORDER   1 Square = 1 Stitch

COLOR KEY

☐ White	⊞ Red	▨ Brown
Ⓐ Pale Yellow	Ⓓ Medium Blue	◩ Grey
Ⓑ Light Pink	● Deep Blue	■ Black
Ⓒ Medium Pink	☒ Green	

COLOR KEY

⊟ Light Blue long stitch
⊟ White long stitch
▨ 2 rows Yellow continental stitch around entire border

TO ASSEMBLE: Drill ⅜-inch holes through base sides for wheel axles. Drill ¼-inch holes through wheel centers. Glue and nail base to bottom of animal. Insert dowels through base and glue wheels onto dowel ends. Varnish lightly.

Crewel Sheep Pillow
Shown on page 22.

MATERIALS
½ yard *each* of white, closely woven fabric and backing fabric
15 three-ply strands *each* of dark, medium, light, and turquoise blue Persian yarn
3 strands of white Persian yarn
Polyester fiberfill for stuffing
Water-erasable marking pen

INSTRUCTIONS
Enlarge pattern (page 28); transfer design to fabric using a water-erasable marking pen. Embroider design in satin, outline, couching, and seed stitches, referring to photograph for ideas. Add French knots for texture.

Cut out sheep 1 inch from basic outline. Back and stuff. Braid six 45-inch strands of yarn to make piping. Whipstitch piping to pillow edges.

Embroidered Sheep Picture
Shown on pages 22–23.

MATERIALS
One painted sheep design
Embroidery floss
12 yards *each* of peach and blue narrow satin ribbon
Small piece of peach satin fabric
18-inch square quilt batting
White glue

INSTRUCTIONS
Embroider sheep as desired. Embellish latticelike border with 2-inch lengths of satin ribbon. Weave ribbon as pattern suggests, alternating colors; glue ribbon in place. Glue 2-inch squares of peach satin fabric into corners of block. Pad picture with batting and frame as desired.

Needlepoint Cow Pillow
Shown on page 24.

MATERIALS
3-ply strands of Persian wool yarn in pale yellow (background), pale blue (border), medium blue, dark blue, pale pink, dark pink, red, green, black, gray, brown, and white
12-count needlepoint canvas
Water-erasable marking pen
No. 20 tapestry needle
Needlepoint frame; masking tape
Backing fabric
Polyester fiberfill; cording

INSTRUCTIONS
Bind canvas edges with masking tape. To simplify stitching, transfer the chart, *opposite,* to graph paper using colored pencils in place of symbols. Mount canvas in a frame to minimize distortion. Using 2-ply strands of yarn, work design in basket-weave and continental stitches.

After stitching, remove canvas from frame and block. Trim canvas, leaving 2 inches around the edges. Baste fabric-covered cording to pillow front. Back and stuff.

Cross-Stitch Bear
Shown on page 25.

MATERIALS
⅓ yard of light blue fabric
Pink embroidery floss
White rickrack; fiberfill
Iron-on interfacing (to back bear fronts)
Water-erasable marking pen

INSTRUCTIONS
Trace pattern directly from the book, or size as desired. (The blue bear in the basket measures 12 inches tall.) Transfer design onto fabric, using a water-erasable marking pen.

Press a layer of iron-on interfacing onto the wrong side of the fabric for extra support while stitching. Stay-stitch perimeter of bear.

Work the design in cross-stitches, using pink floss or colors of your choice. Embroider the facial features and work the outline of the bear in stem stitches.

Sew rickrack around perimeter of bear. With right sides facing, sew backing fabric to bear front along stay stitching; leave opening for turning. Trim seam; clip corners and curves. Turn bear right side out, stuff, and sew opening closed.

Knitted Cat
Shown on page 25.

MATERIALS
For small, 12-inch-tall cat
Size 3 sixteen-inch circular knitting needle
Sizes 3 and 5 double-pointed needles
3 stitch holders
1 skein *each* of Brunswick Pomfret sport yarn in No. 5000 ecru (MC), No. 567 jade heather (A), No. 516 wisteria (B), No. 509 larkspur (C), No. 589 mauve heather (D), No. 569 horizon blue heather (E), No. 503 yellow (F), and No. 563 Cambridge heather (G)
Black and blue Persian wool yarn (for facial features)

For large, 15-inch-tall cat
Size 5 sixteen-inch circular knitting needle
Sizes 5 and 7 double-pointed needles
3 stitch holders
1 skein *each* of Brunswick Germantown in No. 460 black (MC), No. 467 jade heather (A), No. 424 cardinal (B), No. 4281 sea oats heather (C), No. 496 pastel heather (D), No. 469 horizon blue heather (E), No. 490 curry heather (F), and No. 463 Cambridge heather (G)
Gray and green Persian wool yarn (for facial features)

Abbreviations: See page 35.

continued

continued from page 33
A Sampler of Traditional Designs

INSTRUCTIONS
Beg at bottom with MC with circular needle, cast on 100 sts; join.

Rnd 1: Place marker on needle, k 50, place marker, k 50. *Note:* All increases and decreases are done in pattern. All sts are knitted throughout. *Rnd 2:* * 3 A, 1 MC. Rep from * across to marker, sl marker, * 1 MC, 1 A. Rep from * to end.

Rnd 3: 2 A, * 1 MC, 3 A. Rep from * across 48 sts; inc in next st, k 1, sl marker, k 1, inc 1, * 1 MC, 1 A. Rep from * across to end.

Rnd 4: With MC, k to 2 sts before marker, inc 1, k 1, sl marker, k 1, inc 1, k to end. *Rnd 5:* Rep Rnd 4.

Rnd 6: * 1 C, 2 MC, 2 C, 1 MC, 2 C, 2 MC, 1 C, 1 MC. Rep from * to within 2 sts of marker, inc 1, k 1, sl marker, 1 MC, inc 1, 1 MC, * 1 C, 1 MC. Rep from * across to end. *Rnd 7:* * 3 MC, 2 C, 1 MC, 2 C, 3 MC, 1 C. Rep from * across to last 2 sts before marker, inc 1, k 1, sl marker, k 1, inc 1; * 1 MC, 1 C. Rep from * to end. *Rnd 8:* 1 MC, 2 C, 1 MC, 3 C, 1 MC, 2 C, 2 MC, rep from * to marker, sl marker, * 1 C, 1 MC. Rep from * to end.

Rnd 9: * 1 D, 3 B, 1 D, 1 B, 1 D, 3 B, 2 D. Rep from * to last 2 sts before marker, inc in next st, k 1, sl marker, k 1, inc 1, * 1 B, 1 D, rep from * to end. *Rnd 10:* 1 D, k 2 tog D, * 2 B, 1 D, 2 B, 3 D, 1 B, 3 D. Rep from * to marker, sl marker, * 1 D, 1 B. Rep from * to last 3 sts, sl 1, k 1, psso, k 1.

Rnd 11: 1 D, 2 B, * 1 D, 1 B, 1 D, 3 B, 3 D, 3 B. Rep from * to marker, sl marker, * 1 B, 1 D. Rep from * to end. *Rnd 12:* 1 MC, k 2 tog MC, * 3 C, 1 MC, 2 C, 3 MC, 2 C, 1 MC. Rep from * to marker, sl marker, * 1 MC, 1 C. Rep from * to last 3 sts, sl 1, k 1, psso, k 1. *Rnd 13:* * 1 MC, 2 C, 1 MC, 2 C, 3 MC, 1 C, 2 MC. Rep from * to marker, sl marker, * 1 C, 1 MC, rep from * to end.

Rnd 14: 1 MC, k 1 tog C, * 1 MC, 2 C, 2 MC, 1 C, 1 MC, 1 C, 2 MC, 2 C. Rep from * to marker, sl marker, * 1 MC, 1 C. Rep from * to last 3 sts, sl 1, k 1, psso, k 1.

Rnd 15: K even with MC.

Rnd 16: With MC, k 1, k 2 tog, k to last 3 sts, sl 1, k 1, psso, k 1.

Rnd 17: 2 A, * 1 MC, 3 A. Rep from * to marker, sl marker, * 1 MC, 1 A. Rep from * to end. *Rnd 18:* * 3 A, 1 MC. Rep from * to marker, sl marker, * 1 A, 1 MC. Rep from * to end. *Rnd 19:* K even in MC. *Rnd 20:* 1 F, inc 1, 1 MC, * 1 F, 3 MC. Rep from * to marker, sl marker, * 1 F, 1 MC. Rep from * to last 2 sts, inc 1, k 1.

Rnd 21: 1 F, * 1 MC, 3 F. Rep from * to marker, sl marker, * 1 MC, 1 F. Rep from * to end. *Rnd 22:* 1 MC, inc 1 F, 2 MC, * 1 F, 3 MC. Rep from * to marker, sl marker, * 1 F, 1 MC. Rep from * to last 2 sts, inc 1, k 1. *Rnd 23:* K even in MC.

Rnd 24: With MC k 1, inc 1, k to last 2 sts, inc 1, k 1. *Rnd 25:* * 1 E, 1 MC. Rep from * around. *Rnd 26:* K with E, inc 1 st in second and next-to-last st. *Rnd 27:* K even with MC. *Rnd 28:* With MC k 1, inc 1, k to last 2 sts, inc 1, k 1. *Rnd 29:* With MC k even.

Rnd 30: 1 MC, inc 1 MC, * 9 G, 2 MC. Rep from * to marker, sl marker, * 1 MC, 1 G. Rep from * to last 2 sts, inc 1, k 1.

Rnd 31: 2 MC, * 1 G, 2 MC, 3 G, 1 D, 2 G, 2 MC. Rep from * to marker, drop D, sl marker, * 1 G, 1 MC. Rep from * to end.

Rnd 32: 1 MC, inc 1 G, * 3 MC, 5 G, 2 MC, 1 G. Rep from * to marker, sl marker, * 1 MC, 1 G. Rep from * to last 2 sts, inc 1, k 1.

Rnd 33: 2 MC, * 3 G, 2 MC, 3 G, 3 MC. Rep from * to marker, sl marker, * 1 G, 1 MC. Rep from * to end. *Rnd 34:* K with MC, inc in second and next-to-last st.

Rnd 35: K even with MC. *Rnd 36:* Rep Rnd 34. *Rnd 37:* With E, k even. *Rnd 38:* With E, k 1, inc 1, * 1 MC, 1 E. Rep from * to next to last 2 st, inc 1, k 1. *Rnd 39:* K even with MC.

Rnd 40: 1 MC, inc 1 MC, * 3 MC, * 1 B, 1 MC, 1 B, 5 MC. Rep from * to marker, sl marker, * k 1 B, k 1 MC. Rep from * to last 2 sts, inc 1.

Rnd 41: 1 B, 3 MC, * 2 B, 1 MC, 2 B, 3 MC. Rep from * to marker, sl marker, 1 MC, 1 B. Rep from * to end. *Rnd 42:* 1 MC, inc 1 MC, 1 MC, * 1 C, 3 MC. Rep from * to marker, sl marker, * 1 C, 1 MC. Rep from * to last 2 sts, inc 1, k 1.

Rnd 43: * 2 B, 3 MC, 2 B, 1 MC, rep from * to marker, sl marker, * 1 MC, 1 B. Rep from * to end.

Rnd 44: 1 B, inc 1 MC, * 5 MC, 1 B, 1 MC, 1 B. Rep from * to marker, sl marker, * 1 B, 1 MC. Rep from * to last 2 sts, inc 1, k 1.

Rnd 45: K even with MC. *Rnd 46:* * 3 MC, 3 A. Rep from * to 3 sts before marker, k 2 tog, k 1, sl marker, 1 A, with MC sl 1, k 1, psso, * 1 B, 1 MC. Rep from * to end.

Rnd 47: * 2 MC, 1 A, 2 E, 1 A. Rep from * to marker, drop MC, sl marker, 1 A, sl 1, 1 E, psso with A, * 1 A, 1 E, rep from * to end.

Rnd 48: 2 A, * 3 E, 3 A. Rep from * to within 3 sts of marker, k 2 tog, k 1, sl marker, k 1, sl 1, k 1, psso, with A, * 1 E, 1 A. Rep from * to end. *Rnd 49:* K even with E.

Rnd 50: With E, k to 3 sts before marker, k 2 tog, k 1, sl marker, k 1, sl 1, k 1, psso, k to end.

Rnd 51: * 1 F, 3 E, 2 F, 5 E, rep from * to marker, sl marker, * 1 E, 1 F. Rep from * to end.

Rnd 52: * 2 F, 1 E, 5 F, 3 E. Rep from * to last 3 sts before marker, k 2 tog, k 1, sl marker, 1 F, sl 1, k 1, psso, * 1 E, 1 F. Rep from * to end.

Rnd 53: 1 E, 8 F, * 3 E, 8 F. Rep from * to marker, sl marker, * 1 E, 1 F. Rep from * to end.

Rnd 54: Rep Rnd 52. *Rnd 55:* Rep Rnd 51. *Rnd 56:* With E, k to 3 sts before marker, k 2 tog, k 1, sl marker, k 1, sl 1, k 1, psso, k to end.

Rnd 57: Rep Rnd 56. *Rnd 58:* 1 A, * 3 E, 3 A. Rep from * to marker, sl marker, * 1 E, 1 A. Rep from * to end. *Rnd 59:* * 2 MC, 1 A, 2 E, 1 A. Rep from * to marker, sl marker, 1 A, sl 1, 1 E, psso with A, * 1 A, 1 E. Rep from * to end.

Rnd 60: * 3 MC, 3 A. Rep from * to marker, sl marker, * 1 A, 1 MC. Rep from * to end.

Rnd 61: K with MC to within 4 sts of marker, k 3 tog, k 1, sl marker, k 1, sl 2, k 1, psso, k to end.

Rnd 62: Rep Rnd 61. Change to No. 3 (No. 5) double-pointed needles; divide stitches as follows: 34 sts on first needle, 36 sts on second needle, and 34 sts on third needle. Drop marker at *beg* of rnd.

Rnd 63: * 5 MC, 1 D. Rep from * to 4 sts before marker, k 3 tog, k 1, sl marker, sl 2, k 1, psso, * 1 MC, 1 D. Rep from * to end.

Rnd 64: 1 D, * 3 MC, 3 D rep from * to 4 sts before marker, k 3 tog, k 1, sl marker, 1 D, sl 2, k 1, psso, * 1 MC, 1 D. Rep from * to end.

Rnd 65: 2 D, * 1 MC, 5 D. Rep from * to 4 sts before marker, k 3 tog, k 1, sl marker, with MC k 1, sl 2, k 1, psso, * 1 D, 1 MC. Rep from * to end. *Rnd 66:* Rep Rnd 65 to marker, sl marker, with D sl 2, k 1, psso * 1 MC, 1 D. Rep from * to end.

Rnd 67: * 1 D, 3 MC, 1 D, 1 MC. Rep from * to 4 sts before marker, k 3 tog, sl marker, with MC, sl 2, k 1, psso, * 1 D, 1 MC. Rep from * to end. *Rnd 68:* With MC k around making dec before and after marker as on Rnd 67. *Rnd 69:* Rep Rnd 68.

Rnd 70: * 1 B, 1 MC. Rep from * across to 4 sts before marker, k 3 tog, sl marker, with MC, sl 2, k 1, psso, * 1 B, 1 MC. Rep from * to end.

Redistribute rem sts on 3 needles keeping beg and end of rnds bet first and third needle—24 sts on each needle; drop marker.

Rnd 71: * 1 B, 1 MC. Rep from * around. *Rnd 72:* * 1 C, 1 B. Rep from * around. *Rnd 73:* * 1 B, 1 MC. Rep from * around. Break off all colors except MC. *Rnd 74:* K even.

Rnd 75: * K 2 tog, yo, rep from * around end k 1. *Rnd 76:* K even.

Rnd 77: * K 2, inc in next st. Rep from * to marker, k 1, inc, * k 3, inc in next st. Rep from * around (92 sts).

HEAD: Work head as follows with No. 5 (No. 7) double-pointed needles. *Rnd 1:* * K 1, sl 1 as if to purl. Rep from * around, knitting the first and last st tog, and leave on third needle. *Rnd 2:* * K 1, sl as if to purl. Rep from * around. *Rnd 3:* Sl 1 as if to p, k 1. Rep from * around. Rep last 2 rnds until head is 3 (4) inches above eyelet row.

EARS: *Rnd 1:* K 3 tog, k 40, sl 2, k 1, psso, k 40, sl 2, k 1, p2sso.

Rnd 2: K

Rnd 3: Inc in first st, k 8, inc in next st, k 22 and put last 22 sts on holder, inc in next st, k 8, inc in next 2 sts, (k 2 inc in next st) 3 times, put last 26 sts on second holder for right ear, k 22 and put on third holder (inc in next st, k 2) 3 times, inc in next st. Weave 22 sts on first holder to 22 sts on third holder for top of head.

Work left ear as follows: K 10, with second needle k 2, pick up 2 sts along side of top of head, place marker, pick up 3 more sts along side of top of head; complete rnd.

Redistribute sts as follows: Place 11 sts before marker on first needle; 9 sts after marker on second needle; 7 sts, a marker, and last 4 sts on third needle.

Rnd 2: (first needle) k 9, k 2 tog, (second needle) sl 1, k 1, psso, k 7 (third needle). *Rnds 3–5:* Work same as for Rnd 2, having 1 less st on first and second needle each rnd.

Rnd 6: K even. *Rnd 7:* * K 2 tog. Rep from * around, end k 1.

Rnd 8: Rep as for Rnd 7. *Rnd 9:* (K 2 tog) twice; k 1, break yarn, run end through last 3 sts, draw up tightly and pull end to inside.

For the right ear—*Rnd 1:* Beg at left edge of center top of head, pick up 1 st with same needle, k 10 sts from holder (front of ear), with second needle k next 9 sts from holder, with third needle k last 7 sts and pick up 4 more sts at center top of cat's head.

Rnd 2: Sl 1, k 1, psso, k even on second needle, k to last 2 sts on third needle, k 2 tog. Rep Rnd 2 three times more. *Rnd 6:* K even. *Rnd 7:* K 2 tog, around, end k 1. *Rnd 8:* Rep Rnd 7. *Rnd 9:* (K 2 tog) twice; k 1, finish off as for left ear.

TO FINISH HEAD: Embroider facial features as desired. Stuff the head and ears, shaping as you stuff. Thread ribbon through eyelet row and tie a bow to shape the neck.

TAIL: With No. 3 (No. 5) double-pointed needles and MC cast on 22 sts, put marker at beg of rnd, distribute on 3 knitting needles, work for 1 (2) inches.

Rnd 1: K to last 2 sts, put sts on holder, place marker on holder.

Rnd 2: Place 2 sts on holder, k to last 2 sts, put sts on holder.

Rnd 3: Place 2 sts on holder, making 8 sts on holder, k to the last 2 sts, place sts on holder.

KNITTING ABBREVIATIONS

beg	begin(ning)
bet	between
dec	decrease
dp	double pointed
grp	group
inc	increase
k	knit
lp(s)	loop(s)
MC	main color
p	purl
pat	pattern
psso	pass slip st over
rem	remaining
rep	repeat
rnd	round
sk	skip
sl st	slip stitch
sp(s)	space(s)
st(s)	stitch(es)
st st	stockinette stitch
tog	together
yo	yarn over
*	repeat from * as indicated

Rnd 4: Place 2 sts on holder, making 12 sts on holder, k around, k sts on holder. *Rnd 5:* K to marker.

Rnd 6: Work in st st rnd for 2 inches, rep 5 rows of short row shaping. Work 2 inches more in st st round. Continue rep short row shaping and 2 inches of st st rnd until knitted tail measures 12 (14) inches.

Rnd 1: K 2 tog, across. *Rnd 2:* K. *Rnd 3:* Rep as for Rnd 1. *Rnd 4:* Rep as for Rnd 2. Cut yarn and run end through all rem sts; pull up tightly.

TO ASSEMBLE: Block the knitted pieces and trim all ends. (To block, pin knitted pieces to a clean, padded surface so each piece is smooth and flat. Steam-press lightly using a moderate temperature setting. Let pieces dry thoroughly.) Pin tail in place on front of cat. Using overcast st, sew tail to front of body along both sides; stuff lightly through open cast-on edge. Sew closed. Stuff body lightly; weave bottom closed.

A ROOMFUL
OF WHIMSY
FOR KIDS

Six special animals grace this fanciful coverlet and inspire a room filled with kid-pleasing designs you can craft.

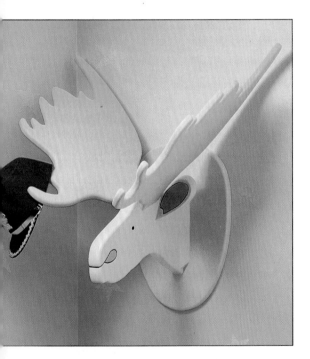

The make-believe moose hat rack, *above,* is just one of seven imaginative projects designed to coordinate with this style-setting, stitched and painted comforter.

Other projects include the wood appliqué rooster on the bureau, the hooked cow rug, the Cheshire cat lamp, the floppy-eared rabbit table, and the lavishly stenciled walls, headboard, and bed linens.

For a closer look, please turn the page. Instructions begin on page 44.

A ROOMFUL OF WHIMSY FOR KIDS

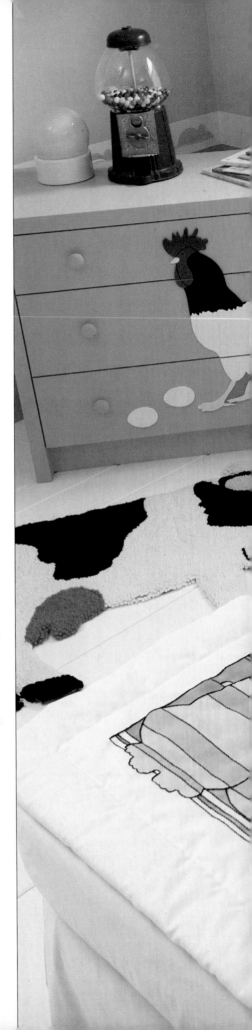

Each of the 16-inch squares on the single-size coverlet, *right,* features a different furred or feathered friend— all guaranteed to delight your favorite young animal lover.

To make your own animal quilt, trace designs onto white cotton squares and color them with bright fabric paints. Accent each animal with black embroidery floss, then join the squares using a sewing machine. Add batting and backing, and quilt along the seams.

On the bureau, *background,* simple shapes cut from hardboard and splashed with paint turn an unfinished chest of drawers into something to really crow about.

A cozy cow rug cushions the floor, *below.* It's a snap to craft when you work with a punch needle tool and use cotton yarns on burlap backing.

A ROOMFUL OF WHIMSY FOR KIDS

Here are more witty designs to craft from wood, using variations on two of the basic animal patterns.

Pictured at left is a closeup view of the bunny-based night table—an absolutely delightful and thoroughly functional piece that has built-in appeal for kids of all ages.

Constructed from ¾-inch-thick particleboard and braced about the ears with triangular supports cut from scrap pine, this simple-to-build table does require the use of a jigsaw and modest familiarity with basic carpentry techniques.

The endearing Cheshire cat lamp (back and front views are pictured *above*) also is cut from particleboard. It is adorned with stripes of bright acrylic paint. The minimal hardware and wiring materials needed to complete this project are readily available in most hardware stores.

Color schemes for both these projects take their cues from the coverlet on the preceding pages, but of course any of the designs may be adapted to suit your personal preferences or to harmonize with an existing decor.

A ROOMFUL OF WHIMSY FOR KIDS

Stenciled walls, headboards, and bed linens are a breeze when you borrow motifs from the blocks on the animal quilt. Stars are cribbed from the cow pasture, mice from the cat square, and plump carrots from the rabbit design.

Cut stencil patterns of your choice from heavy waxed paper or acrylic sheets (both available from art supply stores). Use latex paint and flat kitchen sponges to stencil walls, chair rail borders, and headboard. Switch to fabric paints or acrylics thinned with water to stencil designs on sheets, pillowcases, and other textile projects—curtains or window shades, for example.

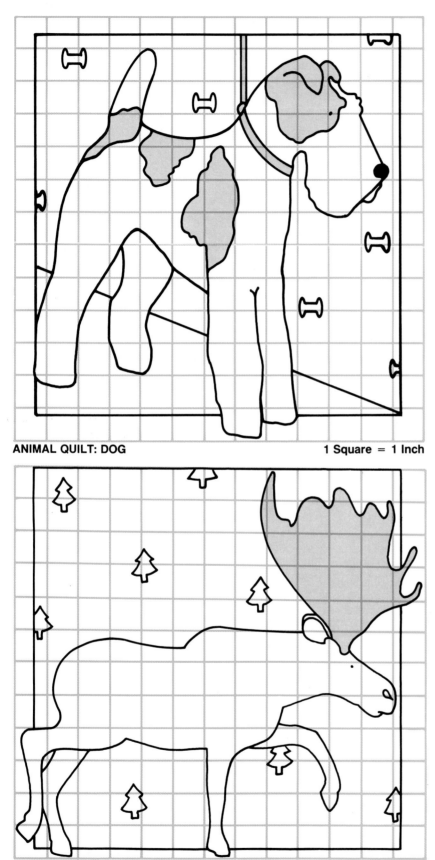

ANIMAL QUILT: DOG   1 Square = 1 Inch

ANIMAL QUILT: MOOSE   1 Square = 1 Inch

Animal Quilt
Shown on pages 36–39.
Finished quilt is 39x54 inches.

MATERIALS
5 yards of 36-inch-wide white
    cotton
Acrylics or fabric paints in these
    colors: blue, green, red, black,
    brown, gold, white, orange, and
    yellow
Black embroidery floss
Quilt batting
Kraft paper
Washable fabric marker

INSTRUCTIONS
From white cotton, cut six 16½-inch
squares for quilt blocks. Cut two
6½x55-inch and two 6½x40-inch
strips for borders. For the quilt back,
cut one piece 35x50 inches.

Note: To adjust the size of the
quilt, add squares or increase the
width of the border. Adjust fabric
amounts accordingly.

Enlarge the designs for the six animal quilt squares (*at left and on the
following pages*) onto paper; trace
them onto preshrunk white cotton
squares.

TO PAINT: Before beginning, practice painting on a scrap of fabric.
Paint up to but not over pattern
lines. Use acrylics or textile paints.
Refer to photographs for colors.

Thin acrylics with water to the
consistency of light cream. For suc-
cessful application and setting of
textile paints, follow the manufacturer's directions.

TO EMBELLISH: Use outline stitches and three strands of embroidery
floss to embroider along the outline
of each design. Add French knot
eyes, then stem-stitch whiskers.

TO ASSEMBLE: With right sides
facing, sew blocks together; use ¼-
inch seams. Fold border strips in
half lengthwise and press. Stitch

one long edge to pieced top; miter corners, and sew to fold line. Repeat for remaining borders.

Turn borders at fold line to the back, over batting and backing; miter the back side of the corners. Turn the raw edges under, and blindstitch to back. Quilt along seam lines.

Moose Hat Rack
Shown on page 36.

MATERIALS
4x4 feet of ¾-inch-thick
  particleboard
Scraps of pine for supports
Wood glue
Butcher paper
Two *each* of 2-inch No. 8 and
  1-inch No. 5 wood screws
1-inch finishing nails
C-clamps
Acrylic paints; brushes

INSTRUCTIONS
Enlarge design, *right,* onto paper; transfer all patterns except the head to particleboard. Head is made of a double thickness of particleboard. Cut two 11x16-inch pieces. Transfer the head pattern to one piece; glue and nail pieces together. Clamp until dry; cut out head. Cut out remaining pieces. Cut a 45-degree bevel on ends of ears and antlers to make a left and right of each. Round over edges; sand.

Cut two 2½-inch-long triangular wedges ⅝ inch to a side with a 45-degree angle. Position antlers. Add wedges as supports; fasten with glue and 1-inch screws. Attach ears.

Make two 9¼-inch-long right-angle support strips with 1-inch sides. Bevel ends to make a right and left piece. With 2-inch screws and glue, fasten head on back piece; reinforce with strips at sides.

Paint to match moose quilt block design, using good quality acrylic paint. Hang on wall by screwing through top of back into stud; fill holes and touch up with paint.

continued

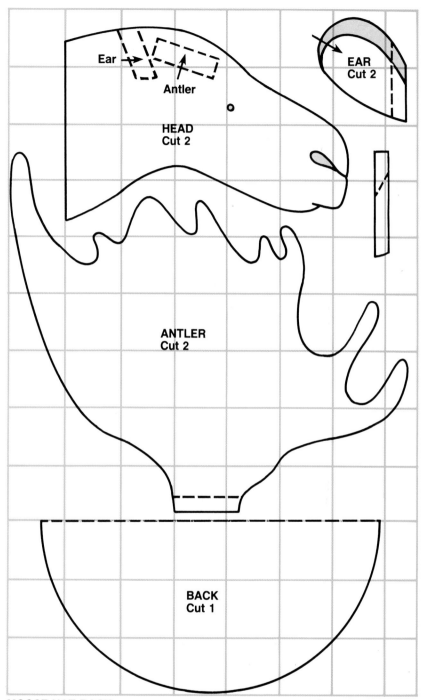

MOOSE HAT RACK

1 Square = 3 Inches

45

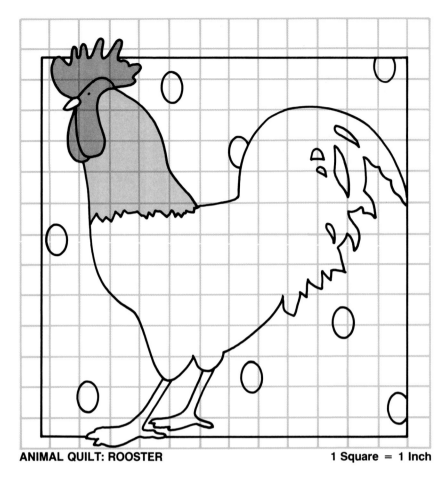

ANIMAL QUILT: ROOSTER   **1 Square = 1 Inch**

continued from page 45
**A Roomful of
Whimsy for Kids**

Wood Appliqué
Rooster on Chest
Shown on pages 38–39.

MATERIALS
Unpainted chest with a plain front
¼-inch-thick hardboard
Wood glue; brads

INSTRUCTIONS
Enlarge chicken and egg patterns
from quilt block design, *left,* to fit
dresser front; transfer to hardboard.

Cut pieces from hardboard. Position chicken on dresser front and
draw lines across the body where
the drawers separate; cut and sand
edges. Attach with glue and brads;
paint. Drill holes for drawer pulls;
attach handles.

Hooked Cow Rug
Shown on pages 38–39.

MATERIALS
3½x4½-foot piece of burlap
Permanent marker
Stretcher strips or rug frame to fit
    burlap
Cotton rug yarn in the following
    colors and amounts (in skeins):
    1 dark pink, 1 light pink, 4 black,
    and 8 white
Speed tufting or punch rug hooking
    tool (available in craft supply
    shops)
Latex rug backing
Butcher paper

INSTRUCTIONS
Enlarge cow pattern, *left,* onto paper
using a scale of 1 square equals 3½
inches; transfer to burlap with permanent marker.

Stretch burlap on frame. Work areas with punch hooking tool, referring to photograph for colors.

Remove rug from frame; trim burlap to within 2 inches of stitching.
Turn edge under; hem. Finish the rug
with a coating of latex painted on
the underside.

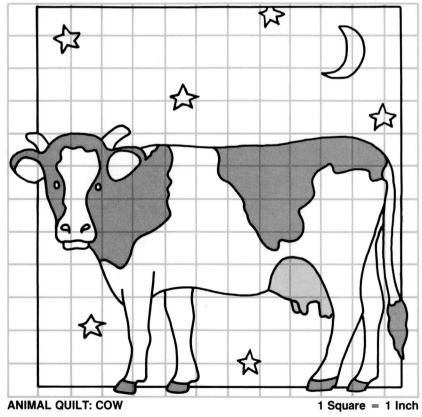

ANIMAL QUILT: COW   **1 Square = 1 Inch**

Rabbit Table
Shown on page 40.

MATERIALS
4x4 feet of ¾-inch-thick
   particleboard
Scraps of pine for supports
Wood glue; wood putty
Sandpaper
Five 2-inch and nine 1-inch No. 8
   wood screws
Finishing nails; butcher paper

INSTRUCTIONS
Enlarge pattern pieces for rabbit table (*below* and on page 48); transfer
to particleboard. Cut out a 21x30-
inch top, a 14x20-inch base, and rabbit pieces.

Bevel back edge of crooked ear to
30 degrees and top two back edges
to 60 degrees. Bevel bottom inside
edge of straight ear to 60 degrees
and top inside edge to 30 degrees.

Round edges; sand lightly. Glue
tail in place. Using 1-inch screws
and glue, fasten ears to body.

continued

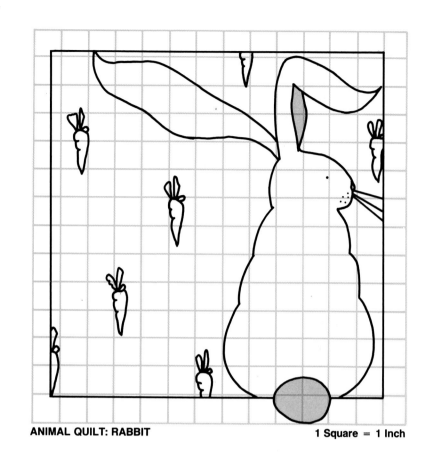

ANIMAL QUILT: RABBIT　　　　**1 Square = 1 Inch**

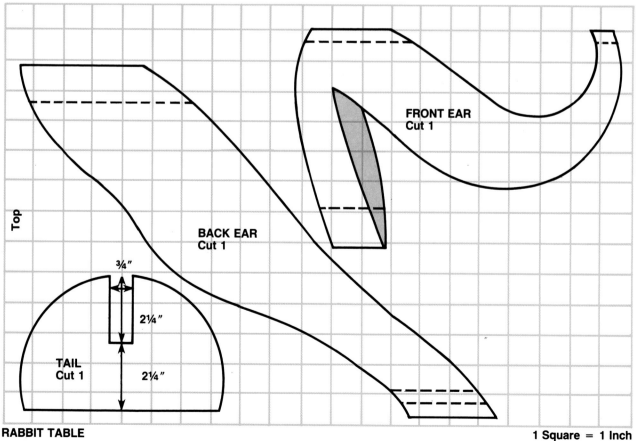

Top

FRONT EAR
Cut 1

BACK EAR
Cut 1

¾"

2¼"

2¼"

TAIL
Cut 1

RABBIT TABLE　　　　**1 Square = 1 Inch**

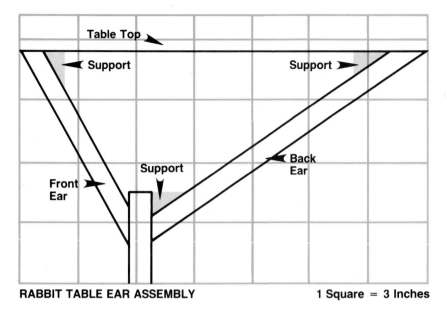

RABBIT TABLE EAR ASSEMBLY

1 Square = 3 Inches

continued from page 47
A Roomful of Whimsy for Kids

Cut a triangular wood support strip with 30-degree and 60-degree angles; the shortest side should be ⅜ inch long. Cut supports to fit inside back ear and tabletop joints at both ears (see diagram, *left*).

Fasten supports in place using glue and brads. Attach top and base with wood screws. (See assembly diagram, *left.*)

Paint the bunny table as shown in the photograph on page 40; use white for tabletop.

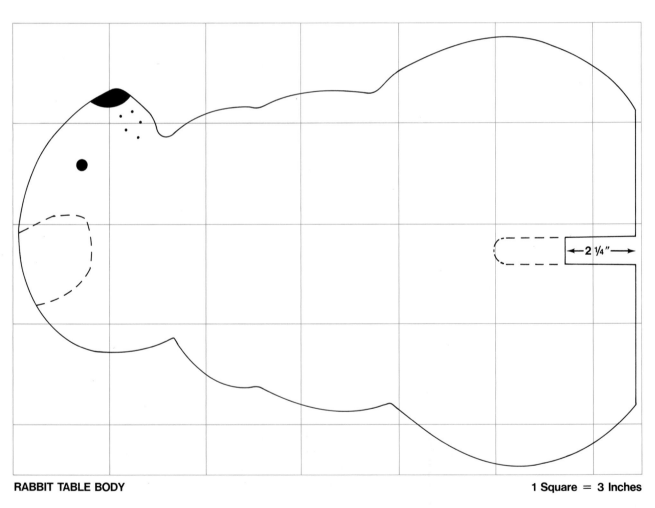

RABBIT TABLE BODY

1 Square = 3 Inches

Cat Lamp

Shown on page 41.

MATERIALS

2x3-foot piece of ¾-inch
   particleboard; wood glue
1-inch wood screws
Light socket; electrical cord; plug
2-inch threaded nipple
2 threaded locknuts

INSTRUCTIONS

Enlarge quilt pattern design, *right,*
using scale of 1 square equals 1⅛
inches; transfer to particleboard.
Enlarge and transfer lamp base pattern, *below right.* Cut out cat, lamp
base, and 3½x3⅝-inch socket holder. Round one short end of holder
(see pattern, *below right*). Drill hole
in holder, centered 1¾ inches from
rounded edge, to size of threaded
nipple. Round over edges; sand.

    Attach base to bottom of cat. Fasten socket holder to back, 3 to 5
inches from the bottom; brace with
scrap lumber. Paint all wood pieces,
then assemble light fixture.

Fantasy Stars on Wall and Pillowcases

Shown on pages 36–39.

MATERIALS

Flat sponges
Acetate or heavy paper for
   stencils
Latex wall paint
Acrylic or fabric paints
Plate or tray for paint
Utility knife

INSTRUCTIONS

Enlarge background motifs from
quilt squares for stencil patterns:
stars from cow square, mice from
cat square, or others of your choice.
Cut designs from paper or acetate to
make stencils.

    Practice on scrap of fabric. Dip
sponge in plate or tray of paint. Position the stencil on wall or fabric;
stamp the cutout area with sponge.
(Refer to photograph on page 42.)

continued

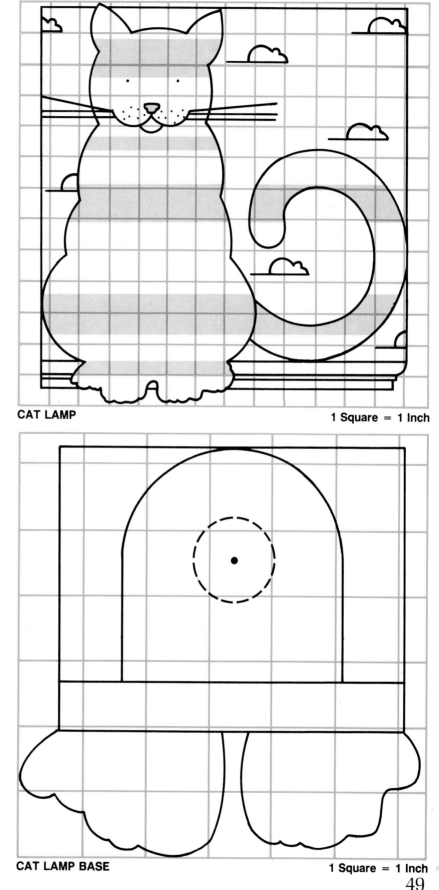

CAT LAMP   1 Square = 1 Inch

CAT LAMP BASE   1 Square = 1 Inch

49

continued from page 49

A Roomful of
Whimsy for Kids

COLOR KEY

1 Black	6 Green
2 Medium Gray	7 Blue
3 Light Gray	8 Red
4 Medium Pink	9 Yellow
5 Light Pink	

CAT AND MOUSE CHAIR

1 Square = 1 Inch

Fantasy Chair Rail And Headboard

Shown on pages 36–37.

MATERIALS

Acetate or heavy paper for
  stencils
Latex wall paint
Utility knife
Flat sponges
Artist's paintbrush

INSTRUCTIONS

For stencil designs, enlarge background motifs (stars, mice, and so forth) from quilt squares. Transfer to stencil paper or acetate; cut out shapes using a utility knife.

Paint stripes on the wall. The fool-the-eye chair rail is 4 inches deep; the top of the rail is 28 inches above the floor. Star border is 5 inches deep. Carrot center of headboard is 31 inches wide.

Note: Plan placement of stencils carefully to avoid half stencils at corners.

Paint star borders according to instructions for wall stencils, page 49. For mice and carrots, trace outline of stencil, then paint motifs the desired color.

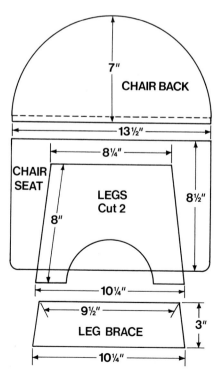

Child's Cat-and-Mouse Chair

Shown on page 15.

MATERIALS

½-inch-thick pine lumber
  or particleboard; nails
Graphite paper; sandpaper
Pink, white, gray, and black
  semigloss paint
Enamel paints in assorted colors
  (green, red, yellow, blue) for
  ribbon bows
Clear acrylic spray; wood glue

INSTRUCTIONS

Enlarge patterns, *opposite and below left.* Transfer outline of chair onto pine or particleboard, using graphite paper. Cut out all pieces; sand edges smooth. Apply two coats of white semigloss paint to all pieces, allowing paint to dry thoroughly between coats.

Transfer designs to chair back and seat using graphite paper; see photograph for placement. Paint designs; allow each color to dry before painting adjacent areas. Use assorted colors to paint ribbons around necks and tails of mice.

To assemble, glue and nail leg sections to bottom of seat; glue and nail cross brace between leg sections. Glue and nail chair back to seat so designs align when joined. Finish with clear acrylic spray.

Heart and Hand Quilt

Shown on pages 16–17.
Finished quilt is 33x42 inches.

MATERIALS

Twelve 10-inch squares of
  assorted print cotton fabrics
Red print fabrics for hearts
Two or more different pink fabrics
  for hands
Scraps of solid green and assorted
  print fabrics for leaves,
  butterflies, and other motifs
¼ yard *each* of four border fabrics
1 yard backing fabric
Lightweight interfacing or muslin
Batting; polyester fiberfill

INSTRUCTIONS

Trace children's hands onto medium-weight cardboard to make patterns. Also sketch simple heart, leaf, and butterfly motifs (as suggested by designs on the quilt), or other motifs of your choice. Make cardboard patterns for these shapes as well.

Cut all motifs from appropriate fabrics (do not add seam allowances), then back each shape with a layer of lightweight interfacing or muslin to prevent see-through and to give added strength when the motifs are machine-appliquéd.

Compose each square individually, arranging hearts, hands, stems and leaves, butterflies, and so forth, on each 10-inch background square until you are pleased with the design. Allow space for ½-inch seams around each square.

When the design is complete, pin or baste shapes in place. Machine-appliqué around edges. Lightly stuff some shapes with fiberfill to give a trapunto effect, if desired.

When all squares are complete, piece blocks together into four horizontal rows of three squares each. Piece rows together to form quilt top, carefully matching seams.

Cut 7-inch-wide strips of four different fabrics to size for borders (includes ½-inch seam allowances). Pin and stitch borders in place, mitering corners. Press quilt top.

Cut a 33x42-inch rectangle of batting and a matching rectangle of backing fabric. Center and layer backing, batting, and appliquéd top; baste all layers together. Turn under raw edges on border strips and slip-stitch to back of quilt.

Cut out four small hearts, pad each one lightly, and machine-appliqué one in each corner of quilt borders (see photograph).

Using embroidery floss, tuft or tie through all layers of the quilt at corners of each block; or, machine-quilt around each square, as desired.

51

STAMP PRINTING

Make a spectacular impression on any room with this ingenious technique. Using easy-to-make foam-rubber stamps, you can print colorful patterns on floors, walls, furniture, and fabrics in next to no time.

STAMP PRINTING

Stamps and a bit of stitching transformed a plain white sheet into the colorful quilt *at left*.

With a little more stamping, you can create trellis- and tulip-patterned fabrics for throw pillows like those at the head of the bed. Then use a small, square stamp to print checked fabric for the pillow ruffles. Extend the look by printing additional yardage in the checked pattern for curtains or a dust ruffle, if you like.

To create the tulip-garden tablecloth, *above,* stamp giant tulip blossoms and butterflies around the edges of a purchased cloth or a circle of sheeting fabric, then paint the stems by hand. Finish the cloth with a deep ruffle of fabric embellished with stamped checks.

For another view of the tablecloth and even more stamp-printing ideas, please turn the page.

55

A splashy checkerboard "rug," bordered with hearts and diamonds, sets the pace in this boldly patterned sun porch.

The squares and Xs in the floor pattern are used lavishly elsewhere in the room to achieve the lattice design on the upholstery, the cable border around the windows, and a patchworklike pattern on the cabinet front.

The stamps that produced these patterns are made from sturdy upholstery foam, are washable and reusable, and work well on almost any material.

For printing on walls, floors, or wooden furniture, begin with light-colored, fresh-painted surfaces. Do your stampings with latex paints in contrasting colors. Then coat freshly printed floors with polyurethane to save on wear and tear.

Prewashed white cotton sheeting and fabric paints or dyes are ideal for pillows, table skirts, upholstery fabrics, and other soft furnishings.

STAMP PRINTING

1 Follow these step-by-step instructions to create any or all of the stamp-printed projects shown on these pages.

On lightweight cardboard, draw a simple shape, such as a heart, a square, or an X. Cut out the shape, then draw around it with a pen onto a piece of high-density upholstery foam.

2 With sharp scissors or a crafts knife, cut out the foam shape. If necessary, trim with clips of the scissors or with a single-edge razor blade until the edges of the shape are smooth. *Note:* For firm foam, you may prefer to use an electric carving knife to cut out the stamp shape.

3 Cut a base for the stamp from a sheet of ⅛-inch-thick acrylic plastic by scoring the plastic with a knife, then breaking it along the scored lines.

Glue the foam cutout to the plastic with superstrength adhesive or crafts glue. Let the glue dry thoroughly before use.

4 Spoon paint onto a leftover piece of plastic or a flat cookie sheet, then roll it out with a brayer or small paint roller.

Dab your stamp into the paint, *above,* until the bottom of the printing surface is well coated, but not saturated. Wipe off excess.

5 Practice printing on newspaper to build your confidence.

Then proceed to stamp your pattern on floors (*below*), walls, furniture, or fabric. The see-through plastic base enables you to position the foam stamp properly for each impression.

INSTRUCTIONS FOR STAMP PRINTING

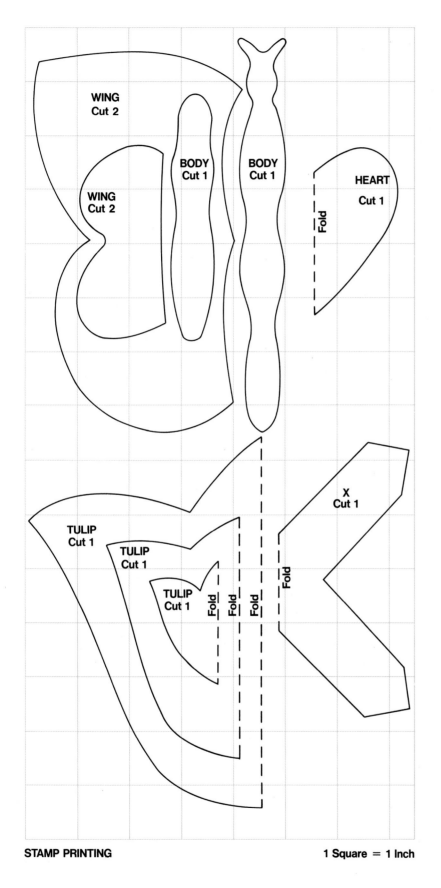

WING
Cut 2

WING
Cut 2

BODY
Cut 1

BODY
Cut 1

HEART
Cut 1

Fold

X
Cut 1

TULIP
Cut 1

TULIP
Cut 1

TULIP
Cut 1

Fold

Fold

Fold

Fold

STAMP PRINTING

1 Square = 1 Inch

Stamp-Printed Projects
Shown on pages 52–57.

MATERIALS
Scraps of ¼- to ½-inch-thick, high-density upholstery foam
Lightweight cardboard
Felt-tip pen; masking tape
Several sheets of ⅛-inch-thick clear acrylic plastic
Superstrength adhesive or crafts glue; scissors; crafts knife
Single-edge razor blade
Short-napped paint roller or printer's brayer; cookie sheet
Interior latex paint for walls and furniture; exterior latex paint for floors; prewashed, white cotton sheeting and fabric paints or dyes for soft furnishings
Polyurethane or varnish for floors
Small artist's brushes for touch-ups

INSTRUCTIONS
Enlarge patterns, *left;* transfer to lightweight cardboard. Cut out patterns or designs of your choice; trace onto foam, using a felt pen. With sharp scissors, crafts knife, or single-edge razor blade, cut out all foam shapes. Also cut three foam squares: 1¾x1¾ inches, 3x3 inches, and 5¼x5¼ inches. If necessary, trim edges of foam squares with scissors or razor blade until each outline is smooth on at least one side (the printing surface).

Next, cut a base for each shape from a sheet of ⅛-inch-thick clear acrylic plastic. Glue foam shapes to plastic bases with superstrength adhesive or crafts glue. (*Note:* Do *not* use water-soluble glue; you will want to be able to wash and reuse stamps. Dry stamps thoroughly before proceeding.)

To print, spoon paint onto a scrap of plastic or a flat cookie sheet; roll paint out with a short-napped paint roller or printer's brayer. Dab bottom of stamp (printing surface) into paint until it is evenly coated. Do *not* saturate the stamp.

Practice printing on newspaper sheets, or on fabric or wood scraps. Clean stamps between printings by patting with newspapers or wiping with a clean cloth. Wash stamps thoroughly after using and before changing color of paint or dye. Use soap and water and press stamp on clean paper towels to remove excess moisture.

Follow specific instructions, *below,* for the stamp-printed projects.

For the tulip quilt

Using patterns, *opposite,* as well as Xs, hearts, and 3-inch squares, plot a design for the top. Refer to diagram, *right,* for ideas. Adapt design to suit your bed size. Make foam stamps for each shape.

Mark center and border areas of the design using a water-soluble pen. Print borders first, allowing each color to dry before moving to next section. Spread newspaper beneath fabric as you print to absorb excess dye or fabric paint.

For the center of the design, print tulip heads first. Paint stems by hand. Use masking tape to mask off ½- to ¾-inch-wide stems; use an artist's brush to paint stems directly on the fabric with fabric paint or dye.

Print butterflies by masking portions of flower stems with tape and printing over them; remove tape so butterflies appear to be behind the stems. (See diagram.)

When design is completed and paint is dry, heat-set designs following the manufacturer's directions.

Back the quilt top with a layer of batting and backing; machine-quilt around stamped shapes. Bind edges or finish as desired.

For pillows and upholstery fabric

Following instructions for printing on fabric, *above,* print fabric yardage with closely spaced Xs (latticework) or with tulip heads and small (1¾-inch) squares.

Print check-patterned yardage for ruffles using the 3x3-inch stamp. Heat-set designs following manufacturer's directions. Sew pillows and add ruffles; upholster furniture.

For the tablecloth

Cut a circle of sheeting to desired size; print large tulips and butterflies around edges, with flower heads

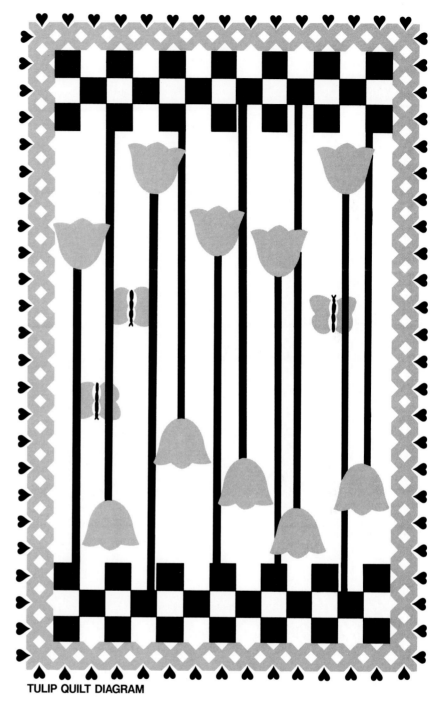

TULIP QUILT DIAGRAM

pointing toward the center of cloth. Heat-set. Hem cloth, or add a ruffle of check-printed fabric.

For the stamped "rug"

Plan a pattern using basic design elements: the heart, 5-inch square, X, or motifs of your choice. Use masking tape to outline area of pattern. Paint background first, using white exterior paint; dry thoroughly.

Paint one section of color at a time. Repair any drips or smudges using an artist's brush and dabs of paint. When the floor is completely dry, protect it with several coats of polyurethane.

For the wall and furniture designs

Tailor designs to suit the space. Touch up printed designs with an artist's brush, if necessary.

CROSS-STITCH FAVORITES

Whether you own a cottage in the country or a sleek urban loft, these witty cross-stitch designs make colorful conversation pieces that are at home in any setting.

Alphabet samplers and sentimental mottoes are staples of the cross-stitch repertoire. They also are part of an embroidery heritage dating back to colonial days and beyond.

Although the pillow and rug designs pictured here are based on these familiar cross-stitch themes, the larger scale of the motifs and the use of new-style yarns and fabrics breathe bright new life into this old tradition.

The stunning area rug, *opposite*, features conventional cross-stitch motifs translated onto seven-count, quick-point canvas and worked in woolen rug yarns. The effect is undeniably dramatic.

Quotation pillows like those on the chair and sofa, *right* and *opposite*, make a delightfully personal decorating statement. This trio displays three of the stitcher's favorite sayings, spelled out in bold letters on quick-to-stitch even-weave fabrics.

You can stitch these designs or create original versions, incorporating your own favorite aphorisms and cross-stitch motifs. Directions begin on page 68.

CROSS-STITCH FAVORITES

In days gone by, young girls practiced their letters and numbers and needlework skills at the same time, by stitching samplers like this one.

Cross-stitch this traditional Tree of Life design—complete with alphabet, numbers, borders, and fanciful motifs—in just five colors of floss to make a charming 12x15-inch picture.

CROSS-STITCH FAVORITES

Cheerful as a country garden—that's the charm of this rose-patterned cloth.

Embroidered here on a 50-inch square of linen, these blossoms and border motifs adapt easily to any size cloth, and are suitable for any number of other projects as well.

When working counted cross-stitch designs such as these on fabrics other than even weaves, you may find it helpful to stitch the designs over waste canvas. Available in most needlework shops, waste canvas is a lightweight, disposable mesh with evenly spaced horizontal and vertical threads.

Basted to the background fabric, waste canvas acts as a grid. With it, your counted cross-stitches will be uniform, both on fabrics so finely woven that you cannot count stitches and on fabrics that are not woven evenly at all.

Two appealing designs illustrate how one cross-stitch pattern can provide inspiration for altogether different projects.

The child's afghan, *opposite,* boasts repeat motifs plucked from the "Home Sweet Home" sampler shown *above.* Bears at tea, hearts, flowers, and border designs are cross-stitched on the crocheted background, following a simple adaptation of the charted design for the sampler figures.

Motifs from any of the other cross-stitch designs in this chapter—or elsewhere in the book—can be similarly adapted.

INSTRUCTIONS FOR CROSS-STITCH FAVORITES

General Instructions

All of the projects shown on pages 60–67 are made with one embroidery stitch—the cross-stitch. If this stitch is new to you, practice making some on scrap fabric before beginning a design. (You may wish to refer to an embroidery book for a diagram and instructions on this stitch.)

To make your stitching easier, you may wish to chart complete patterns in color on grid paper, using colored pencils or felt-tip pens. If you make an error when charting the pattern, cover up the mistake with white typewriter correction fluid. If the error is over a large area, cut out the mistake with an artist's

SAMPLER PILLOW

COLOR KEY

⊠	Wine	☑	Lavender
⊡	Green	⊞	Blue
◉	Rose	■	Navy

1 Square = 1 Stitch

knife and patch the hole with additional graph paper taped to the wrong side of the pattern. (Match squares carefully.)

It is useful to have a supply of tapestry needles so you can thread one with each color of floss or pearl cotton that you plan to use in the design. Also, it's a good idea to wrap your embroidery in a scrap of muslin or a plastic bag to keep it from getting soiled when you are not working on it.

If you have selected dark threads or fabrics for your stitchery, you may wish to check for colorfastness. Most materials will not bleed, but occasionally some do. You can set dyes by dipping fabric or floss into a weak solution of salt and water, or vinegar and water. Allow them to dry thoroughly before stitching.

Specific instructions and patterns for the projects follow below.

"Kind Words" Sampler Pillow

Shown on page 60.
Finished size is 13x13 inches.

MATERIALS
½ yard of 18-count white Aida cloth
No. 5 pearl cotton in the following amounts and colors: 2 skeins of wine; 1 skein *each* of green, rose, lavender, blue, and navy
Tapestry needles
Embroidery hoop
Masking tape
Water-erasable marking pen
½ yard of floral fabric for backing
1½ yards of eyelet lace trim
Polyester fiberfill

INSTRUCTIONS
Bind the edges of the Aida cloth with masking tape to prevent ravel-ing. Find the center of the fabric by locating the center horizontal and vertical threads; mark with a water-erasable pen.

Mount the fabric in an embroidery hoop and thread a 32-inch length of wine-colored pearl cotton through the needle. Draw the thread from back to front, leaving a 2-inch tail on the back; catch the tail in the first several stitches to secure it.

(After stitching, secure the thread end by weaving the thread through four or five stitches on the back of the fabric. *Do not* carry the thread across the back of the fabric because it may create a shadow on the front side.)

Find the center of the diagram, *opposite,* and, using the center of the fabric as your point of reference, stitch the letters. Work each cross-stitch over two threads of the fabric.

continued

SAMPLER PILLOW

1 Square = 1 Stitch

COLOR KEY
⊠ Green
■ Red
⊡ Light Blue
◉ Coral
⊘ Gold

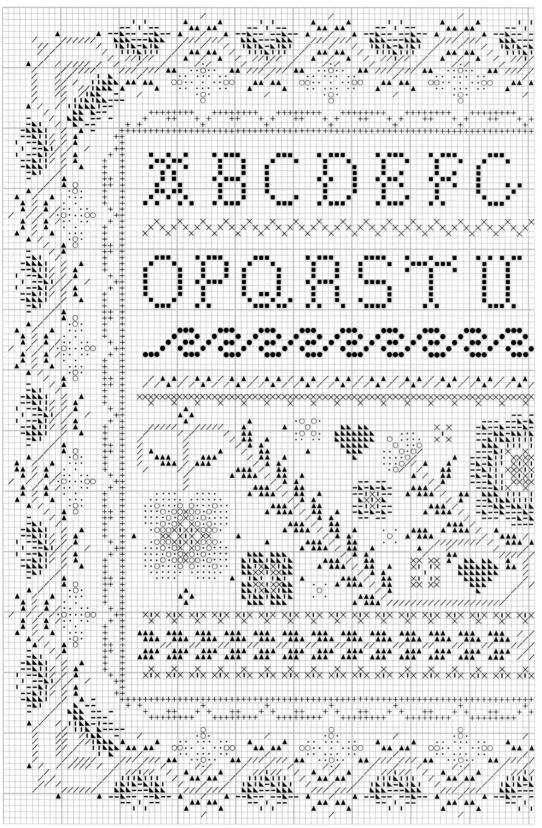

KEEPSAKE SAMPLER RUG

COLOR KEY
- ■ Brown
- ⊠ Antique Gold
- ▲ Leaf Green
- ⁄ Stem Green
- ⊞ Turquoise
- ◉ Bold Blue
- ⊙ Medium Blue
- · Light Blue
- ⊡ Wine
- ◣ Rose
- ⊟ Pink

1 Square = 1 Cross-Stitch

continued from page 69
Cross-Stitch Favorites

When letters are completed, refer to the diagram on page 68 and carefully position the flower basket and wreath motifs; work cross-stitches according to the color key. Then embroider the border as shown, using one color at a time.

To finish, press the fabric lightly, using a clean, damp towel. Trim the outside edges to within 1½ inches of the design and cut a matching-size piece of backing fabric.

For the ruffle, cut and piece a 4-inch-wide strip of fabric and fold it in half lengthwise. Baste the long ends together and gently pull the stitches to gather the fabric.

Baste the ruffle and the eyelet lace to the pillow front. With right sides facing, sew front and back together, using a ½-inch seam. Leave a 6-inch opening on one side; turn right side out. Stuff, and slip-stitch the opening closed.

"A True Friend" Sampler Pillow
Shown on page 61.
Finished size is 9x14 inches.

MATERIALS
½ yard of 22-count white hardanger cloth
½ yard of floral fabric
No. 5 pearl cotton in the following amounts and colors: 2 skeins of green; 1 skein *each* of red, light blue, coral, and gold
1⅔ yards of eyelet lace
Tapestry needle
Embroidery hoop
Masking tape
Water-erasable marking pen
Polyester fiberfill

INSTRUCTIONS
Follow instructions for the "Kind Words" sampler, page 69, working each cross-stitch over two threads of the fabric. Refer to the diagram on page 69 for color and placement of the stitches.

To finish, see instructions for the "Kind Words" sampler.

Sampler Rug
Shown on page 61.
Finished size is 36x52 inches.

MATERIALS
1⅔ yards of 40-inch-wide, 7-count quick-point canvas
1⅔ yards of white felt for backing
70-yard skeins of acrylic rug yarn in the following colors and amounts: 1 *each* of brown, antique gold, turquoise, bold blue, medium blue, light blue, wine, rose, and pink; 2 *each* of leaf green and stem green; 12 skeins of white
No. 17 tapestry needle
Masking tape; water-erasable pen
Liquid latex rug backing
Needlepoint frame (optional)

INSTRUCTIONS
Bind the edges of the canvas with masking tape to prevent raveling. Find the center of the canvas by locating the center horizontal and vertical threads; mark with a water-erasable pen. If desired, mount the canvas in a needlepoint frame to minimize distortion.

Cut 30-inch lengths of rug yarn; thread yarn through a needle. (If the yarn begins to look worn during stitching, cut shorter pieces.) Stitch the center rose motif first, using the center of the canvas to position the motif. Refer to diagram, pages 70–71, for colors and placement.

To begin stitching, draw the yarn to the front of the canvas, leaving a 1-inch tail on the back. Hold the tail in back and catch it in the first several stitches to secure it. Clip ends. Count the threads in your canvas carefully to assure that each cross-stitch is uniform in size.

Work each cross-stitch over two threads of canvas, leaving an empty mesh in the center of each stitch. Work one color at a time. To end, weave the yarn through four or five stitches on the back of the canvas.

After completing the center rose motif, work the antique gold horizontal row directly above the rose, following the pattern shown. Then begin stitching the leaf green and stem green horizontal rows, referring to the pattern. Work complete rows, one at a time, so the crossing threads fall in the same direction.

Complete the wavelike row of bold blue stitches. Then work the bottom row of letters, placing each letter as shown in the pattern.

Begin stitching the antique gold zigzag row and then work the top row of letters.

Finish working all of the design inside the turquoise border. Then stitch the outer floral border, working the white background last.

Block the rug on a clean, padded blocking board and let the rug dry overnight. Press it lightly on the wrong side for a smooth texture.

Turn the 2-inch canvas borders under on each side, and slip-stitch the canvas to the back of the rug. Apply liquid latex rug backing to the stitched area and let dry.

Slip-stitch a white felt backing to the back of the rug, turning the raw edges under. Place a rug pad under the sampler rug so it will wear longer and look better.

Tree of Life Sampler
Shown on pages 62–63.
Finished size is 12x15 inches.

MATERIALS
½ yard of 11-count ecru Aida cloth or even-weave linen
2 skeins *each* of embroidery floss in blue, red, yellow, green, and brown
Tapestry needle and embroidery hoop
Masking tape
Water-erasable marking pen

INSTRUCTIONS
Bind edges of fabric with masking tape. Locate the center of the fabric—where center horizontal and vertical threads meet—and mark with a water-erasable pen.

Mount the fabric in an embroidery hoop. Cut 32-inch lengths of embroidery floss; thread the needle with two strands of brown floss.
continued

TREE OF LIFE SAMPLER

1 Square = 1 Stitch

COLOR KEY ⊠ Blue   ⊡ Red   ⊘ Yellow   ⊙ Green   ■ Brown

CROSS-STITCH DOLLHOUSE

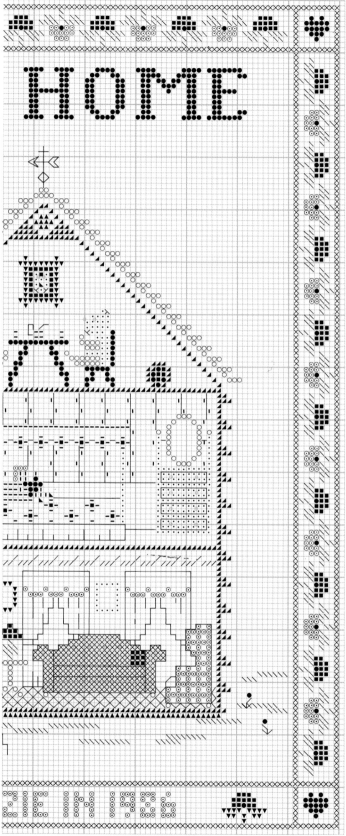

1 Square = 1 Stitch

continued from page 72
Cross-Stitch Favorites

Stitch the brown horizontal row going through center of design (see diagram, page 73), taking each stitch over one thread of fabric. Use two strands of floss throughout.

Work entire center design. Then work outer blue border, stitching a letter or design in each square. (See diagram for colors and placement.)

Block fabric lightly, using a clean, damp towel. Frame as desired.

Cross-Stitch Rose Tablecloth

Shown on pages 64–65.
Finished size of the cloth shown is 49 inches square.

MATERIALS

50-inch square of linen or other tablecloth fabric

1¼ yards of 27-inch-wide, 8½-count waste canvas

DMC embroidery floss in No. 813 blue, No. 318 gray, No. 701 dark green, No. 955 light green, No. 433 brown, No. 353 light coral, No. 3328 dark coral, and No. 321 red

Embroidery needle; sewing thread

Water-erasable marking pen

Felt-tip pens in colors shown on color key; graph paper

continued

COLOR KEY

⊠ Blue
◪ Dark Blue
◿ Light Blue
▲ Gray
◣ Dark Gray
⊙ Brown
⊡ Light Brown
◉ Orange
■ Yellow
▼ Dark Green
◺ Light Green
● Red-Orange
⊞ Rust
⊟ Aqua
Ⅰ Pink

continued from page 75
Cross-Stitch Favorites

INSTRUCTIONS

Using felt-tip pens, chart patterns given on page 78 for outer border corner, outer border center, and inner border corner. Complete the tablecloth design by placing the floral motifs according to the instructions below; then connect them with a narrow border of circles (refer to photograph).

Using water-erasable pen, draw the 49-inch square for the finished cloth. Then find the center of the cloth and draw horizontal and vertical lines intersecting at this point; draw diagonal lines to each corner.

Refer to photograph for placement of motifs. Draw a line 1⅜ inches from the finished edge line for the bottom of the outer border (circle motifs). Mark a line 10 inches from the center of the cloth for the top of the inner border (circle motifs).

OUTER BORDER: Cut waste canvas to size of area to be worked; baste in place. Use three strands of floss over one thread of canvas.

With bottom circles (at edges of corner motif) placed 1⅜ inches from line, work corner motifs.

Center single floral motif between corner motifs, then work narrow border (circles) to connect motifs.

INNER BORDER: Cut waste canvas and baste to fabric. Begin with narrow border (circles), working seven on each side of the vertical line. Work corner motifs.

FINISHING: When cross-stitching is completed, dampen fabric and remove threads of waste canvas. Turn under edge on fold line; hem.

Dollhouse Sampler
Shown on page 66.
Finished size of Dollhouse Sampler is 16¼x19¼ inches, framed.

MATERIALS
24x27 inches of white hardanger
Embroidery floss (see color key)
Graph paper; felt-tip pens

INSTRUCTIONS
Transfer design, pages 74–75, onto graph paper using felt-tip pens.

Begin stitching in the center of the pattern and the center of the fabric. Using two strands of floss, work cross-stitches over two threads of fabric. Also use two strands of floss to outline all areas indicated on chart, *except* use one strand of dark green for diamond-patterned floors in the dining room, living room, and upstairs hall.

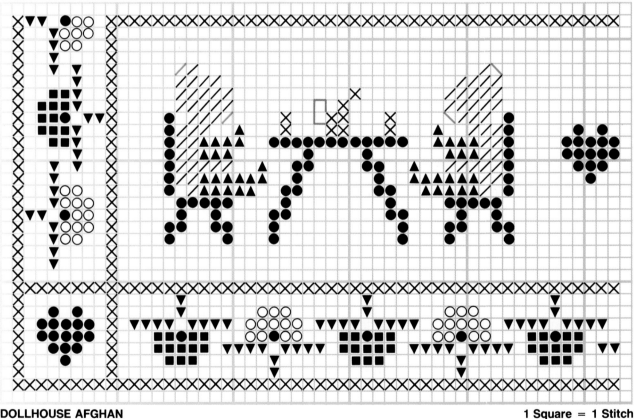

DOLLHOUSE AFGHAN

1 Square = 1 Stitch

COLOR KEY

⊠ Blue	⊡ Coral
▼ Green	⊿ Light Brown
● Red	▲ Dark Brown
■ Yellow	

76

Use gray on tire-swing rope, window and bathtub in bathroom, windows in attic, upstairs hall, kitchen, and front door. Use dark gray on weather vane, attic window (web), hanging pot rope, and sofa.

Use light brown for cafe curtain and cradle in nursery, upper curtain and lamp cord in dining room, and living room chair. Use dark brown for roof and dresser drawers.

With light blue, outline tablecloth in dining room and curtains in living room. Use aqua for dust ruffle on bed, and pitchers in attic and bathroom. Use dark green for bathroom walls, valance, and towels, and for flower stems. Use light green for wall stripes in bedroom.

Use orange for the wall detail, curtains, and floor in nursery, lower curtains in dining room, and facial features on the sun.

Lightly press and block sampler. Frame as desired.

Dollhouse Afghan

Shown on page 67.
Finished size is 37x56 inches, including border.

MATERIALS

Unger Roly Poly (3.5-ounce balls):
   8 balls of No. 8001 white; 1 ball
   each of No. 8352 green, No. 4556
   blue, No. 2277 yellow, No. 6411
   red, No. 9381 coral, No. 3845
   rust, and No. 2532 brown
Size H aluminum crochet hook
Size J afghan hook with a 22-inch
   extender, or size to obtain gauge
Blunt-end tapestry needle

Abbreviations: See page 92.
Gauge: 4 afghan stitches = 1 inch.

INSTRUCTIONS

With Size J afghan hook and white, ch 143.
First Half of Row 1: Leaving all lps on hook, sk first ch, * insert hook in next ch, yo, draw up lp; rep from * in each ch across—143 lps on hook. *Second Half of Row 1:* Yo and draw through first lp on hook, * yo, draw through next 2 lps on hook; rep from * until 1 lp rem on hook.

First Half of Row 2: Insert hook under *second* vertical bar of Row 1, yo, draw up lp and leave on hook; * insert hook in next vertical bar, yo, draw up lp and leave on hook; rep from * across row to within 1 bar of end; insert hook under last bar and thread behind it, yo, draw up lp—143 lps on hook. *Second Half of Row 2:* Rep Second Half of Row 1.

Rep Row 2 (first and second halves) until 56 rows are completed—1 lp on hook.
First Half of Row 57: With white, work as for First Half of Row 2 until 10 sts on hook, drop white to wrong side of work; with green, work next 123 sts—133 lps on hook. Drop green to wrong side of work. With second ball of white, work rem 10 sts—143 lps on hook.
Second Half of Row 57: With white, work as for Second Half of Row 2 until 1 lp before the next green lp. Drop white; pick up green from *underneath* the white (to prevent holes) and work across with green until 1 lp before the next white lp; drop green, pick up white from underneath the green and complete row with white. Fasten off green.
Row 58: Rep Row 57 with white and red. *Row 59:* Rep Row 57 with white and coral. *Row 60:* Rep Row 57 with white and yellow. *Row 61:* Rep Row 57 with white and blue.

Row 62: Rep Row 60. *Row 63:* Rep Row 59. *Row 64:* Rep Row 58. *Row 65:* Rep Row 57. *Rows 66–90:* With white, rep Row 2.

Rep rows 57–90 once more. Then rep rows 57–65. With white, rep Row 2 for 55 more rows.
Last row: Draw up lp under second vertical bar and draw through lp on hook—1 lp on hook; * draw up lp in next vertical bar and draw through lp on hook—1 lp on hook; rep from * across to within 1 bar of end; insert hook under last bar and thread behind it, draw up lp and draw through lp on hook. Do not fasten off.

EDGING: *Rnd 1:* With white and Size H hook, ch 1; work sc evenly spaced around entire afghan, working 3 sc in each corner stitch; join with sl st to first sc. *Next 2 rnds:* Rep Rnd 1; fasten off. Weave in all ends and block.

CROSS-STITCH BORDER DESIGN: Refer to diagram and color chart, *opposite,* to work each cross-stitch over one afghan stitch using one strand of yarn.

Begin working blue-lined border (enclosing flowers) around entire afghan. Work hearts in corners. Work short edges, beginning one stitch from edge; begin and end with a yellow flower. On long edges, begin and end with a coral flower, one stitch from end.

Referring to diagram, *opposite,* stitch bears as follows: from left inner border, skip four stitches; begin first bear motif. Work the motifs across, ending final bear three stitches from right inner border. Use half cross-stitches for chins and tops of bears' heads. Backstitch pitcher handle. Repeat for other end.

Cross-Stitch Towels

Shown on pages 8–9.

MATERIALS

Purchased linen towels or even-weave linen fabric
Scraps of waste canvas
Embroidery floss in two colors of your choice
Embroidery hoop
Embroidery needle

INSTRUCTIONS

Select initials from the chart on page 79; transfer them to graph paper. Determine the placement of letters on even-weave linen fabric. Secure in a hoop and cross-stitch the initials, using two strands of floss over two threads of the fabric.

To stitch onto purchased linens (which are not necessarily even weave), baste a section of waste canvas to fabric. Work the design over canvas. After cross-stitches are completed, dampen the canvas and gently pull out threads.

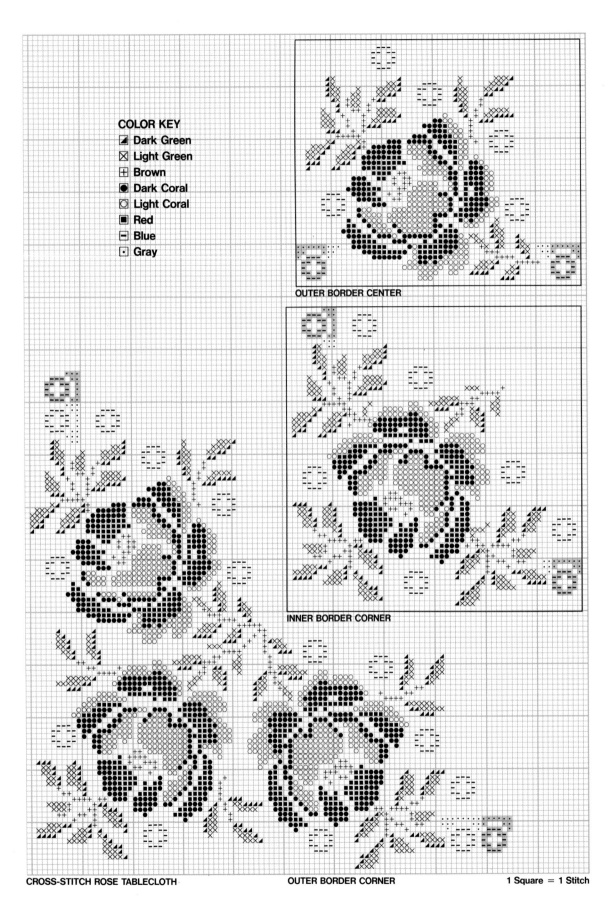

COLOR KEY
◨ Dark Green
⊠ Light Green
⊞ Brown
● Dark Coral
○ Light Coral
■ Red
⊟ Blue
⊡ Gray

OUTER BORDER CENTER

INNER BORDER CORNER

CROSS-STITCH ROSE TABLECLOTH   OUTER BORDER CORNER   1 Square = 1 Stitch

78

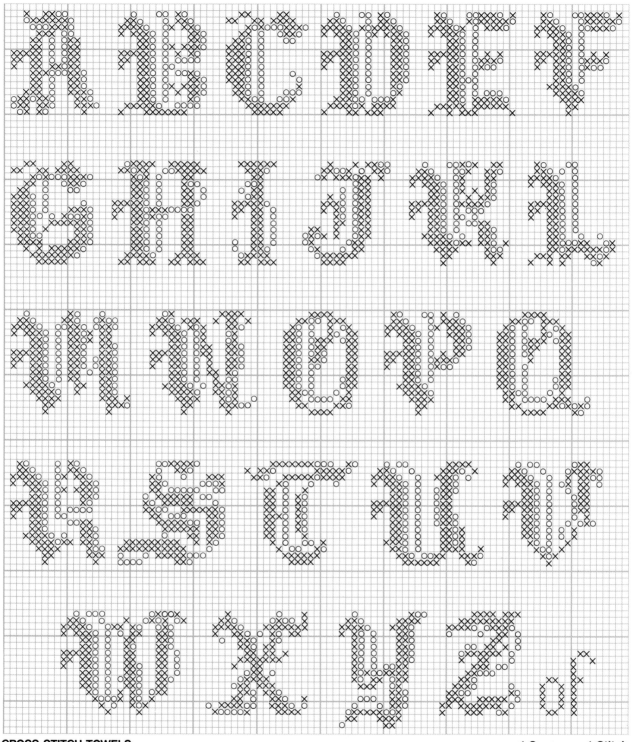

CROSS-STITCH TOWELS

1 Square = 1 Stitch

COUNTRY PLEASURES

A knitted afghan, crocheted pillows, handcrafted rugs, colorful patchwork projects, and unique folk art accessories are among the delights in this country-fresh collection.

Extend a gracious welcome to guests with these handcrafted signs of hospitality.

Pictured *above* is an easy-to-craft, ripple-patterned throw rug. It was hooked by hand, using narrow strips of woolen remnants and fabrics culled from cast-off pieces of family clothing.

To create your own welcome mat, use strips of fabric or lengths of rug-weight woolen yarn. Alter the color scheme of the rug to suit available materials or to complement your decor.

The elegant "Welcome" sign, *opposite—*

embroidered in satin stitches, straight stitches, and cross-stitches on perforated paper—is an up-to-date version of a favorite 19th century stitchery technique. Bright colors and crisp framing lend a contemporary air.

Instructions begin on page 90.

80

COUNTRY PLEASURES

A cozy corner to curl up in—that's part of what country comfort is all about. Here are a pair of projects designed to make any corner of your home snug and inviting.

The sculptured afghan, *opposite,* is knitted of worsted wool and is a perfect warmer-upper for chilly afternoons on the porch or long winter evenings by the fire. Measuring a generous 48x59

inches, this softly textured beauty is suitable as a lap throw, or you might enlarge it slightly (by working additional blocks of the pattern) for use as a single-bed coverlet.

With a little practice, even a novice can crochet the inviting quintet of cushions, *above.* Pretty pearl cotton thread makes them quick and easy to stitch, as well as long wearing.

Crochet a single cushion to nestle in a favorite chair, or turn out a row of bright-colored pillows for a window seat.

COUNTRY PLEASURES

Nothing says "country" quite like a collection of patchwork. Perhaps the most familiar hallmark of country style is a traditional pieced quilt, such as the Nine-Patch design, *left*.

Stitched and hand-quilted from gingham, polka dot, and calico fabrics, this 65x76-inch coverlet embodies the essence of country.

To appreciate the versatility of traditional patchwork designs and techniques, compare this classic quilt with the decidedly un-traditional place mats, *above*. Pieced from contemporary decorator fabrics and entirely machine-stitched, these handsome mats take an up-to-date approach to this old-fashioned craft.

Although the Goose Tracks design, *top*, and the Double Square pattern, *bottom*, are simply variations of two time-honored patterns, the colors and fabrics give them a new look. Place mats like these are just as at home on chrome and glass as they are atop pine or oak.

When planning your own patch-work projects, keep in mind that the character of any design is influenced by the fabrics used in the pattern. Don't hesitate to experiment with colors and prints to discover those you like best.

COUNTRY PLEASURES

Traditional folk art motifs—used on the hooked rug, *right*—look fresh and new when they are worked in bright pastels.

Pennsylvania Dutch designs inspired the seven patterns found on this striking rug. Using wool yarn, work the designs into sturdy background fabric. (Mount the fabric in a wooden frame to keep it taut.) For hooking, use a rug punch tool.

This inexpensive tool will enable you to create a rug in less than half the time it takes to hook a rug by hand. Punch tools, as well as rug hooking frames, are available from specialty craft shops.

The rug shown measures approximately 27x44 inches. Each design motif is 7 inches square, excluding the borders. You can adjust the size or shape of the rug by altering the number or arrangement of the squares. Colors, as always, can be adjusted to suit your taste.

To make this rug a focal point for a room in your home, enlarge several of the motifs to use as appliqué patterns for companion pillows. Small versions of individual design elements—such as hearts, tulips, or birds—might be adapted for stenciled borders around a window frame or along a chair back.

For example, a portion of the heart motif in the lower right corner of the rug appears on the table runner shown on pages 6 and 7. Other appropriate applications for these delightful patterns are sure to occur to you as your rug project progresses.

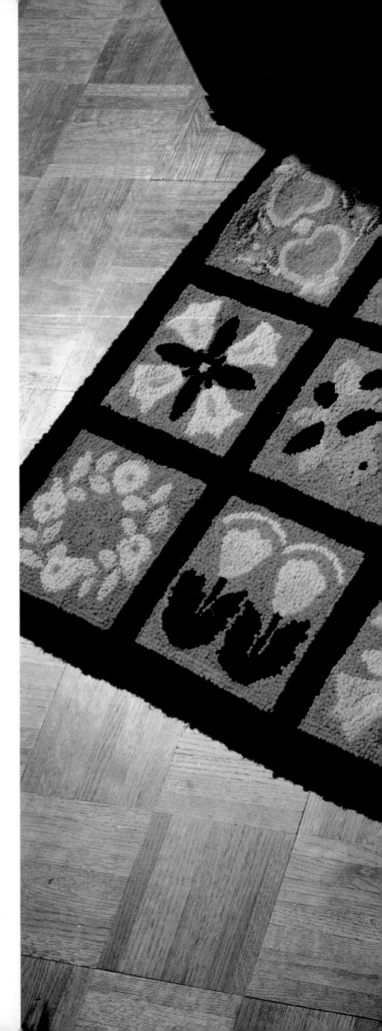

COUNTRY PLEASURES

Gift your home at holiday time with folk-art-inspired accessories to enjoy throughout the year.

The wooden checkerboard, *left,* for example, serves as a festive tray for party snacks at Christmas, then does daily duty for family games the rest of the year. The painted ships and ocean-wave border on this handsome, 17x22-inch board are adapted from a traditional cross-stitch sampler. (You'll find full-size patterns to trace in the instructions.)

Dress up your hearth for the holidays with the charming cross-stitch rug, *above,* another sampler-inspired design. Work narrow strips of calico fabric into No. 4 rug canvas to create this 28x51-inch country carpet with season-spanning appeal. Stitch the design as shown, or create your own using any cross-stitch pattern you like.

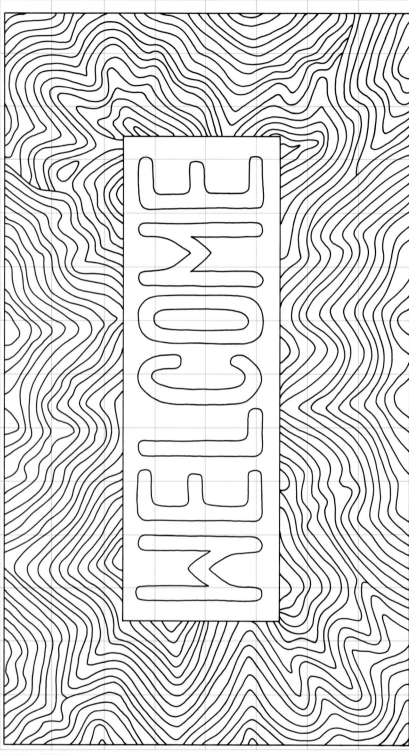

HAND-HOOKED WELCOME RUG   1 Square = 2 Inches

"Welcome" Rug

Shown on page 80.
Finished size is 16x27½ inches.

MATERIALS

⅔ yard of closely woven burlap or monk's cloth (backing)
Strips (¼ to ½ inch wide) of medium-weight wool fabrics
Permanent marking pen
Rug hooking tool and frame
Rug binding tape
Liquid latex rug backing (optional)

INSTRUCTIONS

Enlarge pattern, *left;* each ripple in the design is about ¼ inch wide. Transfer design, centered, onto 24x35 inches of backing fabric; trace outlines with permanent pen.

Hem backing fabric to prevent raveling. Mount onto a rug frame, making sure that horizontal and vertical threads are perpendicular and parallel to edges of the frame.

Begin by hooking the WELCOME letters in double rows of gray wool strips. Work with one hand above the frame, hooking the strips; place the other hand, holding the strips, beneath the frame.

To start a strip, slip the hook through the top of the backing and pull the end of a wool strip through to the top so it extends about ½ inch (trim end later). Next, about two threads away from previous stitch, slip hook through top again. Pick up wool strip and pull it up and through the backing, making a loop about ⅜ inch above backing.

Repeat the hook-down-and-pull-up motion, keeping loops a uniform ⅜ inch high, until strip is finished, or until line of design is completed.

After hooking WELCOME letters (each letter is two rows wide), work background color of center rectangle. Then, working from the center of the design toward the edges, hook ripples of color; each ripple is one row of loops wide.

When hooking is completed, remove rug from frame. Trim ends to match height of hooked pile. Trim unhooked fabric backing to within 1 inch of hooked edges of design. Tack raw edges to back; cover with

1-inch-wide strips of rug binding tape. Prevent strips from pulling out of rug by applying two coats of liquid latex to back, if desired.

"Welcome" Sign

Shown on page 81.
Finished size is 8½x11½ inches.

MATERIALS

9x12-inch piece of perforated paper (available in crafts shops or from Astor Place, Ltd., 239 Main Ave., Stirling, NJ 07980)
Embroidery floss in red, purple, lavender, celery, olive, brown, and yellow; tapestry needle
Graph paper; colored pencils

INSTRUCTIONS

Transfer design, *right,* onto graph paper using colored pencils. Complete design by flopping the border pattern. To simplify stitching, transfer the design onto perforated paper using colored pencils.

Using six strands of floss, work satin stitches, cross-stitches, and small straight stitches as indicated on diagram. Frame as desired.

Knitted Afghan

Shown on page 82.
Finished size is 48x59 inches.

MATERIALS

Unger Aries (100-gram balls) knitting worsted: 6 balls of No. 560 white (MC), and 2 balls *each* of No. 417 light blue (A), No. 415 dark blue (B), No. 427 light green (C), and No. 426 teal (D)
Size 8 knitting needles, or size needed to obtain gauge
Size 8 circular knitting needles, 29 inches long

Abbreviations: See page 35.
Gauge: Motif is a 5½-inch square.

INSTRUCTIONS

MOTIF (Make 80): With MC cast on 3 sts. *Row 1* (right side): K in front *continued*

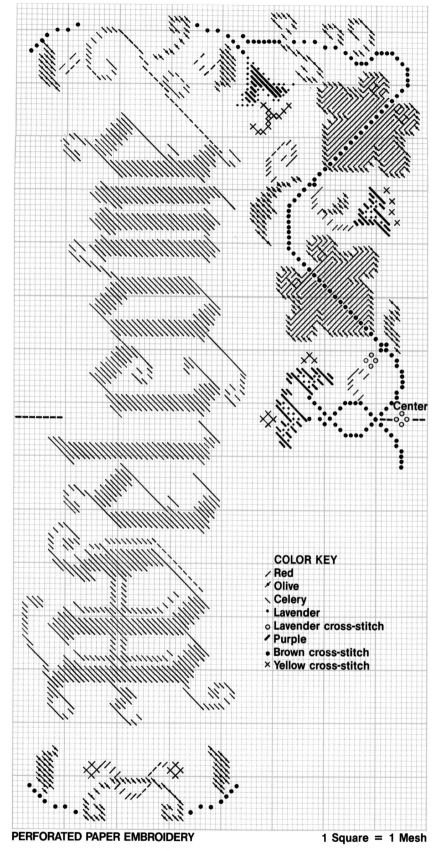

COLOR KEY
⟋ Red
⟋ Olive
⟍ Celery
· Lavender
○ Lavender cross-stitch
⟋ Purple
● Brown cross-stitch
✕ Yellow cross-stitch

PERFORATED PAPER EMBROIDERY   **1 Square = 1 Mesh**

continued from page 91
Country Pleasures

and back of first st (inc made), yo, k 1, yo, inc in last st—7 sts. *Row 2:* K 2, p 3, k 2. *Row 3:* Inc 1, k 2, yo, k 1, yo, k 2, inc 1—11 sts. *Row 4:* K 3, p 5, k 3. *Row 5:* Inc 1, k 4, yo, k 1, yo, k 4, inc 1—15 sts. *Row 6:* K 4, p 7, k 4. *Row 7:* Inc, k 6, yo, k 1, yo, k 6, inc—19 sts. *Row 8:* K 5, p 9, k 5. *Row 9:* Inc, k 8, yo, k 1, yo, k 8, inc—23 sts.

Row 10: K 6, p 11, k 6. *Row 11:* Inc, k 5, sl 1, k 1, psso, k 3, yo, k 1, yo, k 3, k 2 tog, k 5, inc—25 sts. *Row 12:* K 7, p 11, k 7. *Row 13:* Inc, k 6, sl 1, k 1, psso, k 7, k 2 tog, k 6, inc.

Row 14: K 8, p 9, k 8. *Row 15:* Inc, k 7, sl 1, k 1, psso, k 5, k 2 tog, k 7, inc. *Row 16:* K 9, p 7, k 9. *Row 17:* Inc, k 8, sl 1, k 1, psso, k 3, k 2 tog, k 8, inc. *Row 18:* K 10, p 5, k 10. *Row 19:* Inc, k 9, sl 1, k 1, psso, k 1, k 2 tog, k 9, inc. *Row 20:* K 11, p 3, k 11. *Row 21:* Inc, k 10, sl 1, k 1, psso, k 11, inc—26 sts. *Row 22:* K 12, p 2, k 12. *Row 23:* Inc, k 11, sl 1, k 1, psso, k 11, inc—27 sts.

Row 24: K. Change to contrasting color. Complete motifs as follows, making 20 each with A, B, C, and D.

Row 25: K across dec 1 st each end (to dec, work 2 sts tog)—25 sts. *Row 26:* P. *Row 27:* Rep Row 25—23 sts. *Row 28:* K. *Row 29:* P across dec 1 st each end—21 sts. *Row 30:* K. *Rows 31–48:* Rep rows 25–30 three times—3 sts on last row. *Row 49:* Sl 1, k 2 tog, psso. Fasten off.

With leaves at center, arrange motifs in groups of four (five across by four down), having one section of each color at points where color sections meet.

BORDER (Work each side separately): *Row 1:* With right side facing, circular needle, and C, pick up and k across a side having 24 sts across each motif and 2 sts in each corner st (inc made at each end). Continuing to inc 1 st at each end of every row, work as follows: *Row 2:* P. *Row 3:* K. *Row 4:* With D, p across. *Row 5:* P. *Row 6:* K. *Row 7:* P. *Row 8:* With A, p across. *Row 9:* K. *Row 10:* P. *Row 11:* With B, k across. *Row 12:* K. *Row 13:* P. *Row 14:* K. *Row 15:* P. *Row 16:* K. *Row 17:* P. Bind off. Sew border ends tog for mitered corner.

Crocheted Pillows

Shown on page 83.
Pillow top is 18 inches square.

MATERIALS
DMC No. 3 pearl cotton (147-yard balls): 3 balls of one color for *each* pillow top
Size 3 steel crochet hook
1 yard of polished cotton, or other durable contrasting fabric
2¼ yards of cording
Fiberfill or pillow form

Abbreviations: See right.
Gauge: 6 trc = 1 inch; 2 rows = 1 inch.

INSTRUCTIONS
Ch 8, join with sl st to form ring.

Rnd 1: Ch 4, 3 trc in ring, (ch 5, 4 trc in ring) 3 times; ch 3, dc in top of ch-4. (*Note:* When working following rows, beginning ch-4 of previous row will be considered a trc.)

Rnds 2–4: Ch 4, 2 trc over dc, * trc over each trc, (3 trc, ch 5, 3 trc) in next space for corner. Rep from * around, ending with 3 trc in last corner space, ch 3, dc in top of beg ch-4. (*Note:* Hereafter, last corner on each rnd will be finished this way.)

Rnd 5: Ch 4, 2 trc over dc, * trc in first trc, ch 10, sk 7 trc, sc in each of next 6 trc, ch 10, sk 7 trc, trc in last trc, make (3 trc, ch 5, 3 trc) in corner. Rep from * around.

Rnd 6: Ch 4, 2 trc over dc, * trc in first trc, ch 15, sk 2 sts, trc in last trc of same group, 3 trc over lp, ch 9, sk first sc, make sc in 4 center sc, ch 9, 3 trc over lp, trc in first trc, ch 15, sk 2 sts, trc in last trc, make (3 trc, ch 5, 3 trc) in corner. Rep from * around.

Rnd 7: Ch 4, 2 trc over dc, * trc in first trc, ch 7, 2 sc over lp, ch 7, trc in fourth trc of next group, 3 trc over lp, ch 10, sc in each of 2 center sc, ch 10, 3 trc over lp, trc in first trc, ch 7, 2 sc over lp, ch 7, trc in fourth trc of next group, make (3 trc, ch 5, 3 trc) in corner. Rep from * around.

Rnd 8: Ch 4, 2 trc over dc, * trc in first trc, ch 8, sc over lp, sc in each of 2 sc, sc over next lp, ch 8, trc in fourth trc of next group, 3 trc over lp, ch 2, 3 trc over next lp, trc in first trc, ch 8, sc over lp, sc in each of 2 sc, sc

CROCHET ABBREVIATIONS

beg	begin(ning)
bl	block
ch	chain
cl	cluster
dc	double crochet
dec	decrease
dtr	double triple crochet
fol	following
grp	group
hdc	half double crochet
inc	increase
lp(s)	loop(s)
MC	Main Color
pat	pattern
pc	popcorn
rem	remaining
rep	repeat
rnd(s)	round(s)
sc	single crochet
sk	skip
sl st	slip stitch
sp(s)	space(s)
st(s)	stitch(es)
tog	together
trc	triple crochet
yo	wrap yarn over hook
*	repeat from * as indicated
( )	repeat between ( )'s as indicated
[ ]	repeat between [ ]'s as indicated

over next lp, ch 8, trc in fourth trc of next group, make (3 trc, ch 5, 3 trc) in corner sp. Rep from * around.

Rnd 9: Ch 4, 2 trc over dc, * trc in first trc, ch 10, sc over lp, sc in each of 4 sc, sc over lp, ch 10, trc in fourth trc of next group. Make 2 trc in sp and rep from * across side, with (3 trc, ch 5, 3 trc) in corner. Work other sides to correspond. *Rnds 10–13:* Work same as rnds 6–9; make reps for additional spiderwebs. *Rnd 14:* Ch 4, 2 trc over dc, * trc in each of 4 trc, 3 trc over lp, ch 9, sk first sc, make sc in 4 center sc, ch 9, 3 trc over lp. Rep from * twice more, trc in last 4 trc, make (3 trc, ch 5, 3 trc) in corner. Work other sides same way.

Rnd 15: Ch 4, 2 trc over dc, * trc in each of 10 trc, 3 trc over lp, ch 10, sc in each of 2 center sc, ch 10, 3 trc over lp. Rep from * twice more, trc in last 10 trc, make (3 trc, ch 5, 3 trc) in corner. Work other sides same way.

Rnd 16: Ch 4, 2 trc over dc, * trc in 16 trc, 3 trc over lp, ch 2, 3 trc over next lp. Rep from * twice more, trc in 16 trc, make (3 trc, ch 5, 3 trc) in corner. Work other sides same way.

Rnd 17: Ch 4, 2 trc over dc, trc in first trc, * ch 2, sk 2 trc, trc in next 4 sts. Rep from * across side, make trc in last trc and (3 trc, ch 5, 3 trc) in corner. Work other sides same way. (Ch-3 sps may be used instead of ch-2 sps on this row to keep work from being too tight.) *Rnd 18:* Ch 4, 2 trc over dc. Make trc in each trc around, with 2 trc over each sp and (3 trc, ch 5, 3 trc) in corners. Fasten off.

TO BLOCK: Draw an 18-inch square on heavy cardboard. Dampen crochet; pin facedown on cardboard, carefully stretching crochet to size. Steam-press; leave flat until dry.

TO ASSEMBLE: Cut two 20-inch squares from the contrasting fabric; cover cording with bias fabric. Center and tack crocheted top to right side of one fabric square, using matching thread.

Sew cording to top, ¼ inch from edge of crochet. With right sides facing, sew cushion front to back; leave one side open. Clip corners, turn, and stuff. Sew opening closed.

Nine-Patch Quilt

Shown on page 84.
Finished size is 65½x76 inches.

MATERIALS

2 yards of dark pindotted fabric (solid squares)
1 yard *each* of light and dark fabric scraps; ⅔ yard of light fabric (inner border); 1½ yards of dark fabric (outer border)
4¼ yards of backing fabric
Quilt batting; ½ yard of dark fabric *or* 8 yards of wide bias tape; cardboard; thread
Water-erasable marking pen

NINE-PATCH QUILT ASSEMBLY DIAGRAM

INSTRUCTIONS

This quilt consists of 4½-inch-square Nine-Patch blocks and plain blocks arranged diagonally. Frame rows with narrow and wide borders; bind in contrasting fabric.

To make a similar quilt, follow the instructions below. Refer to the photograph for color and placement suggestions. Use ¼-inch seams.

TO CUT BLOCKS: Make a 5x5-inch cardboard template. (Measurement includes ¼-inch seam allowance.) Cut 56 squares from dark pindotted fabric.

Cut a 4½-inch-square template in half diagonally for edging triangles; add seam allowances. Use one piece to cut 30 triangles from dark pindotted fabric. For corner triangles, cut remaining triangle template in half (add seam allowances) and use one piece to cut four from dark pindotted fabric. Set pieces aside.

Each Nine-Patch block has four dark- and five light-colored squares. Cut a 2x2-inch template. (Measurement includes seam allowance.) Cut 288 squares from dark fabrics, 360 squares from light fabrics.

TO PIECE BLOCKS: Sew a strip of three squares (light, dark, light). Sew another strip of three (dark, light, dark). Sew a third strip the same as the first. Piece the three strips together to make a checkerboard pattern. Repeat for 72 blocks.

continued

93

continued from page 93
Country Pleasures

TO ASSEMBLE: Following diagram on page 93, join blocks. When diagonal rows are completed, piece rows.

For inner border, cut two 2½x51-inch and two 2½x60-inch strips; piece if necessary. Join to edges of pieced top. For outer border, cut two 6½x76-inch and two 8½x54½-inch strips; piece if necessary. Join to edges of inner border.

TO FINISH: Piece backing to size. Layer backing, batting, and top. Baste together, then quilt as desired. Bind edges with bias tape or 2-inch-wide fabric strips.

Goose Tracks Place Mat
Shown on page 85.
Finished size is 12x17¾ inches.

MATERIALS
For six place mats
1⅛ yards *each* of muslin, fleece, and light print fabric
½ yard *each* of medium and dark print fabrics

INSTRUCTIONS
Trace patterns, *above right.* Cut templates for pattern pieces; add ¼-inch seam allowances. Trace templates on wrong side of fabrics. Cut 18 large (medium print) and 36 small triangles (light print); when tracing small triangles, flop template for other half. Sew small triangles to large ones, forming rectangles (see photograph); make 18. Piece two strips of nine rectangles each.

From light fabric, cut mat center 6½x18½ inches. From dark fabric, cut two ¾x18½-inch strips for piping. Fold strips in half, wrong sides facing; baste to center, raw edges together. Sew pieced strips to center, triangles facing opposite directions. (See diagram, *far right.*)

Cut both muslin and fleece to 12½x18½ inches. Pin muslin to mat, right sides facing, atop fleece. Sew edges; leave opening. Turn; sew opening. Quilt.

Double Square Place Mat
Shown on page 85.
Finished size is 12x17¾ inches.

MATERIALS
For six place mats
1⅛ yards *each* of muslin and fleece
⅝ yard *each* of light and dark print fabrics
½ yard medium print fabric

INSTRUCTIONS
Cut two 1½-inch-square cardboard templates. Cut one square in half diagonally; use one of the triangles for the second template. When cutting from fabrics, trace around templates on the wrong side; add ¼-inch seam allowances to all edges and cut out.

Cut four small squares and eight small triangles from the light print. From the medium print, cut eight small triangles. With right sides facing, sew light and medium triangles into squares.

Cut dark print 3½x9½ inches for the center; also cut two strips 2x6½ inches and two strips 2x12½ inches. From medium print, cut two strips 2x3½ inches and two strips 2x9½ inches.

Follow the diagram, *below left,* to sew mat together, beginning with the center rectangle. (*Note:* Join short strips to short ends of rectangle, then long strips to the long side.)

Finish same as Goose Tracks Place Mat, *left.* *continued*

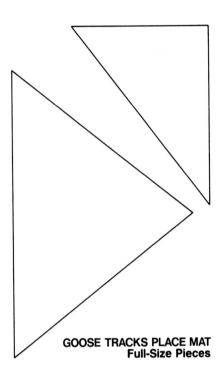

GOOSE TRACKS PLACE MAT
Full-Size Pieces

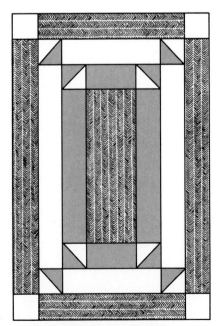

DOUBLE SQUARE PLACE MAT
ASSEMBLY DIAGRAM

GOOSE TRACKS PLACE MAT
ASSEMBLY DIAGRAM

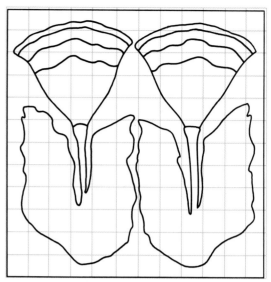

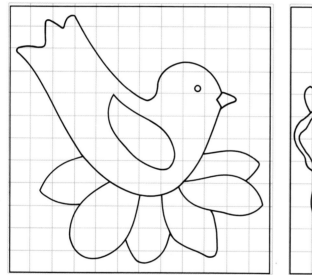

FOLK ART HOOKED RUG

1 Square = 1 Inch

95

LOVE AND JOY RUG

1 Square = 1 Stitch

continued from page 94
Country Pleasures

Folk Art Hooked Rug

Shown on pages 86–87.
Finished size is 27x44 inches.

MATERIALS

Burlap backing; rug punching tool; rug frame; masking tape
Wool yarn or fabric strips in desired colors
Permanent felt-tip marker; paper
Dressmaker's carbon paper
Rug binding; latex rug backing

INSTRUCTIONS

Mark burlap with 15 squares (7x7 inches), leaving 1¼ inches between squares and a 1¾-inch-wide border. Enlarge and transfer patterns from page 95 to squares using dressmaker's carbon paper, or sketch motifs of your choice. Trace lines with permanent marker. Bind edges with masking tape; mount in frame. For hooking, see instructions for "Welcome" Rug, page 90. When hooking is completed, finish edges with rug binding; apply latex to rug back.

Checkerboard

Shown on page 88.

MATERIALS

¾x17x22-inch plywood
Screen molding (edging for board)
Wood glue; small finishing nails
Blue antiquing finish; brush
Acrylic paints; fine brushes
Clear varnish; sandpaper
Tracing and carbon papers

INSTRUCTIONS

Sand board. Cut molding to fit edge; glue and nail in place. Antique the board following kit instructions.

Draw a 13¼-inch square for the checkerboard; center between sides and place bottom of the square 2⅜ inches from the bottom edge of the board. Divide the square into eight rows of eight blocks, each 1⅝x1⅝ inches. Paint blocks, alternating light and dark colors.

Trace border design, pages 98–99. Position top border ⅞ inch from top edge of board and ⅜ inch from checkerboard. Transfer design to board using carbon paper.

COLOR KEY

☐ Background (Cream)	◩ Navy Blue
☑ Light Brown	⊞ Dark Teal
▼ Brown	⊠ Gray
⊟ Light Green	◎ Wine
◉ Dark Green	· Yellow
◼ Blue	▲ Red

For bottom border, refer to photograph and position the water design ¾ inch from bottom of checkerboard; transfer to board.

Refer to the photograph for color placement; paint designs and checkerboard with fine brushes and acrylics. When dry, apply clear varnish.

"Love and Joy" Rug

Shown on page 89.

MATERIALS

No. 4 rug canvas, 31½x54 inches
1¼ yards of backing fabric (optional)
1-inch-wide fabric strips in colors to match color key
Graph paper; colored markers

INSTRUCTIONS

Note: Fabric amounts will vary according to size of rug and designs used; ½ yard of 44-inch-wide fabric will yield 18 strips. Each strip makes about 14 *worked* cross-stitches. For accurate yardages, count number of stitches required for each color.

Refer to diagram, *opposite,* and chart designs onto graph paper using colored markers.

To prepare strips, fold raw edges of 1-inch strips to center; fold in half again and press. Work rug in hand (rather than on a frame) for flexibility. Cross-stitch motifs following charted design, then fill background.

To finish, turn raw edges of canvas under and baste to rug back. Add backing fabric, if desired.

Woodburned Table

Shown on pages 18–19.
Finished tabletop is a 42-inch-diameter circle.

MATERIALS

42-inch-diameter unfinished pine tabletop or round of plywood
Woodburning tool
Watercolors in assorted colors
Artist's brushes; varnish or polyurethane finish
Sandpaper; carbon paper

INSTRUCTIONS

Sand tabletop lightly in one direction, following the grain of the wood. A quadrant of the design is given on page 100. Enlarge the design and transfer to the table using carbon paper.

Practice woodburning on scrap lumber, holding the woodburning tool like a pencil. Practice pressure control by developing a floating touch. The slower the stroke, the darker the tool will burn. Experiment with different effects, then work the design on the tabletop.

Test watercolor paints on scrap wood to determine whether colors will run. Then paint wreath, referring to photograph. Allow each color area to dry thoroughly before adding the next color. Clean and dry brushes between colors.

When tabletop is completely dry, sand edges again; varnish entire top. When dry, sand lightly and apply varnish or clear polyurethane.

Woodburned Robins

Shown on page 18.
Finished bird is 2⅛x5½ inches.

MATERIALS

½-inch pine
Drill with ¼-inch bit
¼-inch dowels
Watercolors; polyurethane
Carbon paper; wood glue
Woodburning tool; jigsaw

INSTRUCTIONS

Trace pattern, page 100, onto pine board. If making more than one, leave 1-inch spaces between birds. Wood-burn all lines of design. Paint with watercolors, referring to photograph for colors. Using jigsaw, cut robin ⅛ inch outside woodburned lines. Sand and varnish. Drill holes along bottoms of robins for dowels.

Sunshine and Shadow Quilt

Shown on page 7.
Finished size is approximately 42 inches square.

MATERIALS

⅛ yard *each* of brown, dark green, light green, pink, red, and light blue fabrics
⅜ yard *each* of gray-purple and bright purple fabrics
1 yard of gray-blue fabric
1¼ yards of backing fabric
5 yards of wide black bias tape
Quilt batting; curtain rings

INSTRUCTIONS

Preshrink all fabrics. Using the diagram on page 101 for reference, cut 1½-inch squares in colors indicated; piece to make the center of the quilt. Use ¼-inch seams throughout.

Next, cut four 3-inch squares of gray-purple fabric for corner blocks of the first border; cut four 3x21½-inch strips of bright purple. Sew squares onto short ends of two strips; set aside. Sew remaining two strips to top and bottom of pieced center square. Stitch the pieced borders to sides of center.

For the outer border, cut four 8-inch squares of gray-purple and four 8x26½-inch strips of gray-blue fabric. Join two squares to short ends of two strips; set aside. Stitch remaining strips to top and bottom of first border, then add pieced outer borders to sides.

Cut quilt backing and batting to size. Sandwich batting between top and backing; quilt as desired. Bind edges of quilt with black bias tape.

If desired, stitch curtain rings to the top back of the quilt for hanging.

Crocheted Afghan

Shown on pages 6–7.
Finished size is 54x65 inches.

MATERIALS

Unger Aries knitting worsted (3.5-ounce balls): 10 balls of No. 423 green; 3 balls of No. 570 bright blue; 4 balls of No. 474 fuchsia
Size H aluminum crochet hook

Abbreviations: See page 92.
Gauge: 16 sc = 5 inches.

INSTRUCTIONS

Note: Turning chains always count as first st of row.

With green, ch 176.

Foundation Row: Dc in fourth ch from hook and in each rem ch; ch 2, turn—174 dc, counting turning-ch as dc. *Row 1* (right side): Sk first dc, dc around post *from front* of each of next 2 dc; * dc around post *from back* of each of next 3 dc; dc around post *from front* of next 3 dc; rep from * across; end dc around post from back of last 2 dc, dc in turning ch-3 lp. *Row 2:* Ch 3, turn; dc in each dc across; end dc in turning ch-lp.

Row 3: Ch 2, turn; sk first dc, dc around post *from back* of each of
continued

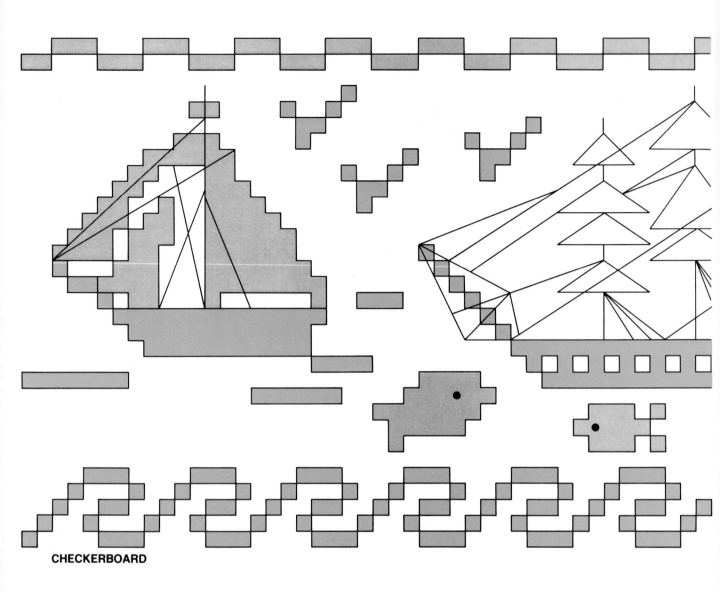

CHECKERBOARD

continued from page 97
Country Pleasures

next 2 dc; * dc around post *from front* of each of next 3 dc; dc around post *from back* of next 3 dc; rep from * across; end dc around post *from front* of last 2 dc, dc in turning ch-lp.

Row 4: Rep Row 2. Rep rows 1–4 for pat 3 times more; then rep Row 1. Continuing with green over next 21 sts only, work until length of strip measures 60 inches from beg; end with even row of pat; fasten off. Join green 21 sts from the end of the horizontal border strip, ch 3; beg with Row 2 of pattern, work the border to correspond with the opposite border strip; fasten off.

BLUE BORDERS: With right side facing, join blue in next unworked dc (22nd dc) of green horizontal border; ch 1, sc in same st as join and in next 131 sts; ch 1, turn—132 sc made. *Row 1:* Sc in first sc; * ch 1, sk next sc, sc in next sc, sc in skipped sc; rep from * across row; end sc in last sc; ch 1, turn.

Row 2: Sc in first sc; in *each* ch-1 sp across work 2 sc; sc in last sc; ch 1, turn—132 sc.

Rep rows 1–2 for a total of 2½ inches, ending with Row 2. Continue with blue over next 9 sc only; work pat as follows: *Row 1:* Sc in first sc, (ch 1, sk next sc, sc in next sc, sc in skipped sc) 4 times; ch 1, turn.

Row 2: (In each ch-1 sp work 2 sc) 4 times; sc in last sc; ch 1, turn.

Rep rows 1–2 until *total* length of blue strip is 50½ inches, ending with Row 1. Fasten off. Join blue 9 sts from the end of unworked green horizontal border strip. Ch 1, work strip to correspond with first blue strip; fasten off.

FUCHSIA PANEL: Join fuchsia in next unworked sc of blue horizontal border. Ch 1, sc in same st as join and in next 15 sts, ch 1, turn—16 sc.

Row 1: Sc in first sc and each sc across row, ch 1, turn.

Rep Row 1 until length of strip is 47 inches; fasten off.

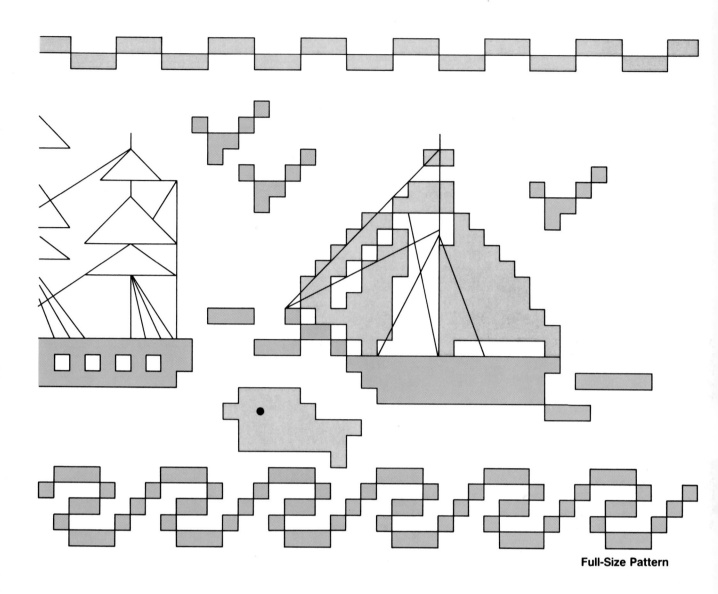

Full-Size Pattern

GREEN PANEL: Join green in next unworked sc of blue horizontal border, ch 2, dc in each of next 15 sc, ch 2, turn.

Row 1: (Sk next dc, dc in next dc, ch 1, dc around post *from front* of skipped dc) 7 times; dc in turning ch-lp; ch 2, turn.

Row 2: Sk first dc, dc in each of next 14 dc (sk all ch-1 sts); end dc in turning ch-lp, ch 2, turn.

Rep rows 1–2 until length of strip is 47 inches; fasten off.

* Decreasing 1 st on first row, repeat Fuchsia Panel over next unworked 17 sc of blue horizontal border—16 sc. Work even over 16 sts for 47 inches.

Rep Green Panel over next unworked 16 sc of blue horizontal border. Rep from * once more.

Rep Fuchsia Panel over rem unworked 16 sc of horizontal blue border. Whipstitch panels tog, keeping patterns aligned. (Green outside border panels should be 3 inches longer than remaining panels.)

Join blue in top of blue strip, and work in pat over 9 stitches. Sc across tops of rem panels, *and at the same time* inc 2 sts and work in pattern over remaining 9 blue border sts—132 sc across row.

Working in pat as established for blue border over 132 sts, rep rows 1 and 2 for 2½ inches. Fasten off.

Whipstitch blue panels to outside green border panels. Join green, and work in green border pattern over 174 sts to correspond to opposite end; fasten off.

BORDER: *Rnd 1:* Join fuchsia in any corner sp; ch 1. Sc evenly spaced around afghan as follows: On short ends, dec over every tenth and eleventh stitches to keep work flat. On long ends, work 2 sc around turning ch-3 sts and 1 sc around turning ch-2 stitches. Join to first sc. *Rnd 2:* Working *clockwise,* ch 1, sc in next sc, * ch 1, sc in next sc, rep from * around; join to sc at beg of rnd; fasten off. Block afghan to finished size.

continued

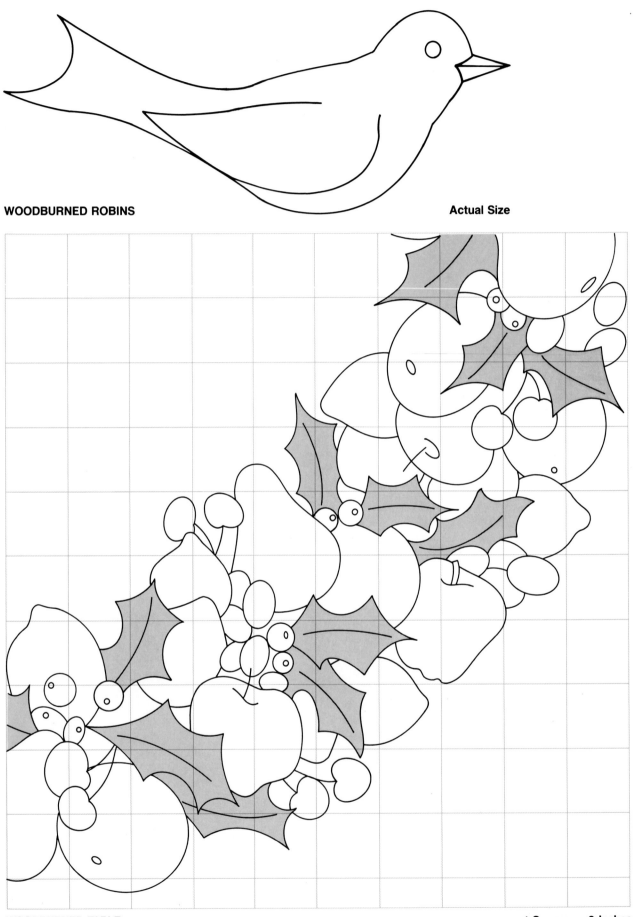

WOODBURNED ROBINS   **Actual Size**

WOODBURNED TABLE   **1 Square = 2 Inches**

COLOR KEY

- ⊞ **Bright Purple**
- ⊙ **Gray Purple**
- ■ **Dark Green**
- ⊡ **Light Green**
- ▲ **Gray Blue**
- ☐ **Light Blue**
- ◢ **Red**
- ⊘ **Pink**
- ⊠ **Brown**

continued from page 99
Country Pleasures

Magazine Rack Cover

Shown on pages 6–7.
Finished design can be adapted to any purchased magazine rack.

MATERIALS

Purchased magazine rack
Cotton fabric and polyester batting in sufficient yardage to cover rack (sling)
Scraps of solid-colored fabric (prairie points, piping)
Cording; thread; heavy paper
Water-erasable marking pen

INSTRUCTIONS

Make a paper pattern from sling included with purchased magazine rack; add 2¾ inches to *each* short end and ¾ inch to *each* long edge (these measurements allow for ¼-inch seams, overlaps on short ends, and quilting). Cut two pieces from cotton fabric and one from batting.

To make prairie points, cut seven (or a sufficient number for width of sling) 2½-inch squares from scrap fabrics. Fold each square in half diagonally, and then fold in half again so that all raw edges align; press. Make a piping strip the width of short end of sling front. Position piping, then prairie points along one short end, with points of triangles facing downward and raw edges aligned. Baste in place.

Layer front and back, right sides facing, atop batting; leave opening on side to turn. Clip corners and turn; blindstitch opening closed.

Mark diamond quilting lines on fabric using water-erasable marking pen. Machine-quilt on lines. Place on rack to mark top fold lines.

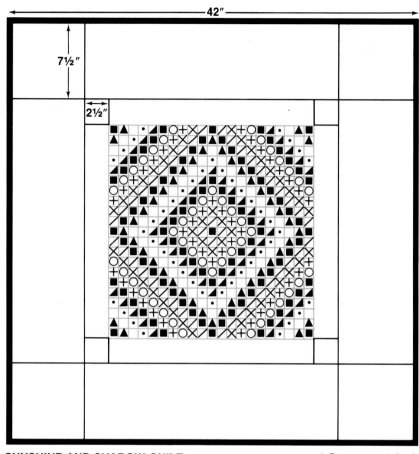

SUNSHINE AND SHADOW QUILT

42"

7½"

2½"

1 Square = 1 Inch

Remove from rack, fold down ends, and stitch in place. Slide dowels into sling and assemble rack.

Table Runner

Shown on page 6.
Finished size may be adapted for any size table.

MATERIALS

2⅓ yards of 45-inch-wide navy cotton fabric; paper
½ yard of light rose cotton fabric
¼ yard of dark rose cotton fabric
⅛ yard *each* of light green, dark green, blue, purple, brown, pink, and black cotton fabric
5 yards of cording
16x80 inches of polyester batting
Sewing and quilting thread
Water-erasable marking pen

INSTRUCTIONS

Use ¼-inch seams throughout.

Make paper pattern for runner. The runner shown is 60 inches on each side with a 9½-inch triangular drop at each end. Cut front and back from navy fabric, adding ¼ inch all around for seams.

Make 74 prairie points (or sufficient amount for your runner), referring to instructions for Magazine Rack Cover, *left*. Make piping; baste on seam line. Tack prairie points in place. Layer front and back, right sides facing, atop batting; sew together, leaving an opening. Trim, turn, close opening, and press.

Sketch your own design, or enlarge one from this book (we used a motif from the Folk Art Hooked Rug, shown on pages 86–87). Cut the design from fabrics, adding ¼-inch seam allowances. Turn edges under; appliqué to runner. Quilt as desired.

PAINT AND PAPER PATCHWORK

For a fresh twist to the country look, translate favorite patchwork patterns into paint or paper designs for your walls or floors. A plus is that each of these no-sew "quilts" is a snap to piece.

PAINT AND PAPER PATCHWORK

To re-create this spectacular cut-and-paste Log Cabin design for your wall, first locate a couple of old wallpaper sample books containing small prints (ask in wallpaper shops for books of discontinued styles).

You'll also need a metal straightedge, a single-edge razor blade or crafts knife, vinyl wallpaper paste, and a brush to apply the paste.

The Straight Furrow Log Cabin design pictured here is 75 inches square.

It consists of thirty-six 12½-inch blocks arranged in six rows containing six blocks each.

Sort the papers into three sets of light colors and three of dark. Collect a stack of medium tones for the block centers.

1 Using a razor or knife and a straightedge, cut thirty-six 3½-inch squares from the medium-tone papers (one for the center of each block). Cut light and dark papers into 1½-inch-wide strips for the logs.

Assemble the squares and strips into 36 Log Cabin blocks. For ease in handling, arrange each block on a 12½-inch tray of paper, *left.*

2 Center and mark a 75-inch square on the wall. With a brush, spread vinyl wallpaper paste in the lower left corner of the penciled square and press the paper pieces of one quilt block in place.

Continue pasting pieces in place, one square at a time, *left,* until the quilt is completely assembled.

Instructions begin on page 108.

PAINT AND PAPER PATCHWORK

Spruce up the front porch or family room with a painted One-Patch-patterned floor design in soothing shades of gray and white, *left*.

For this project you'll need one gallon each of white and dark gray deck paint, brushes, a metal yardstick, pencils, and lots of masking tape.

With pencil and yardstick, measure and mark the perimeter of the design. Paint the porch floor outside the marked area a dark gray, and paint the inside area of the design white.

When the paint is dry, pencil in the squares and borders of the design. Set off the lightest areas with masking tape and paint them first. When these are dry, remove the tape and repeat the taping and painting process for the medium and dark areas of the design. Allow ample drying time between coats.

For subtle color variations on the medium and dark squares, mix the gray and white paints together in different ratios.

For instant impact in a small space, paint a patchwork pattern on a wall. The Diamond-in-a-Square design, *top*, is just 24 inches square, but this traditional Amish pattern can be adjusted to suit any available wall.

1 Begin by planning the pattern on paper pieced to the size of the wall you plan to paint. Then, in pencil, lightly sketch the outlines of the design on the wall, *above left*.

2 Mark the lightest areas of the design with masking tape; paint these first. Remove the tape and allow the paint to dry thoroughly, then repeat the taping and painting steps for medium and then for dark colors, *above right*.

107

PAINT AND PAPER PATCHWORK

Paper-and-Paste Log Cabin Quilt

Shown on page 105.
Finished size is 75x75 inches.

MATERIALS

10–15 pages of vinyl wallpaper samples in each of the following seven color groups: lights, medium lights, dark lights, medium tones (for center squares), light darks, medium darks, and darks
Metal straightedge; pencil
Single-edge razor or crafts knife
Vinyl wallpaper paste and brush
Wallpaper roller or brayer
Molding trim

INSTRUCTIONS

From wallpaper sample books, tear 10–15 pages for each of the seven color groups. To begin, cut thirty-six 3½-inch squares from the *medium-tone* papers for the center squares of the quilt blocks; set aside.

Next, cut the remaining six sets of color-grouped pages into the following strips, using a razor or crafts knife and a metal straightedge to ensure accuracy (you may have to piece the longest strips): Lights: Thirty-six 1½x9½-inch strips and thirty-six 1½x11-inch strips.

Medium lights: 36 strips 1½x6½ inches and 36 strips 1½x8 inches.

Dark lights: Thirty-six 1½x3½-inch strips and thirty-six 1½x5-inch strips.

Light darks: Thirty-six 1½x5-inch strips and thirty-six 1½x6½-inch strips.

Medium darks: Thirty-six 1½x8-inch strips and thirty-six 1½x9½-inch strips.

Darks: 36 strips 1½x11 inches and 36 strips 1½x12½ inches.

Note: All measurements *must* be exact for the paper-quilt blocks to fit together perfectly.

Referring to the diagram, *above right,* arrange the center squares (medium tones) and light and dark strips into 36 quilt blocks. For ease in handling, assemble each block on a 12½x12½-inch piece of paper.

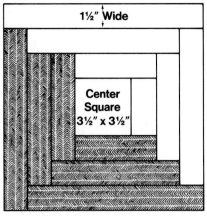

LOG CABIN SQUARE BLOCK

To transfer the quilt design to the wall, pencil thirty-six 12½-inch-square blocks on the wall, arranged in six rows of six blocks each.

With a paintbrush, spread a thin coat of vinyl wallpaper paste in the lower left corner block on the wall. Beginning with the center square and the light strips of one paper-quilt block, press the square and strips into the paste. Work quickly to complete the block before the paste dries. Adjust the position of the strips by pushing them into place with your fingers.

Work diagonally from the lower left corner toward the upper right corner of the design, placing the dark halves of the blocks adjacent to the dark halves of the preceding row. Place the light halves against the light halves for the next row. (See photograph, page 105.)

Make sure the edges of the paper strips are perfectly aligned. Press each completed quilt block with a dry paint roller or brayer to make sure the strips lie absolutely flat.

Frame the completed paper quilt with strips of molding that are cut to size. Paint these strips white or a color of your choice. Then nail or glue them directly onto the wall.

Diamond-in-a-Square Painted Wall Quilt

Shown on page 107.
Finished size is 24 inches square.

MATERIALS

Quick-drying latex interior paints in 3 colors of your choice
1-inch-wide brushes
Masking tape; level; pencil
Metal yardstick
Artist's brushes for touch-ups

INSTRUCTIONS

This design works best on a light background. To paint a pattern on a dark wall, paint the area the design is to cover with white primer.

To begin, mark a 24-inch square on the wall, using the metal yardstick, level, and pencil. Next, mark 3-inch-wide bars inside the square. Then mark 1¾-inch-wide bars inside the first set. Mark the center of the innermost line on all sides of the square; connect these four dots to form the center diamond in the pattern. (See diagram, *below left.*)

Use good-quality masking tape to mask off the lightest areas of the pattern first, pressing the edges of the tape firmly to prevent paint from seeping beneath them.

Brush on the lightest color paint with smooth, even strokes. Within 3 minutes of painting, carefully pull away the tape. Allow the first color to dry, then repeat the procedure for the medium color, then the dark color. Allow ample drying time between the coats. When painting is completed and all tape has been removed, touch up the quilt design with artist's brushes, if necessary.

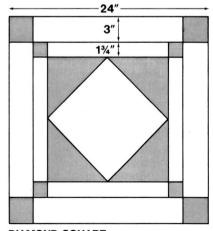

DIAMOND SQUARE

Painted One-Patch Porch Floor

Shown on page 106.

MATERIALS

Graph paper
One gallon each of latex porch and deck paint in gray and white (or colors of your choice)
Brushes; metal yardstick
Pencil; masking tape
Tin cans or plastic containers for mixing colors; varnish

INSTRUCTIONS

First, work out the dimensions of the floor design on graph paper to suit the available space. (See diagram, *below,* for pattern and proportions.)

With yardstick and pencil, measure and mark the perimeter of your design on the floor. Paint the floor around the design dark gray; paint the inside of the design area white. When paint is dry, mark the lines of all the elements within the design.

To paint the design, use masking tape to mask off the lightest areas; paint gray squares and borders. For color variations, mix gray and white paints in slightly different proportions for each patch of the design.

When all tape has been removed and paint is dry, touch up any drips or smudges with an artist's brush.

Protect the painted area with several coats of polyurethane varnish.

ONE-PATCH DIAGRAM

OTHER USES FOR PATCHWORK DESIGNS

Dozens of other quilt patterns lend themselves to cut-and-paste or paint techniques. Simple geometric patterns are most suitable for both types of projects. Straight-edge shapes (squares, rectangles, strips, and triangles) are the easiest to cut and piece, or to paint. The success of projects like these depends on your patience and accuracy.

Color also is crucial. You might first work out your design on graph paper using colored pencils. This will give you an idea of your design and the interplay of colors.

Or work out various color schemes to suit your decorating taste. Consider shades of one color, a two-color pattern, or a multicolored pattern.

Before painting a design, paint sheets of poster board using latex paints in the colors you've selected. Cut out the appropriate shapes from each of the painted boards and arrange them into your pattern to check the way the colors relate to each other. If necessary, change colors, or their values, to enhance your project.

Work the same way with paper. Using samples of the papers you've selected, create a miniature design before you begin the large project.

If you're a bit timid about pasting or painting a design directly onto a wall or floor, create your pattern on plywood or foam-core board (for paper quilts) or artist's canvas (for painted patchwork). Designs painted on canvas can be stretched and mounted on walls. Or, properly primed and protected with several coats of polyurethane, they can be used as floorcloths.

Cut-and-paste patchwork might also be used to embellish a tabletop, tray inserts, cabinet fronts, a toy chest, or other furniture. Protect papered surfaces, such as tabletops, with several coats of polyurethane if they will be subjected to wear and tear.

In addition to whole quilts, such as those pictured on pages 106–107, consider using individual quilt-block patterns. You can highlight architectural details by painting patterns on stair risers and above a ceiling beam. Or paint different but complementary quilt-block patterns on each side of a wooden-cube table.

OLD-FASHIONED FLORALS

Flowers of every size, shape, and shade have offered abundant inspiration to stitchery enthusiasts through the years. Here is a fresh bouquet of designs— in appliqué, embroidery, needlepoint, and crochet— for you to choose from.

Reminiscent of a more graceful era, the lovely floral bedspread, *right,* lends an irresistible air of romance to any setting. The soft pastels and beguiling mix of embroidery and appliqué techniques are typical of designs popular in the 1920s and '30s.

To re-create this single-bed-size summer spread, stitch the designs on a purchased coverlet or a good-quality muslin sheet, using pastel fabrics with a slightly faded look for the blossoms.

To adapt the design for a larger spread, enlarge the pattern pieces or add more flowers to the design.

You also can rearrange these delightful blossoms to suit other projects for your home. For example, the vaseful of flowers would make a beautiful stitchery wall hanging, and the floral spray at the head of the spread might easily be pruned to fit a pillow top.

Directions begin on page 122.

OLD-FASHIONED FLORALS

Gracing the table, *opposite,* and shown close up *at left* is a dainty ribbon-work runner. It probably was stitched around the turn of the century as a pretty window panel or fancy dresser scarf.

With the help of a charted pattern and modern materials, you can reproduce this lovely bit of stitchery for any number of decorative uses.

Stitched on nylon net with narrow silk or rayon ribbons in various pastel tints, the panel would make an elegant curtain for a special window or a glass panel in a door.

Or, for a beautiful table runner, you might work the design in floss on fine linen or cotton.

All of the embroidery is worked in simple straight and satin stitches. So even if you are new to needlework, you'll find this an easy project to stitch.

OLD-FASHIONED FLORALS

Intricate floral patterns are perennial favorites with many crocheters, and pictured here is one of the prettiest.

This exquisitely patterned cloth could almost be called a crocheted variation on the familiar Grandmother's Flower Garden quilt pattern. Each circular block of the design looks like a nosegay of eight dainty blossoms clustered around a single white flower (see detail, *above*).

The flowers are linked by filler motifs reminiscent of stepping-stones in the garden. A lacy scalloped border completes this 45-inch-square tablecloth.

OLD-
FASHIONED
FLORALS

Fine filet crochet captures the ruffled petals and slender foliage of graceful carnations on the panel inserts for these handsome, handcrafted shutters, *right*.

The pair of inserts on the left is a mirror image of the pair on the right, so there are only two parts to the pattern. Also, the motif on one half of the design is an extension of the motif on the adjoining half.

Many filet crochet patterns of appropriate size may be adapted for similar window treatment. Simply divide the design into insert-size slices, and crochet each slice separately.

These crocheted panels were designed specifically for the shutters in which they're used. But you could easily adapt any design to suit the dimensions of purchased shutters. Simply extend or reduce the background mesh along the top, bottom, and sides of the motif.

116

OLD-FASHIONED FLORALS

No matter what the season, the view from *this* window is always filled with flowers, thanks to the clever fool-the-eye shade, *above*.

To make a scene-stealer like this one, embroider the design on a translucent curtain panel in a special version of the outline stitch (see instructions). Even the delicate strings of fringe and the gathers in the shade are stitched on.

Lush poppies, leaves, and a lacing of ribbons—worked in running and stem stitches—pattern the cloth, *opposite*.

Embroider this 35x45-inch design on white fabric using bright-colored thread. Or stitch it in pale thread atop a darker ground.

OLD-FASHIONED FLORALS

It took Grace Snyder 16 months to piece the remarkable Flower Basket quilt shown *at right.* Based on a floral motif found on a favorite set of china, this museum-quality quilt is a one-of-a-kind tour de force. But even a beginning needlepointer can create the striking rug and matching pillow, *opposite,* from a pattern based on Grace's exquisite design.

Scotch stitches—worked over 10-count canvas for the rug and 14-count canvas for the pillow—mimic the intricate detail of the patchwork. And rich wool yarns in jewellike tones capture the vibrant colors of the original fabrics.

A closeup view, *left,* of this quilt reveals that the design is composed of small, postage-stamp-size blocks of fabric. Each of the blocks is pieced from two tiny right triangles, usually representing a light and a dark shade of the same color.

INSTRUCTIONS FOR OLD-FASHIONED FLORALS

Appliquéd Coverlet
Shown on pages 110–111.

MATERIALS
Twin-size muslin sheet (66x96 inches), or sufficient yardage to piece coverlet

Cotton broadcloth in the following amounts and colors: ⅜ yard *each* of blue and tan; ¼ yard *each* of pink and green

Embroidery floss in colors shown on the color key

Embroidery needle

Embroidery hoop

INSTRUCTIONS
Two patterns are given for the coverlet—one for the center, *below,* and one for the top, *opposite.* Connect marks around designs to make a grid; enlarge both patterns.

Turn up 1½-inch hem all around on coverlet or along sheet sides.

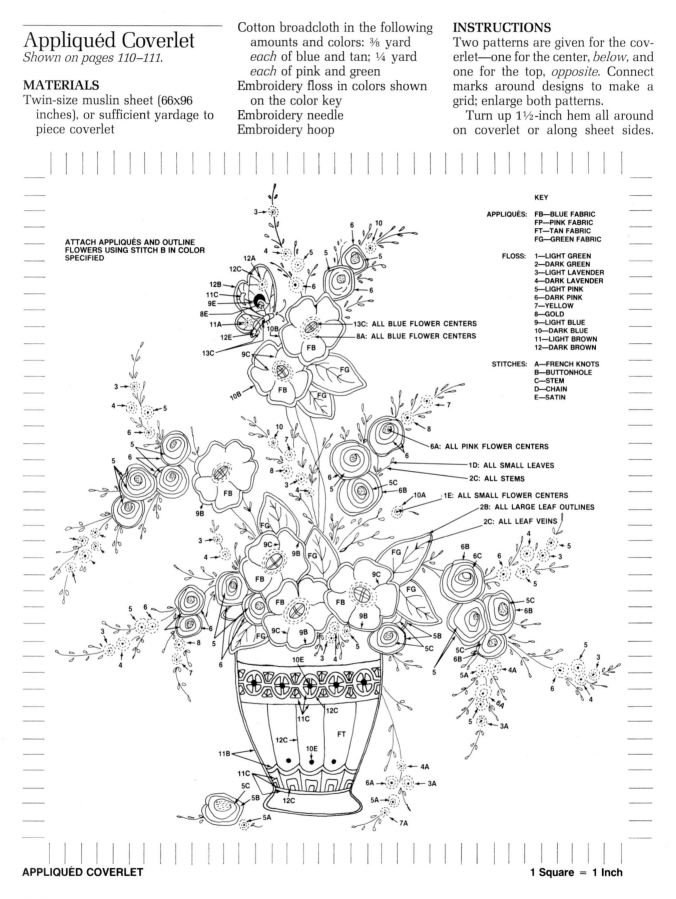

ATTACH APPLIQUÉS AND OUTLINE FLOWERS USING STITCH B IN COLOR SPECIFIED

KEY

APPLIQUÉS: FB—BLUE FABRIC
FP—PINK FABRIC
FT—TAN FABRIC
FG—GREEN FABRIC

FLOSS: 1—LIGHT GREEN
2—DARK GREEN
3—LIGHT LAVENDER
4—DARK LAVENDER
5—LIGHT PINK
6—DARK PINK
7—YELLOW
8—GOLD
9—LIGHT BLUE
10—DARK BLUE
11—LIGHT BROWN
12—DARK BROWN

STITCHES: A—FRENCH KNOTS
B—BUTTONHOLE
C—STEM
D—CHAIN
E—SATIN

13C: ALL BLUE FLOWER CENTERS
8A: ALL BLUE FLOWER CENTERS

6A: ALL PINK FLOWER CENTERS
1D: ALL SMALL LEAVES
2C: ALL STEMS
1E: ALL SMALL FLOWER CENTERS
2B: ALL LARGE LEAF OUTLINES
2C: ALL LEAF VEINS

APPLIQUÉD COVERLET

1 Square = 1 Inch

122

Transfer the designs, centered on the width, to the sheet or coverlet. Position the base of the urn about 29 inches above the lower edge of the fabric. Place the topmost branches of the upper motif about 5½ inches below the upper edge of the fabric.

Trace the appliqués onto tissue paper; cut from fabric, adding ¼-inch seam allowances. Cut the overlapping designs from a single piece of fabric. For example, the three blue flowers in the urn can be cut as one; the embroidery stitches will define the shapes of the individual blossoms.

Turn under seam allowances; appliqué flowers and leaves, using buttonhole stitches. After appliqués are in place, embroider flower centers, leaf veins, and so forth, following color and stitch key.

When all embroidery on the coverlet is completed, work dark blue stem stitches along hemlines.

Ribbon Table Runner

Shown on pages 112–113.
Finished size is 19x53 inches.

MATERIALS
19x53-inch piece of 10-count netting mesh

Tapestry needle
⅛-inch-wide silk or satin ribbon in coral, medium rose, pale green, light green, medium green, medium yellow, pale yellow, violet, and off-white
Permanent needlepoint markers or acrylic paints to match ribbons
Heavy paper

INSTRUCTIONS
To re-create the antique runner as shown in the photographs, first extend the lines at the side and bottom edges of the design on page 124 to make a grid; then enlarge the half-pattern onto heavy paper and place it under the piece of netting mesh.

Referring to the photographs for color placement, color the designs with diluted acrylic paints or needlepoint markers. Transfer the remaining half of the design to the netting mesh.

Thread a tapestry needle with silk or satin ribbon. Embroider long satin stitches over the mesh, following painted design. Keep all embroidery stitches horizontal, and break long areas of pattern into shorter stitches to minimize snagging.

To finish the embroidered runner, bind the cut edges of the netting mesh with ribbon; then press lightly from the back.

Crocheted Nosegay Cloth

Shown on pages 114–115.
Finished size is 45 inches square.

MATERIALS
DMC Brilliant crochet cotton (218-yard balls): 7 balls of white (MC); 3 balls *each* of No. 210 lavender (A) and No. 955 green (B); and 2 balls *each* of No. 748 yellow (C), No. 745 peach (D), No. 818 pink (E), and No. 828 blue (F)
Size 7 steel crochet hook, or size to obtain gauge

Abbreviations: See page 92.
Gauge: Main motif measures 6½ inches in diameter including edging round of MC.

INSTRUCTIONS
CENTER MOTIF (Make 36): With MC, ch 7; join with sl st to form ring.

Rnd 1: Ch 3, work 23 dc in ring; join with sl st to top of beg ch-3.

Rnd 2: Ch 4, dc in same st as join; (ch 1, sk 2 dc, in next dc work dc, ch 1, dc) 7 times; ch 1, join with sl st to third ch of beg ch-4.

Rnd 3: Sl st into next ch-1 sp, ch 3; in same sp work dc, ch 1, 2 dc; (sc in

continued

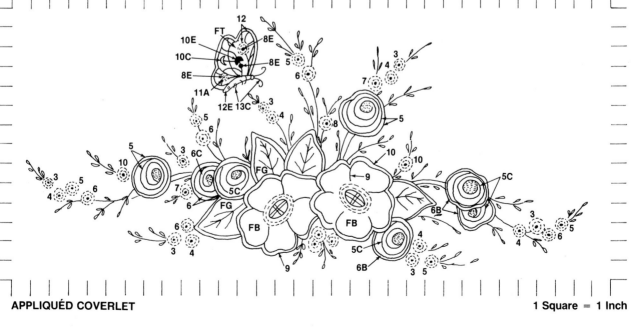

APPLIQUÉD COVERLET

1 Square = 1 Inch

continued from page 123
Old-Fashioned Florals

next ch-1 sp, in next ch-1 sp work 2 dc, ch 1, 2 dc) 7 times; sc in last ch-1 sp, join with sl st to top of beg ch-3.

Rnd 4: Sl st in next dc and into next ch-1 sp; ch 3, in same sp work 2 dc, ch 1, 3 dc; (sc in next sc, in next ch-1 sp work 3 dc, ch 1, 3 dc) 7 times; sc in next sc, join to top of beg ch-3. Fasten off.

FIRST FLOWER: With C, ch 6; join with sl st to form ring.

Rnd 1: Ch 3, in ring work 6 trc, 3 dc, 6 sc, and 2 dc. Change to A and join A with sl st to top of beg ch-3; fasten off C.

Rnd 2: Ch 1, sc in same st as join; (ch 4, sk 2 sts, sc in next st) 5 times; ch 4, join with sl st to sc at beg of rnd.

Rnd 3: **Sl st into next ch-4 lp; in same lp work hdc, dc, 4 trc, dc, hdc—petal 1 made; in next ch-4 lp work hdc, dc, 4 trc, dc, hdc—petal 2 made; in next ch-4 lp work sc, 6 dc, sc—petal 3 made; (in next ch-4 lp work 5 sc) 2 times—petals 4 and 5 made; in next ch-4 lp work sc, 6 dc, sc—petal 6 made;** join with sl st to hdc at beg of rnd. Fasten off. Mark sp between the third and fourth dc of last petal completed.

SECOND FLOWER: *Rnds 1–2:* Work as for First Flower using C for Rnd 1 and E for Rnd 2.

Rnd 3: Continue with E and work petals 1 and 2 as on Rnd 3 of First Flower. In next ch-4 lp work sc, 3 dc; with right sides facing, sl st in marked sp of First Flower (sixth petal); in same ch-4 lp of Second Flower work 3 dc, sc. Complete rem 3 petals as for First Flower. Fasten off.

THIRD–EIGHTH FLOWERS: Work the same as for the Second Flower. Join each flower to the preceding flower made to complete a ring of eight flowers; use the following colors: E and F, F and A, E and C, C and D, E and A, C and F.

RIBBON TABLE RUNNER   1 Square = 1 Inch

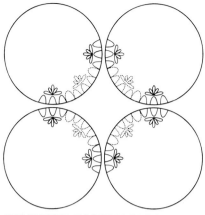

CROCHETED NOSEGAY CLOTH ASSEMBLY DIAGRAM

(*Note:* On Rnd 3 of Eighth Flower, join petal 6 of last flower to petal 3 of First Flower to close ring.)

JOINING FLOWER RING TO CENTER MOTIF: Join B to any sc on last rnd of Center Motif, ch 3; holding back last lp of each dc, work 2 dc in same place as join, yo and draw through all 3 lps on hook; * ch 1, sl st in sp between petals 4 and 5 of any flower on ring, ch 3, sc in next ch-1 sp of Center Motif, ch 3, insert hook through back lp of st before joining of same flower and through back lp of corresponding st of next flower, yo and draw through all lps on hook; ch 2, sk 2 ch of last ch-3 lp worked, sc in next ch of ch-3 lp, sc in side of sc of Center Motif, ch 3. **Holding back last lp of each dc, work 3 dc in next sc of Center Motif, yo and draw through all 4 lps on hook—cl made.** Working joinings in the *next* flower on the ring, rep from * around; join last ch-3 with sl st to top of beg ch-3. Fasten off.

LEAF INSERTS: *Note:* After joining flowers to center, petals 1 and 2 of each flower rem free of all joinings; they run along the outside edges of the assembled piece. Petal 1 lies to the *right* of each flower joining that makes the ring; petal 2 lies to the *left* of each flower joining. Leaf inserts are worked bet these two petals.

With B, ch 5; sl st in sp between second and third trc of petal 1; ch 4, sl st in first ch of beg ch-5; ch 4, sl st in sp between petals 1 and 6 of same flower; ch 4, sl st in first ch of beg ch-

5; ch 4, sl st to flower joining; ch 4, sl st in first ch of beg ch-5; ch 4, sl st in sp between next 2 petals of *next* flower, ch 4, sl st in first ch of beg ch-5; ch 4, sl st in sp between second and third trc of petal 2 on same flower; ch 4, sl st in first ch of beg ch-5. Fasten off.

Rep leaf insert in 7 rem spaces between flowers along outer edge of flower ring.

Finishing rnd: Join MC in any first ch (same ch used to make leaf insert joinings). Ch 3, in same sp as join work 2 dc; * ch 2, in same sp as the *next* leaf joining work **3 dc—dc shell made**; ch 2, in sp bet petals 1 and 2 of same flower work **3 trc—trc shell made**; ch 2, in same sp as the *next* leaf joining work dc shell; ch 2, in center ch of *next* leaf insert work dc shell; rep from * around; join the last ch-2 with sl st in the top of beg ch-3—24 dc shells and 8 trc shells made. Fasten off.

TO ASSEMBLE: Arrange 36 completed motifs, 6 across by 6 down, rotating motifs randomly so flower color varies from motif to motif. Keep alternate leaf inserts at centers of top, bottom, left, and right sides; see illustration, *above left*.

Hold two motifs, right sides tog, and work through the corresponding stitches of both motifs to complete joinings as follows: Join MC in center st of dc shell to right of leaf insert, ch 1, sc in same st as join; (ch 4, sc in center of next dc shell) 2 times. Fasten off. Rep this joining at rem 3 sides of main motif as shown in the illustration.

FILLER MOTIFS (make 25): With MC, ch 4; join with sl st to form ring.

Rnd 1: Ch 3, 2 dc in ring, (ch 2, 3 dc in ring) 3 times; ch 2, join with sl st to top of beg ch-3.

Rnd 2: Ch 3, dc in each of next 2 dc, * **in next ch-2 sp work dc, ch 1, dc, ch 1, dc—corner made;** dc in next 3 dc; rep from * twice more; work corner in last ch-2 sp; join to top of beg ch-3.

Rnd 3: Ch 4, * sk dc, dc in next dc, ch 2, sk dc, **in next dc work dc, ch 1,**

trc, ch 1, dc—corner made; ch 2, sk dc, ** dc in next dc, ch 1; rep from * twice more; then work from * to **; join with sl st to third ch of beg ch-4.

Rnd 4: Sl st into next ch-1 sp, ch 4, dc in same sp; in next ch-2 sp work dc, ch 1, dc; * ch 1, in corner trc work dc, ch 1, dc, ch 1, dc; ch 1, sk next ch-1 sp, ** in next ch-2 sp work dc, ch 1, dc; in next ch-1 sp work dc, ch 1, dc; in next ch-2 sp work dc, ch 1, dc; rep from * twice more; work from * to **; in last ch-2 sp work dc, ch 1, dc; join with sl st to third ch of beg ch-4.

Rnd 5 (joining rnd): Ch 1, sc in first ch-1 sp; * in next ch-1 sp work 3 dc, sl st into ch-2 sp to left of dc-shell worked into leaf insert of main motif; work 3 dc in same ch-1 sp of motif in progress; ch 1, work corner of joining motif as follows: **dc in corner dc of Rnd 4, ch 3, join with sl st to next ch-2 sp of main motif, ch 3, dc in top of last dc made, ch 5, join with sl st to next ch-2 sp of main motif, ch 1, join to adjoining ch-2 sp of *next* main motif, ch 5, sc in top of last dc made; ch 3, join with sl st to next ch-2 sp of main motif, ch 3, dc in top of last dc made, dc in corner dc of Rnd 4 of joining motif—corner of joining motif made;** ch 1, sk next 2 ch-1 sps of the filler motif; in the next ch-1 sp work 3 dc; sl st in the next ch-2 sp of the main motif; 3 dc in the same ch-1 sp of the filler motif; ** sc in the next ch-1 sp; rep from * twice more, then work from * to **; join with sl st to beg sc. Fasten off.

EDGING: *Rnd 1:* With right side facing, join MC in second free ch-2 sp from right at edge of main motif, sc in same place, * (ch 7, sc in next ch-2 sp) 12 times to next motif joining; ch 2, sc in first free ch-2 sp on *next* main motif, ** ch 7, sc in next ch-2 sp; rep from * around, working 21 ch-7 lps on each corner motif; end rnd at **, ch 3, dc in first sc to complete last lp.

Rnd 2: Sc in last lp formed, * ch 7, sc in next ch-7 lp; rep from * to next ch-2 sp; ch 3, in ch-2 sp work dc; ch 3, sc in next ch-7 lp; Working as established, complete rnd. Join last ch-7 with sl st to sc at beg of rnd.

continued

FILET CROCHET SHUTTERS Chart 1

Chart 2 1 Square = 1 Stitch

→3
→1

2→

continued from page 125
Old-Fashioned Florals

Rnd 3: Sl st to center of first ch-7 lp, sc in same lp; * ch 7, sc in next ch-7 lp; rep from * around to next dc; ch 3, dc in dc, ch 3, sc in next ch-7 lp. Working as established, complete rnd. Join with sl st to sc at beg of rnd.

Rnd 4: Sl st into first ch-7 lp, ch 3, in same lp work 2 dc, ch 1, 3 dc; * dc in next sc; in next ch-7 lp work 3 dc, ch 1, 3 dc; rep from * around and, *at same time,* work dc in each dc at top of motif joinings; end with dc in last sc, sl st in top of beg ch-3. Fasten off.

Filet Crochet Shutter Panels

Shown on pages 116–117.
Finished size of each blocked panel is 7¼x16 inches.

MATERIALS
For four panels
DMC Cébélia Size 20 crochet cotton (405-yard balls): 3 balls of white; Size 9 steel crochet hook
Shutters; glass or clear plastic glazing points (optional)

Abbreviations: See page 92.
Gauge: 5 spaces = 1 inch; 5½ rows = 1 inch.

INSTRUCTIONS
To adjust panels to fit shutters, add rows of spaces to top and bottom of panel. Work from charts, *opposite.* (*Note:* Join new ball at beginning or end of row.) For each pair of shutters, make one panel from each chart. Read the charts from right to left for odd-numbered rows and from left to right for even-numbered rows.

FIRST PANEL: Ch 113. *Row 1:* Dc in eighth ch from hook; * ch 2, sk 2 ch, dc in next ch. Rep from * across—36 sps. Ch 5, turn. *Row 2:* **Sk first dc, dc in next dc—beg sp over sp made; * ch 2, dc in next dc—sp over sp made.** Rep from * across to last sp, end **ch 2, sk 2 ch of turning ch, dc**
continued

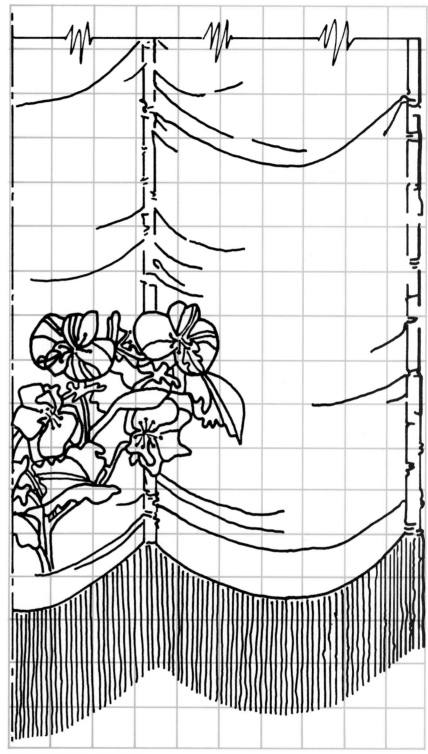

EMBROIDERED CURTAIN

1 Square = 2 Inches

127

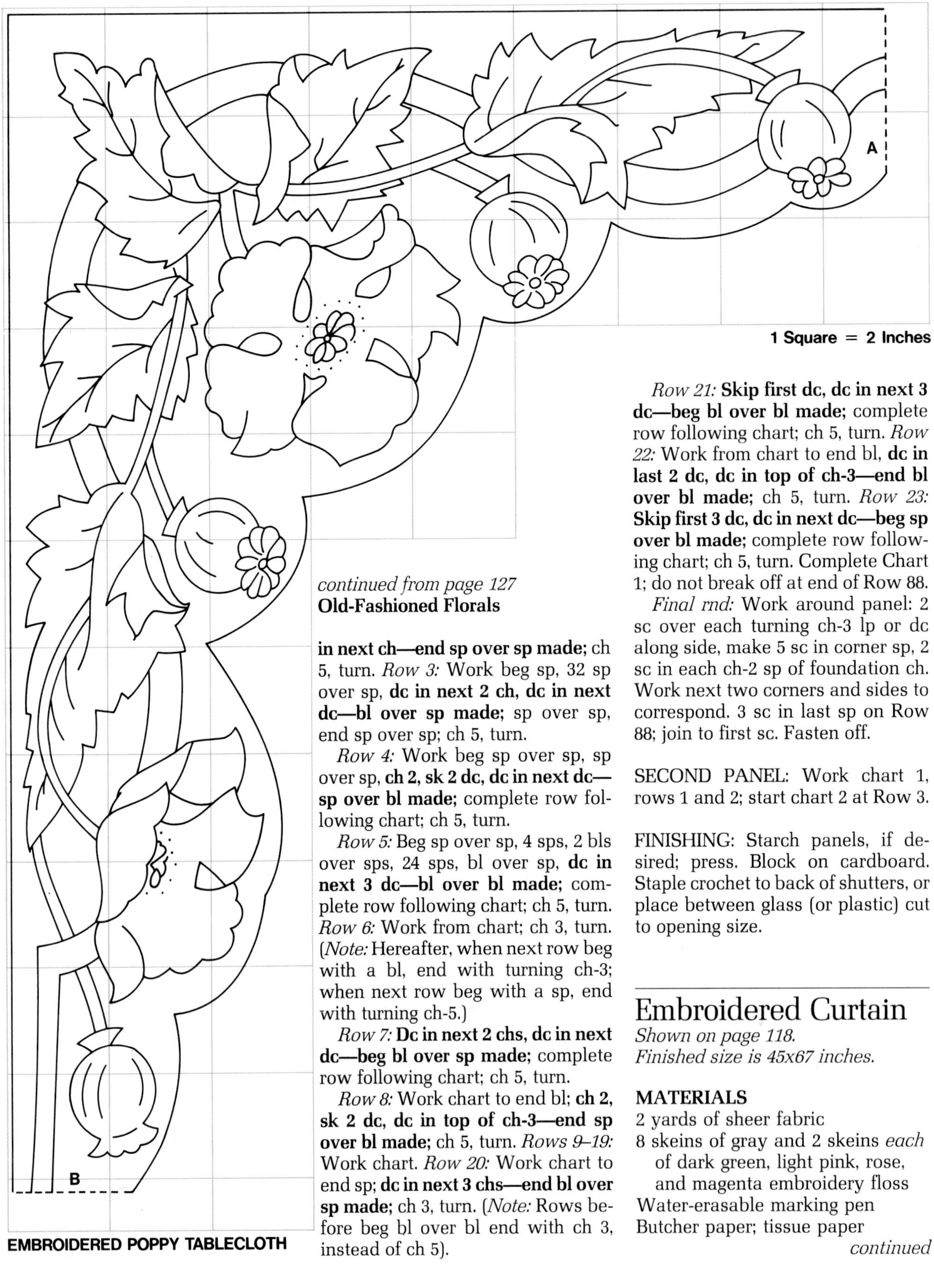

1 Square = 2 Inches

EMBROIDERED POPPY TABLECLOTH

continued from page 127
Old-Fashioned Florals

in next ch—end sp over sp made; ch 5, turn. *Row 3:* Work beg sp, 32 sp over sp, **dc in next 2 ch, dc in next dc—bl over sp made;** sp over sp, end sp over sp; ch 5, turn.

Row 4: Work beg sp over sp, sp over sp, **ch 2, sk 2 dc, dc in next dc— sp over bl made;** complete row following chart; ch 5, turn.

Row 5: Beg sp over sp, 4 sps, 2 bls over sps, 24 sps, bl over sp, **dc in next 3 dc—bl over bl made;** complete row following chart; ch 5, turn. *Row 6:* Work from chart; ch 3, turn. (*Note:* Hereafter, when next row beg with a bl, end with turning ch-3; when next row beg with a sp, end with turning ch-5.)

Row 7: **Dc in next 2 chs, dc in next dc—beg bl over sp made;** complete row following chart; ch 5, turn.

Row 8: Work chart to end bl; **ch 2, sk 2 dc, dc in top of ch-3—end sp over bl made;** ch 5, turn. *Rows 9–19:* Work chart. *Row 20:* Work chart to end sp; **dc in next 3 chs—end bl over sp made;** ch 3, turn. (*Note:* Rows before beg bl over bl end with ch 3, instead of ch 5).

Row 21: **Skip first dc, dc in next 3 dc—beg bl over bl made;** complete row following chart; ch 5, turn. *Row 22:* Work from chart to end bl, **dc in last 2 dc, dc in top of ch-3— end bl over bl made;** ch 5, turn. *Row 23: **Skip first 3 dc, dc in next dc—beg sp over bl made;** complete row following chart; ch 5, turn. Complete Chart 1; do not break off at end of Row 88.

Final rnd: Work around panel: 2 sc over each turning ch-3 lp or dc along side, make 5 sc in corner sp, 2 sc in each ch-2 sp of foundation ch. Work next two corners and sides to correspond. 3 sc in last sp on Row 88; join to first sc. Fasten off.

SECOND PANEL: Work chart 1, rows 1 and 2; start chart 2 at Row 3.

FINISHING: Starch panels, if desired; press. Block on cardboard. Staple crochet to back of shutters, or place between glass (or plastic) cut to opening size.

Embroidered Curtain
Shown on page 118.
Finished size is 45x67 inches.

MATERIALS
2 yards of sheer fabric
8 skeins of gray and 2 skeins *each* of dark green, light pink, rose, and magenta embroidery floss
Water-erasable marking pen
Butcher paper; tissue paper

continued

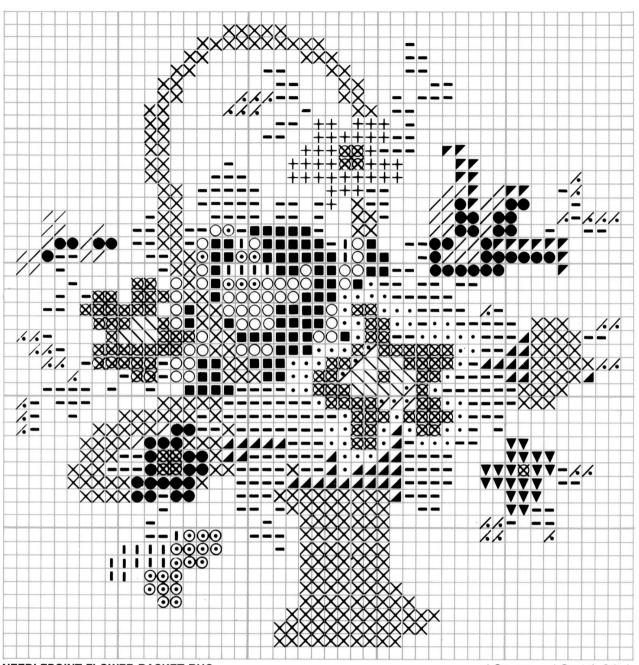

NEEDLEPOINT FLOWER BASKET RUG

1 Square = 1 Scotch Stitch

COLOR KEY

- ■ Red/Red
- ◨ Pink/Red
- ⊙ Light Pink/Dark Pink
- Ⅱ Light Pink/Light Pink
- ◪ Pink/Dark Blue
- ◩ Light Blue/Light Blue
- ● Light Blue/Dark Blue
- ⊞ Lavender/Purple
- ⊡ White

- ⊠ Light Brown/Dark Brown
- ◢ Dark Brown/Caramel
- ⊟ Light Green/Dark Green
- ◪ Gray/Light Green
- ▼ Light Orange/Dark Orange
- ◹ Yellow/Orange
- ⊠ Light Yellow/Dark Yellow
- ◿ Gray/Yellow

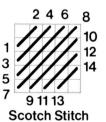

Scotch Stitch

129

continued from page 128
Old-Fashioned Florals

INSTRUCTIONS

Enlarge the pattern, page 127, onto butcher paper. Cut tissue paper to window size; fold vertically in half. Transfer pattern to tissue (broken line on fold). If necessary, extend length of pattern. Place tissue under the fabric, with 2½-inch margins at sides and 10 inches of fabric below fringe. Trace.

Embroider using double running stitches and floss in colors of your choice (see photograph). Sew casings for rods at top and bottom.

Embroidered Poppy Tablecloth
Shown on page 119.
Finished size is 35x44 inches.

MATERIALS
36x45 inches of white fabric
No. 5 pearl cotton in teal

INSTRUCTIONS
Enlarge pattern, page 128. Place design 1½ inches from edges of fabric, positioning A at center of short side and B at center of long side.

Use stem stitches on lines; work rows of running stitches, ⅛ inch apart, between border outlines. Add row of running stitches ¼ inch outside design. (See photograph.) Hem.

Needlepoint Flower Basket Rug
Shown on page 120.
Finished rug is 33x47 inches.

MATERIALS
38x48-inch piece of 10-mesh needlepoint canvas
Tapestry needle; gingham
Three-ply Persian yarn in following colors and amounts (in strands): dark brown (78), light brown (68), light purple (5), medium purple (72), light green (185), dark green (51), light yellow (15), medium yellow (15), orange (4), dark yellow (6), light pink (16), medium pink (16), medium red (54), dark red (4), and white or off-white (1,856)
5 yards of rug binding
Colored pencils to match yarns
Graph paper; masking tape
Needlepoint frame; liquid latex

INSTRUCTIONS
Transfer pattern, page 129, to graph paper using colored pencils. Transfer to canvas. Tape edges; mount in frame.

Using three plies of yarn, work design in Scotch stitches (see diagram, page 129), following color key. Each color combination has a symbol. Use first color to work top three diagonal strands of a single Scotch stitch block; use second color for lower four diagonal stitches.

Add border, if desired. Work entire background in Scotch stitches.

Sprinkle with water to dampen yarn. Cover blocking board with gingham. Tack the needlework face-down, aligning edges on gingham checks; sprinkle again. Dry at least 24 hours; remove. Turn under edges; sew to back with binding. Coat with liquid latex.

Flower Basket Needlepoint Pillow
Shown on page 120.
Finished size is 16x16 inches.

MATERIALS
20x20-inch piece *each* of 14-mesh canvas and backing fabric
Three-ply Persian yarn in following colors and amounts (in strands): dark brown (44), light brown (34), light purple (5), medium purple (5), light green (36), dark green (36), light yellow (13), medium yellow (13), orange (4), dark yellow (5), light pink (9), medium pink (9), medium red (25), dark red (4), and white or off-white (85)
Tapestry needle
Graph paper; masking tape
Colored pencils to match yarns
16-inch square of pillow form or fiberfill; needlepoint frame

INSTRUCTIONS
Transfer pattern, page 129, to graph paper; proceed as for Flower Basket Rug, *below left*. Use Scotch stitches and two plies of yarn. Block as for rug. Cut backing to size. Sew back to front between first and second rows of needlepoint. Leave one side open. Trim, turn, and stuff. Close opening.

Hooked Heirloom Rug
Shown on pages 8–9.
Finished size is 18x34½ inches.

MATERIALS
20x36-inch piece of rug burlap
⅛-inch-wide wool strips in the following colors and amounts (in ounces): white (7), hunter green (5), and brown (4); 2 ounces *each* of cream, gold, yellow-green, sea foam, and avocado green
Size 5 or 6 crochet hook
3 yards of hunter green rug binding; masking tape
Permanent colored markers
Embroidery hoop or rug frame
Liquid latex

INSTRUCTIONS
These directions are for an 18x34½-inch area rug (approximately half the size of the rug shown). Enlarge pattern, *opposite,* and transfer to burlap. Lightly color areas using permanent colored markers.

Tape edges; stretch in hoop or frame. Practice hooking on scrap fabric before beginning project.

Prop hoop or frame, right side up, against table. Hold wool strip underneath. With other hand, push the crochet hook through one mesh of the burlap and pull one end of wool strip up through the hole to a height of 1 inch (end will be trimmed later). Push hook through next mesh; pull up a loop to a height of ⅛ inch.

Continue in this manner. Outline each design area, then fill in flowers and other motifs. Wool strips should be smooth on underside. Trim all ends flush with pile on top of rug. Bind edges. Coat back of finished rug with liquid latex.

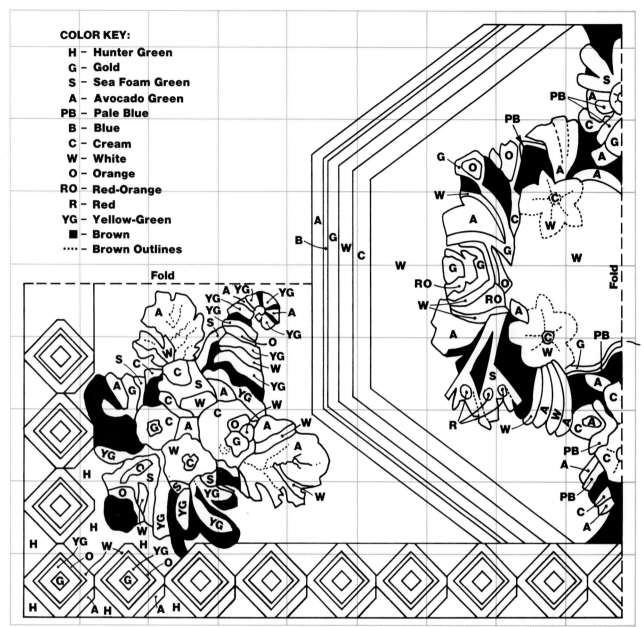

COLOR KEY:

- H – Hunter Green
- G – Gold
- S – Sea Foam Green
- A – Avocado Green
- PB – Pale Blue
- B – Blue
- C – Cream
- W – White
- O – Orange
- RO – Red-Orange
- R – Red
- YG – Yellow-Green
- ■ – Brown
- ···· – Brown Outlines

Fold

Fold

HOOKED HEIRLOOM RUG

1 Square = 2 Inches

131

HOMEWORK
PIERCED PAPER

You and your family can create romantic accents for your home with this simple, old-fashioned craft. Patterns of tiny holes pierced in heavy white paper lend a wonderfully lacy look to decorative borders.

PIERCED PAPER

Paper piercing is a delightfully easy and inexpensive way to embellish paper items of every description, from charming stationery, cards, and bookmarks, *above,* to window shades and shelving borders, *opposite.*

All you'll need are a line drawing of the design, tissue paper for the pattern, a selection of paper to pierce, and a sharp needle or pin. Your local stationery store (or art-supply store) will prove a gold mine of sample papers on which to practice.

Folded note cards of good-quality stock are ready-made to receive a small heart and flower design, *above* and *opposite.*

And pretty bookmarks for yourself, or a book-loving friend, are a snap to make from scraps of paper tied with satin ribbon.

Pierced borders are a graceful touch for shelves or window shades. Satin ribbon woven through the paper adds a special touch.

For illustrated how-to instructions, please turn the page.

PIERCED PAPER

Delicate pierced-paper designs take on extra punch when displayed against contrasting backgrounds. The charming pattern of hearts and flowers on the pierced mat, *left,* shows elegantly against a liner of deep green mat board.

The mat design is based on a 6-inch-wide motif that can be repeated and adapted as necessary to suit almost any size mat or frame opening.

You can develop your own design for a picture mat—or similar project—from almost any line drawing. Choose a simple pattern of hearts, flowers, birds, abstract doodles, or geometric motifs—anything that lends itself to small repeats for a border design.

Or try piercing on dark-colored papers to achieve additional interesting effects. And although paper piercing is usually done from the back, you can add textural interest to your designs by piercing some holes from the front. Feel free to experiment.

1 To duplicate the pierced-paper mat, *opposite,* trace the design, page 141, onto tissue paper. Trace the outline of the mat first, then center and trace the pattern motifs.

Use one colored pencil (green) to indicate areas that are punched from the back, and a second color (red) for holes punched from the front.

2 Tape pattern to wrong side of mat board. Use a pin to pierce the green lines. Space holes evenly, piercing through both tissue and mat paper. (The tool pictured *at left* is an artist's punch from an art-supply shop.)

To complete design, turn mat over, retape the pattern, and punch along the red lines.

3 When the design is finished, trim the inner and outer borders of the mat using an artist's knife, utility blade, or sharp scissors.

For complete how-to instructions for this and other pierced-paper projects, please turn the page.

INSTRUCTIONS FOR PIERCED PAPER

General Instructions

To begin, trace or enlarge designs included here and on the following pages onto tissue paper. Cut tissue the same size as the paper you plan to use for your project.

Paper piercing is usually done from the back side of the paper. For textural interest, pierce some holes from the *front*. As a guide, pierce from the back the areas on the patterns designated by black lines, and pierce from the front the areas designated by blue lines. Space holes about ⅛ inch apart.

Tape tissue pattern on back of paper to be used. Lay paper over a foam pad; begin to evenly pierce holes around the outside edges of drawn shapes. Pierce through both tissue and paper. Refer to photographs, pages 132–136, for piercing ideas.

For large shapes, use an instrument with a large point; for small, delicate shapes, use a finer point.

To pierce dots from the front side, remove tissue pattern and tape pattern to front atop the pierced holes. Pierce areas indicated by blue lines.

Stationery, Note Cards, And Bookmark

Shown on page 134.

MATERIALS
Purchased stationery or note
  cards; masking tape
Narrow ribbon for bookmark
Foam pad; tissue paper
Colored pencils
Sharp needle; scissors

INSTRUCTIONS
Trace heart design, *top right,* or floral motif, *center right,* onto tissue. Place atop stationery or opened note card; follow General Instructions, *above.* For bookmark, cut a 1½x8½-inch piece of paper. Transfer heart design, *bottom right,* to tissue; pierce according to General Instructions, *above.* Round top corners; make hole with punch and tie ribbon in place.

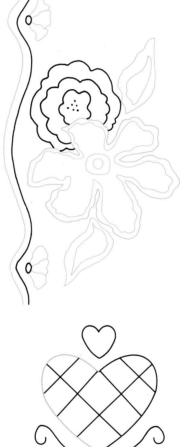

STATIONERY, NOTE CARDS, AND BOOKMARK

Pierced Window Shade
Shown on page 135.

MATERIALS
Window shade
Foam pad; tissue paper
Masking tape
Colored pencils
Sharp needle; scissors

INSTRUCTIONS
Trace and arrange the floral pattern, *right,* onto tissue cut the same size as the area of shade you plan to pierce. Arrange the design along the bottom of shade, adding blooms up the sides if desired. Pierce following the General Instructions, *left.*

Pierced-Paper Shelf Liner
Shown on pages 134–135.

MATERIALS
Medium-weight paper, such as
  index, charcoal drawing, or
  watercolor paper
⅜-inch-wide satin ribbon
Foam pad; tissue paper
Masking tape; colored pencils
Sharp needle; scissors
Crafts glue

INSTRUCTIONS
Cut paper into 10-inch-wide strips of desired length. Trace floral design, *right,* or bird and heart design, page 140; transfer to paper according to General Instructions. Evenly space and repeat the design along the paper strips. (*Note:* Adjust width of strip as desired, allowing for at least a 3-inch fold at the top of the paper to rest on the shelf.) When piercing is completed, cut a scalloped border to follow the pierced design.

For ribbon embellishment, cut ½-inch slits every inch across the strip and 3 inches below the top. Weave ribbon through the slits; fasten with glue. Fold the paper 3 inches from the straight edge; attach to shelf. Cut a piece of paper to cover shelf, if desired. *continued*

SHELF LINER

continued from page 138
Homework
Pierced Paper

Picture Mat

Shown on page 136.
Finished size is 24x24 inches.

MATERIALS

Medium-weight paper, such as
   charcoal drawing, index, or
   watercolor paper
Foam pad; tissue paper
Colored pencils; masking tape
Sharp needle or artist's punch;
   crafts knife or scissors; rubber
   cement
Cardboard mat in contrasting color

INSTRUCTIONS

The mat shown measures 24x24
inches (outside dimensions), with
edges about 5 inches wide. The design itself is about 3 inches wide and
is worked on the inner portion of the
mat. By enlarging or reducing the
pattern, *opposite,* or by adding, sub-
tracting, or repeating motifs, you
can adapt the design to fit a larger or
smaller mat.

PIERCED-PAPER MAT: To begin,
cut four 5x24-inch strips from the
medium-weight paper. Form strips
into a square, with the top and bottom strips overlapping the two side
strips. With crafts knife, miter the
corners of all four strips so they fit
neatly together.

Next, cut a 5x24-inch tissue strip
and trace the design, *opposite,* onto
the strip. (*Note:* The pattern repre-
sents one-half of the design for one
side of the mat. Flop the pattern
along the centerline to complete the
design for one side.)

Tape the tissue pattern to one mat
strip and proceed as described in
the General Instructions, page 138.
Repeat the instructions for all four
strips. (*Note:* Take particular care to
align the one-half-heart design on
the mitered edge at each end of each
strip so that a complete heart is
formed in the corners when the
strips are assembled. Refer to photograph, page 136.)

When piercing is completed, cut
the scalloped edge of each mat strip
with a crafts knife or sharp scissors.
Cut the scalloped edge ⅛ inch from
the pierced scallop design.

CONTRASTING MAT: From cardboard or mat board of a contrasting
color, cut a backing to match the
outside dimensions of the pierced-
paper mat. Determine the inside dimensions of the mat board after
you've selected the photograph or
picture to be framed; then cut out
the center. Fit the pierced strips together atop the backing mat; glue in
place with spots of rubber cement.
Frame the picture as desired.

For smaller picture mats, or for
mats in unusual shapes and sizes
(round, oval, or miniature), you may
prefer to cut the entire pierced mat
from a single sheet of paper.

Trace the design onto tissue paper as usual, then tape pattern atop
the piercing paper and pierce the entire design *before* cutting the mat.
This will ensure a well-centered design, and enable you to control the
inner and outer margins of the design more precisely.

SHELF LINER

If you're feeling adventurous, experiment with a variety of designs to see how each looks on different kinds, weights, textures, or colors of papers. You might also practice piercing the same designs with different size punches, from fine needles to awls, or with any other sharp-pointed tools you might have on hand. Vary the distance between pierced holes—closer together or farther apart—to see which effects you like best. And of course you can turn each of these experiments into a note card or bookmark, so nothing is wasted.

Once you've perfected your paper-piercing technique, with even spacing and regular pressure on the punch, you'll discover other ways to use this craft in your home.

For example, you might create a pierced-paper lampshade from an inexpensive, purchased paper lampshade. To work on a curved surface, spread your foam pad over a tailor's ham placed at the pointed end of your ironing board. You will have to rotate the shade frequently to keep the portion of the design you are pricking centered over the padded surface, but the results will be well worth the effort.

Another spectacular way to enhance your pierced-paper designs is to paint some of the design elements with watercolors before you begin piercing. For best results, work on blocked watercolor paper.

After you have traced the design onto tracing paper, transfer the design to the piercing paper using light pencil markings that can be erased easily. With watercolors, paint portions of the design in tinted pastels or bright primary colors. Allow the paint to dry completely, then carefully erase the pencil lines.

Remove the paper from the block and pierce the paper around the painted designs. Use the tracing-paper pattern to pierce only the unpainted portions.

PIERCED PAPER PICTURE FRAME
Full-Size Pattern

141

VERSATILE ONE-STITCH DESIGNS

Create a spectacular array of pillows, linens, and gifts using just one easy stitch. That's all it takes to embroider this mix-and-match collection of country-fresh designs.

Charming motifs inspired by patterns from old-fashioned pillow shams enhance everything from the lap quilt, pillows, and bed linens, *left,* to the quilted jacket, *above.*

Use each bouquet, garland, or sprig of flowers alone or in combination with other designs. They work up quickly in the easiest embroidery technique—outline stitches.

Directions begin on page 148.

VERSATILE ONE-STITCH DESIGNS

Pictorial designs worked in outline stitches are often referred to as redwork, because traditionally these one-color designs were worked in red embroidery floss, as are most of the patterns in this section.

Single-color stitching does seem to strengthen these designs. But, of course, you can embroider the motifs in a color other than red—or even a mix of hues. Note the charming antimacassar set worked in blue on the easy chair, *far right*.

Playing with scale offers additional possibilities for adapting the patterns. The summery lap quilt airing on the balcony, *near right,* combines an outsize bouquet with a sized-to-match border to stunning effect.

Smaller versions of the various bouquet and garland patterns appear on the pillow, anti-macassars, and table skirt, *far right.*

144

VERSATILE ONE-STITCH DESIGNS

A graceful twining
of blue humming-
birds and red
morning glories
encircles the
birdcage cover,
right. The same
design borders the
quilt, sheets, and
tablecloth shown on
preceding pages.

This versatile
border pattern is
conveniently
broken down into
several horizontal
sections and a
corner. You can
combine and repeat
these elements,
depending on the
dimensions of the
surface you plan to
embroider.

Other ways to
make the most of
this lovely design
include curtain
panels, table
runners, and skirt
hems. You might
also use portions of
the design on place
mats and napkins.

Flowery bouquets can be worked on purchased linen towels in no time at all, *left.* For the perfect house gift, stitch up a bunch of towels like these in shades to match a friend's best powder room. Add borders of pretty lace for an extra-fancy touch.

Here the lily of the valley bouquet appears on a delicate heart-shaped pillow and a terry cloth towel.

If you prefer, you can machine-embroider projects like these. Simply outline the designs, using closely spaced, narrow zigzag stitches.

147

INSTRUCTIONS FOR VERSATILE ONE-STITCH DESIGNS

General Instructions

All of the projects in this section were embroidered using a single, simple stitch: the outline or stem stitch (see diagram, *right*). This stitch is flexible enough to follow any line or curve.

The loop of the stitch may lie *above* or *below* the needle, whichever is comfortable for you. But to create a neat, smooth line of stitches, work all loops in the same way; do not alternate the loops once you have begun to embroider. For graceful curves, you may wish to decrease slightly the length of the stitches on curved lines.

STEM STITCH

Pillow Shams

Shown on page 142.
Finished size is 18x18 inches.

MATERIALS
For each sham
1¼ yards of 45-inch-wide white cotton-blend fabric
½ yard of print fabric for ruffle
3 yards of 2-inch-wide lace edging
Red embroidery floss
Polyester fiberfill or pillow form

LILY OF THE VALLEY

1 Square = 1½ Inches

148

INSTRUCTIONS

Enlarge the Basket of Flowers or the Lily of the Valley design, *below* and *opposite,* to size (use a scale of 1 square equals 1½ inches). Using dressmaker's carbon paper or a water-erasable marking pen, transfer the design to the center of a 20-inch square of white fabric. Using two strands of embroidery floss, work design in outline stitches. When completed, press wrong side of design. Cut pillow backing to match.

From print fabric, cut and piece a 6x144-inch ruffle strip. Join short ends. Fold strip in half lengthwise, wrong sides together; press. Gather along raw edges; pin and baste ruffle to right side of pillow back.

To make white ruffle, cut and piece a 5x144-inch strip of white fabric. Join short ends. Fold the strip in half with wrong sides together and press. Pin lace strip to front of white ruffle, matching raw edges. Gather, fit, and baste double ruffle to pillow front so lace side is next to embroidered side of pillow front.

With right sides facing, and with ruffles carefully tucked in toward center, stitch pillow back to front. Leave opening for turning. Turn, press, stuff, and sew opening closed.

BASKET OF FLOWERS

1 Square = 1½ Inches

BIRDCAGE COVER   1 Square = 2 Inches

continued from page 149
Versatile One-Stitch Designs

Embroidered Jacket
Shown on page 143.

MATERIALS
Purchased jacket pattern
Fabrics as required by pattern
Water-erasable marking pen
Embroidery floss

INSTRUCTIONS
Transfer selected motifs, page 148, onto front sections; embroider. Assemble following pattern directions.

Lap Quilt
Shown on page 144.
Finished size is 48x60 inches.

MATERIALS
2 yards of white cotton-blend
  fabric
½ yard *each* of two red calico
  prints for border triangles
3 yards of print fabric for backing
Red embroidery floss
Quilt batting
White quilting thread

INSTRUCTIONS
Enlarge quilt design, *opposite,* and transfer to center of a 36½x48½-inch piece of white fabric. Work design in outline stitches, using three strands of red floss. When completed, press on wrong side.

To make templates for the border triangles, cut an 8½-inch square of cardboard. Cut square in half diagonally, then cut one of the resulting right-angle triangles in half again. Use the larger (8½x8½x12-inch) triangle as the template for the large border triangles. Use one of the smaller (6x6x8½-inch) triangles as a template for the triangles edging the corner blocks on the border.

Adding ¼-inch seam allowances, trace and cut large triangles as follows: 14 white, six of one red calico print, and seven of a second red calico print. Adding ¼-inch seam allowances, trace and cut four small triangles from the two red prints.

Corner blocks for the quilt are 6½-inch squares (includes ¼-inch seam allowances), embellished with a single rose motif traced from the center bouquet.

Embroider the four corner blocks, then piece top, bottom, and side borders by hand or machine. Press the borders and stitch to edges of the center panel.

To back the quilt, piece backing fabric to measure 51x63 inches (or 3 inches larger all around than completed top). Spread backing on floor or table, wrong side up. Center batting and embroidered top on the backing. Pin and baste all three layers together.

Quilt around triangles, using a running stitch and white quilting thread. Trim edges of batting and top. Fold raw edges of backing up and over top to form a narrow binding. Tuck the raw edges under and hand-stitch edging in place.

Antimacassar Set
Shown on page 145.

MATERIALS
½ yard of white cotton-blend
  fabric
3½ yards of ½-inch-wide lace
Blue embroidery floss

INSTRUCTIONS
For the headrest, use the Basket of Flowers pattern, page 149, enlarged to full size (1 square equals 1 inch). Transfer the design to a fabric sized for your chair, referring to the photograph for placement.

Embroider the design in outline stitches, using two strands of blue floss. After stitching, trim the bottom edge of the fabric into a gentle curve (refer to the photograph).

For the armrests, use the pattern as is, without enlarging it. Trace the design onto two 7x10-inch rectan-

LAP QUILT

1 Square = 3 Inches

gles, referring to the photograph for positioning. Embroider design using two strands of blue floss. Round the corners below the design, as shown in the photograph.

Press the headrests and armrests on the wrong side. Pin and baste narrow lace trim around the edge of each piece. Cut backings to match the headrests and armrests. With right sides facing, sew the fronts to the backs; leave openings for turning. Turn, press, and slip-stitch all openings closed.

BOUQUET

continued from page 151
Versatile One-Stitch Designs

Shaped Pillow
Shown on page 145.

MATERIALS
Two 14-inch squares of white fabric; 1 yard of calico (ruffle)
1½ yards of 2-inch-wide lace edging
Red embroidery floss; fiberfill

INSTRUCTIONS
Enlarge center portion *only* of the Lily of the Valley design, page 148, using a scale of 1 square equals 1 inch. Center and transfer the design onto a square of white fabric. Trace a heart outline around the design (heart should measure 14 inches from top to point and from side to side across fullest portion of design). Do not cut out heart shape until embroidery is completed. Mount fabric in hoop if desired.

Using two strands of floss, work entire design in outline stitches.

When embroidery is complete, cut out heart shape; press on wrong side. Cut backing shape to match.

From calico, cut and piece a 5x60-inch strip of fabric for ruffle. Stitch short ends together, fold strip in half, and press. Gather fabric to fit outside edge of heart. Baste lace ruffle to front of fabric ruffle; pin and baste this double ruffle along perimeter of heart, with lace facing right side of pillow top.

With right sides facing, and ruffles tucked to inside, stitch back to front. Leave opening for turning. Turn, press, stuff, and close opening.

Table Skirt
Shown on page 145.
Table skirt is 67 inches in diameter.

MATERIALS
6 yards of 54-inch-wide white cotton fabric (or enough fabric to cut two 54-inch circles and a border strip pieced to measure 16x216 inches)
Red embroidery floss

INSTRUCTIONS
Note: Adjust cloth size by fitting circle to table. Finished ruffled border is 8 inches wide; length of border equals four times the diameter of the circle.

Cut two fabric circles to size indicated above; set aside. Next, cut and piece a 16-inch-wide strip for ruffle, with length to match size indicated above. Fold in half to make a piece 8 inches wide; press. Unfold.

Enlarge the morning glory edging, page 150, and transfer it to the border, adjusting the design to fit the fabric. (*Note:* The folded edge will be the bottom of the ruffle; position the design about 1 inch above the fold.)

Using two strands of floss, work the vine and bird design in outline stitches. When complete, join short ends of strip, refold to 8 inches wide, and press. With right sides of strip and circle facing, ease border ruffle and gather slightly to fit edge of one fabric circle; baste in place.

With right sides facing, pin and stitch backing circle to top. Leave an opening for turning. Turn, press, and stitch opening closed.

Birdcage Cover
Shown on page 146.
Finished size is 36x36 inches.

MATERIALS
1⅛ yards of white cotton-blend fabric
Red and blue embroidery floss
4⅛ yards of purchased or hand-crocheted lace edging

INSTRUCTIONS
Note: The bird and vine design featured on the birdcage cover (and on the purchased sheet shown on page 142) adjusts easily to suit a tablecloth of almost any dimensions.

To make birdcage cover, cut a 36-inch square from white fabric. Mark exact center of the square; cut from the center of one side into the center of the square. Hem edges of the slit.

Enlarge the morning glory and hummingbird design, page 150, and transfer it to fabric, adjusting the pattern to fit gracefully around the edges of the square.

Work the design in outline stitches, using two strands of floss. Use blue for the birds and red for the remainder of the design.

To finish, press the back of the fabric and hem raw edges. Hand-stitch lace edging along the underside of the hem.

Hand Towels
Shown on page 147.
Finished towel is 14x22 inches.

MATERIALS
For one towel
14½x22½-inch piece of white cotton or linen
⅞ yard of ½-inch-wide lace
Red or blue embroidery floss

INSTRUCTIONS
Trace the Bouquet pattern, *opposite,* onto the center of one end of the fabric rectangle. Embroider the design in outline stitches, using two strands of red or blue floss. Press finished design on wrong side.

Fold raw edges under ⅛ inch and then fold again; press. Stitch hems by hand or machine. Add lace trim to each end of towel.

Terry Cloth Towel
Shown on page 147.

MATERIALS
Purchased terry towel
Embroidery floss
Tissue paper

INSTRUCTIONS
Enlarge the center portion of the Lily of the Valley pattern on page 148, and transfer it to tissue paper (*Note:* Dressmaker's carbon paper and transfer pens will not work on terry cloth). Pin the paper pattern to the right side of the towel. Embroider the design through both tissue and towel; tear the paper away.

ELEGANT TREASURES FOR EVERYDAY USES

Beautiful linens—both new and antique—are made to be seen and enjoyed. Finding ways to bring these treasures out of the "just-for-best" closet and into your daily life is part of the joy of decorating.

This dainty set of cross-stitched towels, *above* and *right,* offers a pretty and practical showcase for your stitchery talents. The set features a different floral design for each day of the week.

You also can use these motifs to personalize your purchased or handmade linens.

Simply substitute cross-stitched initials or a name in the space provided for the day of the week.

Directions begin on page 164.

ELEGANT TREASURES
FOR EVERYDAY USES

A crocheted doily, *above,* provides a warmly inviting backdrop for some of life's simplest pleasures—whether you're penning a postcard or relaxing over a cup of tea. Surprisingly serviceable, delicate doilies also protect fine wood finishes from occasional spills and scratches.

New or old, lovely needlework can be fashioned into dramatic home accessories like the pretty openwork, embroidered pillow tops, *right.*

Turn pieces from your private collection into one-of-a-kind pillows, or try your hand at these handsome, geometrically patterned hardanger designs.

ELEGANT TREASURES FOR EVERYDAY USES

Snow-white linens, ornamented with lace and lavish embroidery, were once a part of every young bride's trousseau. Fine pillow slips like those *at left* were lovingly stitched and stored for the day a young woman would marry and start her own household.

Times have changed, of course, but handmade linens are still highly prized by decorators and needlework aficionados alike. Such touches lend an instant air of grace and luxury to the simplest bedroom setting.

If you are fortunate enough to have a collection of antique cases on hand, don't be afraid to use them. You might want to reserve old or fragile cases for use as removable shams (not to be slept on). But with proper care and hand-washing, pillowcases like these can be beautiful and functional for years.

159

ELEGANT TREASURES FOR EVERYDAY USES

For the ultimate in romantic bedroom furnishing, create this lacy filet crochet spread. Admittedly a labor of love, this exquisite star-patterned coverlet is destined to become a cherished family heirloom.

Measuring a generous 78x94 inches, the spread consists of 48 blocks, each 11 inches square. And it features a graceful 6-inch-deep sawtooth edging that repeats the star pattern in miniature. (The spread, which fits either a twin or double bed, can be made larger by increasing the number of pattern blocks.)

To make an elegant, coordinated bedroom ensemble, repeat the star-patterned edging on the curtains and pillow shams.

160

ELEGANT TREASURES FOR EVERYDAY USES

A beautiful setting turns any gathering into a festive occasion. And these spectacular tablecloths are sure to inspire happy get-togethers—whether it's coffee and dessert with a dozen friends, or an intimate celebration for two.

Near right is a 54-inch-square cloth composed of row upon row of delicate spiderweb motifs. The intricate tracery of this pattern takes on added drama when draped over a solid-colored underskirt.

The same is true of the exquisite wedding-ring cloth, *far right*—so called because of the graceful interlocking rings in the border.

This elaborately patterned circular cloth offers an exciting challenge for the experienced crocheter, and the results are undeniably worth the effort.

162

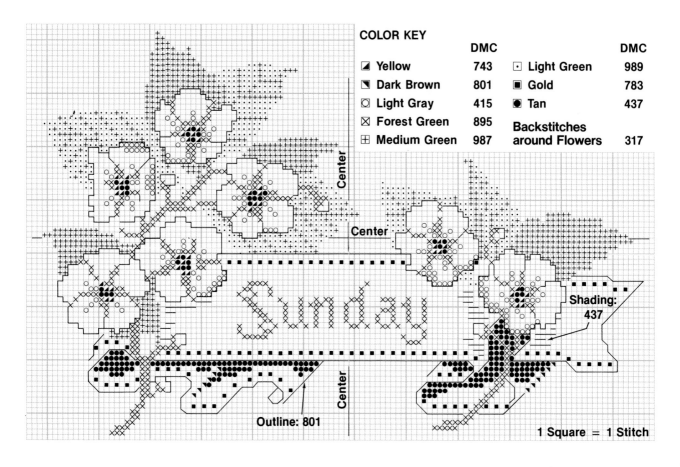

COLOR KEY

		DMC			DMC
◪	Yellow	743	⊡	Light Green	989
◥	Dark Brown	801	◼	Gold	783
◔	Light Gray	415	◕	Tan	437
⊠	Forest Green	895		**Backstitches**	
⊞	Medium Green	987		**around Flowers**	317

Center

Center

Shading: 437

Center

Outline: 801

1 Square = 1 Stitch

Cross-Stitch Wildflower Towels

Shown on pages 154–155.
Finished size is 13½x18½ inches.

MATERIALS
For each towel
16x20 inches of 14-count white
  Aida cloth
DMC six-strand embroidery floss
  (see charts for colors)
½ yard *each* of ⅜-inch-wide satin
  ribbon and ungathered white
  lace
Embroidery hoop; tapestry needle
Graph paper; masking tape
Colored pencils or markers

INSTRUCTIONS
Referring to charts *above* and on
pages 165–167, transfer designs to
graph paper; use pencils or markers
to indicate colors.

    Mark vertical center of cloth with
basting thread. Baste a line 7 inches

above the bottom edge. The points
at which lines cross represent centers on charts. Bind edges with tape.

    Stitch designs over one thread of
fabric using two strands of floss. Fill
flowers with stitches; backstitch
over cross-stitches within petals. To
finish, hem the edges, adding lace
and ribbon (see photograph).

Hardanger Pillows

Shown on pages 156–157.

MATERIALS
For both pillows
Two 16x16-inch squares of ecru
  hardanger fabric; ½ yard *each*
  of lining and backing fabric
Pillow forms or fiberfill
1 ball (95 yards) of No. 8 ecru
  pearl cotton; 1 ball (53 yards) of
  No. 5 ecru pearl cotton
Ecru sewing thread; tweezers
Size 24 or 26 tapestry needles
Small embroidery scissors

INSTRUCTIONS
To prevent raveling, hem raw edges
of each hardanger square. Following
charts, pages 168–169, and beginning at the center of the fabric, work
all kloster blocks using No. 5 pearl
cotton.

    Carefully clip fabric threads
where indicated by shaded blocks
on the charts. For neat openings, cut
as close to the kloster blocks as possible. Cut only the area of embroidery to be worked immediately. Use
tweezers to remove fabric threads.

    After removing threads, embroi-
der woven bars, picots, and loops
(see charts) using No. 8 pearl cotton.

    When embroidery is complete,
trim fabric to 13x13 inches with the
embroidery centered. Cut matching
lining and backing. Baste right side
of the lining to wrong side of embroidered fabric. Stitch front and
back into a pillow. *continued*

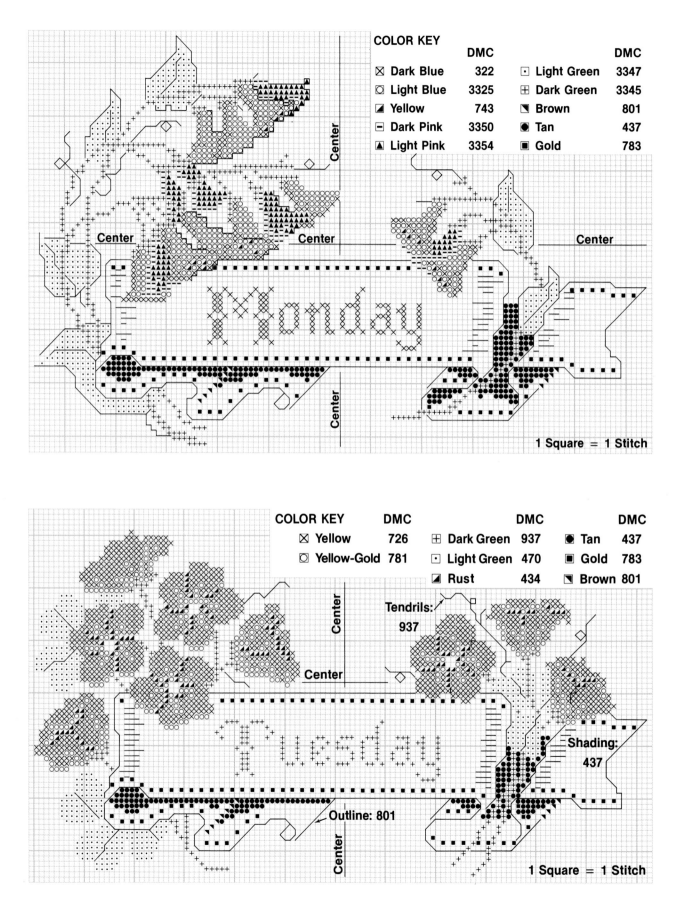

COLOR KEY

		DMC				DMC
⊠	Dark Blue	322	⊡	Light Green	3347
⊘	Light Blue	3325	⊞	Dark Green	3345
◤	Yellow	743	◥	Brown	801
⊟	Dark Pink	3350	⬤	Tan	437
▲	Light Pink	3354	◼	Gold	783

Center

Center Center Center

Center

Center

1 Square = 1 Stitch

COLOR KEY DMC

		DMC				DMC			DMC
⊠	Yellow	726	⊞	Dark Green	937	⬤	Tan	437
⊘	Yellow-Gold	781	⊡	Light Green	470	◼	Gold	783
			◤	Rust	434	◥	Brown	801

Center

Tendrils:
937

Center

Shading:
437

Outline: 801

Center

1 Square = 1 Stitch

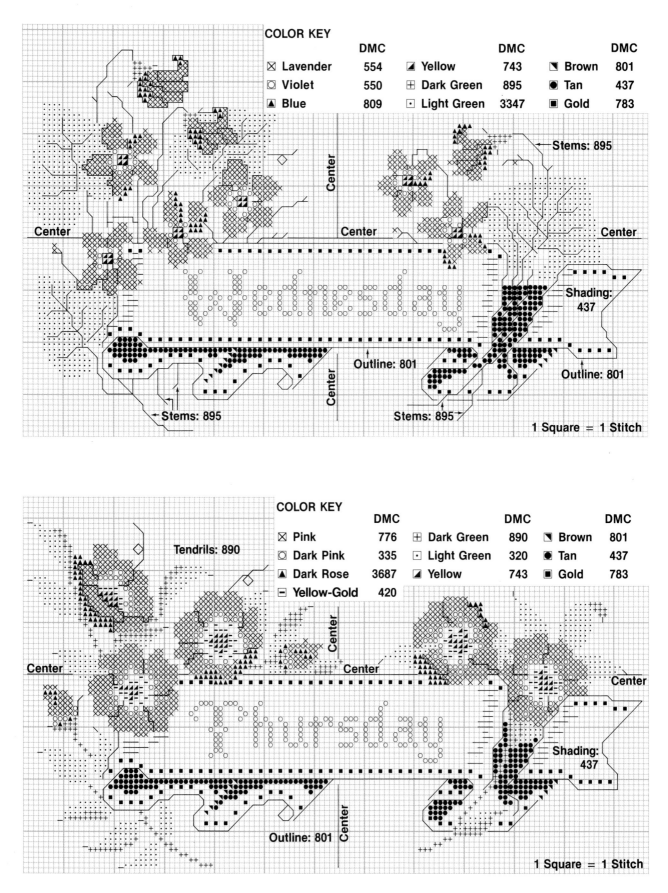

COLOR KEY

		DMC			DMC			DMC
⊠	Lavender	554	◪	Yellow	743	◥	Brown	801
○	Violet	550	⊞	Dark Green	895	●	Tan	437
▲	Blue	809	·	Light Green	3347	■	Gold	783

Stems: 895

Center

Center

Center

Center

Shading: 437

Outline: 801

Outline: 801

Stems: 895

Center

Stems: 895

1 Square = 1 Stitch

COLOR KEY

		DMC			DMC			DMC
⊠	Pink	776	⊞	Dark Green	890	◥	Brown	801
○	Dark Pink	335	·	Light Green	320	●	Tan	437
▲	Dark Rose	3687	◪	Yellow	743	■	Gold	783
−	Yellow-Gold	420						

Tendrils: 890

Center

Center

Center

Shading: 437

Outline: 801

Center

1 Square = 1 Stitch

166

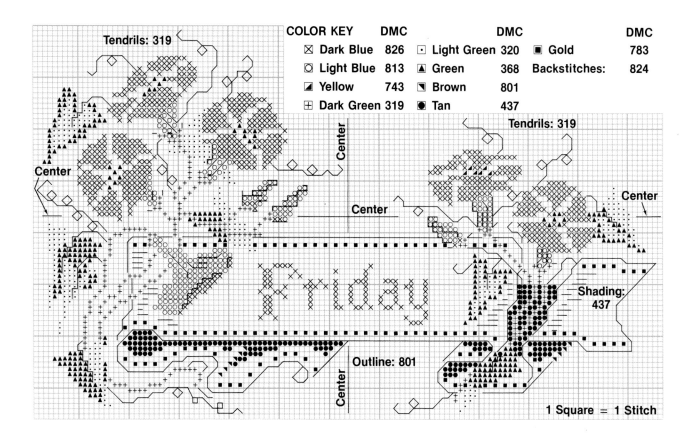

Tendrils: 319

COLOR KEY

		DMC			DMC			DMC
⊠	Dark Blue	826	⊡	Light Green	320	▣	Gold	783
◯	Light Blue	813	▲	Green	368		Backstitches:	824
◤	Yellow	743	◥	Brown	801			
⊞	Dark Green	319	●	Tan	437			

Center

Center

Tendrils: 319

Center

Center

Friday

Shading: 437

Outline: 801

Center

1 Square = 1 Stitch

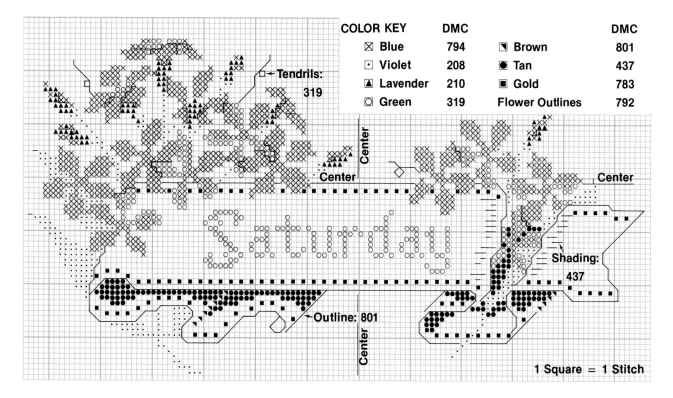

COLOR KEY

		DMC			DMC
⊠	Blue	794	◥	Brown	801
⊡	Violet	208	●	Tan	437
▲	Lavender	210	▣	Gold	783
◯	Green	319		Flower Outlines	792

←Tendrils: 319

Center

Center

Center

Saturday

Shading: 437

Outline: 801

Center

1 Square = 1 Stitch

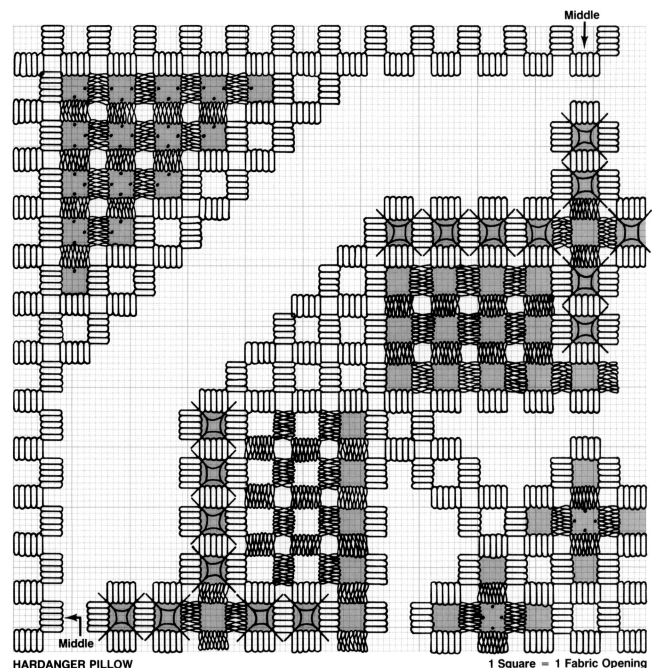

Middle ↑

↖ Middle

HARDANGER PILLOW

1 Square = 1 Fabric Opening

---

continued from page 164
Elegant Treasures for Everyday Uses

Crocheted Doily

Shown on page 156.
Finished size is 9 inches square.

MATERIALS
Size 30 cotton crochet thread: 1 ball of white
Size 9 steel crochet hook

168

Abbreviations: See page 92.
Gauge: Each motif is 3¾ inches square before joining and edging.

INSTRUCTIONS
MOTIF (Make 4): Beg at center, ch 14. Join with sl st to form ring.

Rnd 1: **Ch 4, holding on hook last lp of each st work 2 trc in ring, yo and draw through all lps on hook—beg cluster (cl) made; (ch 4, dc in**

---

ring, ch 4; **holding on hook last lp of each st work 3 trc in ring, yo and draw through all lps—cl made)** 3 times; ch 4, dc in ring, ch 4, join with sl st to top of beg cl.

Rnd 2: Ch 9 (count first 3 chs as dc, rem chs are ch-6 lp), * in next dc work (trc, ch 6, trc), ch 6, ** dc in top of next cl, ch 6; rep from * twice, work from * to **, join with sl st to third ch of beg ch-9. *Rnd 3:* Ch 4, * 5 trc in next ch-6 lp, trc in next trc, ch 6, sc in next ch-6 lp, ch 6, trc in next

HARDANGER PILLOW

1 Square = 1 Fabric Opening

trc, 5 trc in next ch-6 lp, ** trc in next dc; rep from * twice, work from * to **, join with sl st to top of beg ch-4.

Rnd 4: Ch 4, **holding on hook last lp of each st work 2 trc in same sp as joining, yo and draw through all lps on hook—beg cl made,** * ch 7, skip 5 trc, trc in next trc, ch 7, trc in each of next 2 ch-6 lps, ch 7, trc in next trc, ch 7, skip 5 trc, ** cl in next trc; rep from * twice, work from * to **, join with sl st to top of beg cl.

Rnd 5: Ch 8, 4 trc in first ch-7 lp, * trc in next trc, in next ch-7 lp work (4 trc, ch 7, 1 trc), in next ch-7 lp work (trc, ch 7, 4 trc); trc in next trc, 4 trc in next ch-7 lp, ch 4, ** trc in top of cl, ch 4, 4 trc in next ch-7 lp; rep from * twice, work from * to **, join with sl st to fourth ch of beg ch-8.

continued

continued

STITCH GUIDE

Kloster block (5 st over 4 threads)	
Oblique loops	Woven bar
Fabric openings	Woven bar with picot

169

continued from page 169
**Elegant Treasures for
Everyday Uses**

Rnd 6: Ch 4, trc in next trc, * ch 8, skip 3 trc, trc in next 5 trc, in next ch-7 lp work (4 trc, ch 8, trc), in next ch-7 lp work (trc, ch 8, 4 trc), trc in 5 trc, ch 8, skip 3 trc, ** (trc in next trc) 3 times; rep from * twice, work from * to **, trc in next trc, join with sl st to top of beg ch-4. Fasten off.

To finish, sew four motifs tog at side edges, leaving 2 ch-8 lps free at each corner of each motif.

CENTER FILLING: Join thread in a corner ch-8 lp at center of piece, ch 4, trc in each of rem corner ch-8 lps around center—7 trc and beg ch, join with sl st to top of beg ch-4. Fasten off.

EDGING: At top edge of upper left motif join thread in center trc of 3-trc group.

Rnd 1: Ch 4, in next ch-8 lp work (dc, ch 1) 3 times; (dc in next trc, ch 1, skip 1 trc) 4 times; dc in last trc, ch 1, * in next ch-8 lp at corner work (dc, ch 1) 4 times; in next ch-8 lp at same corner work (dc, ch 1) 4 times; (dc in next trc, ch 1, skip 1 trc) 4 times; dc in last trc, ch 1, in next ch-8 lp work (dc, ch 1) 3 times; dc in center trc of 3-trc group, ch 1, in next ch-8 lp work (dc, ch 1) 3 times; (dc in next trc, ch 1, skip 1 trc) 4 times; dc in last trc, ch 1, in next ch-8 lp work (dc, ch 1) 3 times; in next ch-8 lp at same corner work (dc, ch 1) 3 times; in next ch-8 lp of corner of *next motif* work (dc, ch 1) 3 times; in next ch-8 lp of same corner work (dc, ch 1) 3 times; (dc in next trc, ch 1, sk 1 trc) 4 times; dc in last trc, ch 1, in next ch-8 lp work (dc, ch 1) 3 times; ** dc in center trc of 3-trc group, ch 1, in next ch-8 lp work (dc, ch 1) 3 times; (dc in next trc, ch 1, sk 1 trc) 4 times; dc in last trc, ch 1; rep from * twice, work from * to **, join with sl st to third ch of beg ch-4.

Rnd 2: Sl st to first ch-1 sp formed by last ch of beg ch-4 of Rnd 1, ch 4, (dc in next ch-1 sp, ch 1) 11 times; * sc in next ch-1 sp for corner, ch 1, (dc in next ch-1 sp, ch 1) 24 times; (2 sc in next ch-1 sp) 5 times; ** ch 1, (dc in next ch-1 sp, ch 1) 24 times; rep from * twice, work from * to **, ch 1, (dc in next ch-1 sp, ch 1) 12 times, join to third ch of beg ch-4.

Rnd 3: Sl st to first ch-1 sp formed by last ch of beg ch-4 of Rnd 2, ch 4, (dc in next ch-1 sp, ch 1) 10 times; * sc in next ch-1 sp, sc in sc, sc in next ch-1 sp, ch 1, (dc in next ch-1 sp, ch 1) 23 times; skip next sc, sc in next 8 sc, ch 1, skip next sc and ch-1 sp, ** (dc in next ch-1 sp, ch 1) 23 times; rep from * twice, work from * to **, (dc in next ch-1 sp, ch 1) 12 times, join with sl st in third ch of beg ch-4.

Rnd 4: Sl st to first ch-1 sp formed by last ch of beg ch-4 of Rnd 3, ch 8, sl st in fourth ch from hook, trc in same ch-1 sp, [ch 5, skip 1 ch-1 sp, 2 sc in next ch-1 sp, ch 5, skip 1 ch-1 sp, in next ch-1 sp work (trc, **ch 4, sl st in fourth ch from hook—picot made,** trc)] 2 times; ch 5, skip 1 ch-1 sp, * sc in next ch-1 sp, sc in 3 sc, sc in next ch-1 sp, [ch 5, skip 1 ch-1 sp, in next ch-1 sp work (trc, picot, trc), ch 5, skip 1 ch-1 sp, 2 sc in next ch-1 sp] 5 times; ch 5, skip 1 ch-1 sp, in next ch-1 sp work (trc, picot, trc), ch 5, skip 1 ch-1 sp and sc, sc in 6 sc, ch 5, skip 1 sc and 1 ch-1 sp, ** [in next ch-1 sp work (trc, picot, trc), ch 5, skip 1 ch-1 sp, 2 sc in next ch-1 sp, ch 5, skip 1 ch-1 sp] 5 times; in next ch-1 sp work (trc, picot, trc), ch 5, skip 1 ch-1 sp; rep from * twice, work from * to **; [in next ch-1 sp work (trc, picot, trc), ch 5, skip 1 ch-1 sp, 2 sc in next ch-1 sp, ch 5, skip 1 ch-1 sp] 3 times, join with sl st to fourth ch of beg ch-8. Fasten off.

Crocheted Pillowcase Insertion
*Shown on pages 158–159.
Insertion is 1⅞ inches wide.*

MATERIALS
DMC Cébélia Size 30 crochet thread (50-gram balls): 1 ball of white for *each* pillowcase
Size 10 steel crochet hook, or size to obtain gauge; pillowcase

Abbreviations: See page 92.
Gauge: 8 sts = 1 inch; 17 rows = 2 inches.

INSTRUCTIONS
Ch 50. *Row 1:* Dc in eighth ch from hook, * ch 2, skip 2 chs, dc in next ch; rep from * across—15 sps. Ch 5,

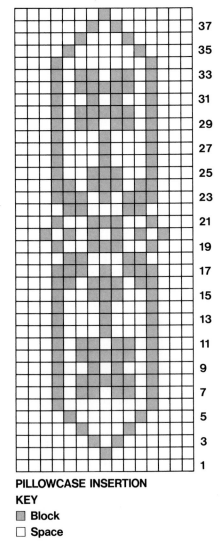

**PILLOWCASE INSERTION
KEY**
■ Block
□ Space

turn. *Row 2:* **Skip first dc, dc in next dc—beg sp over sp made; ch 2, dc in next dc—sp over sp made;** work 5 more sps, **2 dc in next ch-2 sp, dc in next dc—bl over sp made;** 6 sps, **ch 2, sk 2 ch, dc in next ch—end sp over sp made.** Ch 5, turn.

Row 3: Work beg sp over sp, 5 sps, 1 bl, **ch 2, skip 2 dc, dc in next dc—sp over bl made;** 1 bl, 5 sps, 1 end sp. Ch 5, turn. *Rows 4–6:* Follow chart, *opposite. Row 7:* Work beg sp, 2 sps, **dc in next 3 dc—bl over bl made;** (1 sp, 2 bl) 2 times, 1 sp, 1 bl, 2 sps, 1 end sp. Ch 5, turn. Follow chart through Row 38. Rep rows 1–38 until length is 40¼ inches. Fasten off. Sew ends into ring.

To finish, cut and finish a 2-inch-wide faced hem from hem end of purchased pillowcase. Narrowly hem remaining raw edge of case. Sew filet edges to hemmed edges of fabric pieces, matching side seams.

Crocheted Rose Insertion and Border

Shown on pages 158–159.
Insertion is 3¼ inches wide; border is 4 inches at widest point.

MATERIALS
DMC Cébélia Size 30 crochet thread (50-gram balls): 2 balls of white for *each* pillowcase
Size 10 steel crochet hook, or size to obtain gauge; pillowcase

Abbreviations: See page 92.
Gauge: 7 spaces = 1 inch; 7 rows = 1 inch.

INSTRUCTIONS
INSERTION: Ch 74. *Row 1:* Dc in eighth ch from hook, * ch 2, sk 2 ch, dc in next ch; rep from * across—23 sps. Ch 5, turn. *Row 2:* Sk first dc, dc in next dc—beg sp over sp made; ch 2, sk ch-2 sp, dc in next dc—sp over sp made, 8 sps; **2 dc in next ch-2 sp, dc in next dc—bl over sp made;** 11 sps, **ch 2, sk 2 ch, dc in next ch—end sp over sp made.** Ch 5, turn.

Row 3: Work 11 sps, bl; **ch 2, sk 2 dc, dc in next dc—sp over bl made;** 9

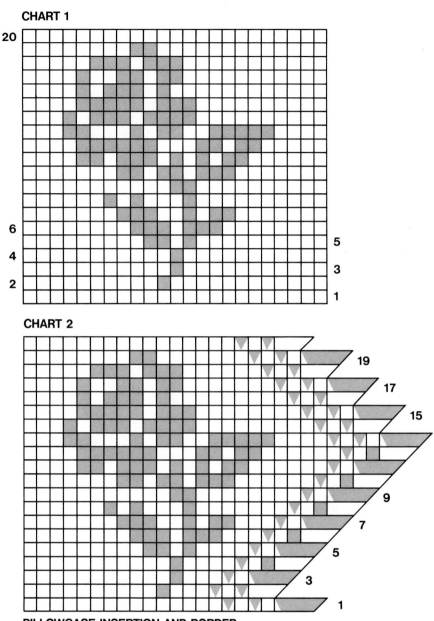

CHART 1

CHART 2

PILLOWCASE INSERTION AND BORDER

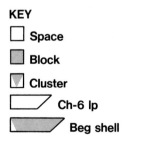

KEY

☐ Space

▨ Block

◩ Cluster

▱ Ch-6 lp

▱ Beg shell

sps, end sp. Ch 5, turn. *Row 4:* Work beg sp, 10 sps, **dc in next 3 dc—bl over bl made,** 10 sps, end sp. Ch 5, turn. Continue following chart 1, *above right,* for rows 5–20.

Rep rows 1–20, working Row 1 into sts of previous row; complete 14 repeats. Fasten off. Join ends.

BORDER: Ch 63. *Row 1:* Sc in second ch from hook, work 14 dc across next 6 ch, (ch 2, sk 3 ch, work 4 dc across next 2 ch) 2 times, ch 2, sk 2 ch, dc in next ch; 14 sps more. Ch 5, turn. *Row 2:* Work beg sp, 9 sps, bl, 2 sps; ch 2, sk next ch-2 sp, **4 dc in next ch-2 sp—cluster (cl) over sp made; ch 2, sk next 4 dc, 4 dc in next ch-2 sp—sp over cl and cl over sp made;** ch 6, sk next cl and ch-2 sp, sc in next dc. Ch 1, turn. *continued*

continued from page 171
Elegant Treasures for Everyday Uses

Row 3: **In first ch-6 lp work sc and 14 dc—beg shell made;** ch 2, sk next cl, cl in next ch-2 sp; **ch 2, sk 3 dc, dc in next dc—sp over cl made;** 2 sps, bl, 10 sps, end sp. Ch 5, turn.

Row 4: Work beg sp, 10 sps, bl, 3 sps, sp over cl and cl over sp; **ch 2, sk next 2 dc, dc in next 4 dc—4 dc bl made;** ch 6, sk next 8 dc, sc in last sc. Ch 1, turn. *Row 5:* Beg shell, ch 2, sk next bl, cl in next ch-2 sp, 4 sps, bl, sp, 2 bls, 8 sps, end sp. Ch 5, turn.

Work rows 6–12 following chart 2. *Row 13:* Beg shell, ch 2, sk next bl, cl in next ch-2 sp, ch 2, sk next cl, cl in next ch-2 sp, 4 sps, 5 bls, 2 sps, 2 bls, sp, bl, 3 sps, 2 bl, 2 sps, end sp. Ch 5, turn. *Row 14:* Beg sp, 2 sps, bl, sp, 3 bls, sp, 4 bls, 9 sps, cl, sp, cl, ch 6, sk next cl, and ch-2 sp, sc in next dc. Ch 1, turn.

Complete rows 15–20 following chart 2, page 171. *Next row (Row 1 of second rep):* Beg shell, (sk next cl, cl in next ch-2 sp) 2 times, 14 sps, end sp. Ch 5, turn. Continue working rows 2–20 following chart 2. Rep

these last 20 rows 12 times more—total of 14 reps. Fasten off. Sew first and last rows together to form ring.

TO FINISH: Open pillowcase hem; cut a 3½-inch-wide ring of fabric from end of case. Narrowly hem edges of ring; topstitch. Sew border and insertion to fabric ring. Hem rem raw edge; topstitch. Sew to remaining edge of insertion.

Embroidered Pillowcase
Shown on pages 158–159.
Finished size is 21x30 inches.

MATERIALS
Purchased pillowcase
Embroidery floss in light blue, dark blue, green, yellow, rose, orange, dark coral, orchid, tan, pink, and black; embroidery needle
Clark's crochet thread: 1 ball (No. 30) *each* of white and variegated blue; sizes 9 and 14 crochet hooks
Dressmaker's carbon paper; paper

INSTRUCTIONS
Trace pattern, *below,* onto paper; flop pattern for other half. Open hem on pillowcase; cut on first fold line. Placing scalloped edge of design on edge of case, transfer the design to pillowcase front using dressmaker's carbon paper. Transfer scalloped line to front and back.

EDGING: Cut pillowcase on scalloped line; sew rolled hem.

Row 1: With Size 14 hook and white, beg at side seam and work sc around edge (7 sts per inch), punching hook through fabric just above hem. Pull up sts so that chain of sc lies on folded edge. Fasten off. *Row 2:* Attach variegated thread in same st as join; with Size 9 hook ch 5, sk 2 sts, dc in next st, * ch 2, sk 2 sts, dc in next st *, rep between * around; join with sl st to third ch of beg ch 5.

Row 3: Sl st in next ch-2 sp, ch 3, make 3 dc in the same sp, 4 dc in the next ch-2 sp, * ch 2, 4 dc in each of the next two ch-2 sps, rep from * around; join with sl st to top of beg ch-3. *Row 4:* Sl st over next 3 dc, sc between the next 2 dc, sk 4 dc, * 4 dc in next ch-2 sp, **ch 5, sl st in first ch**

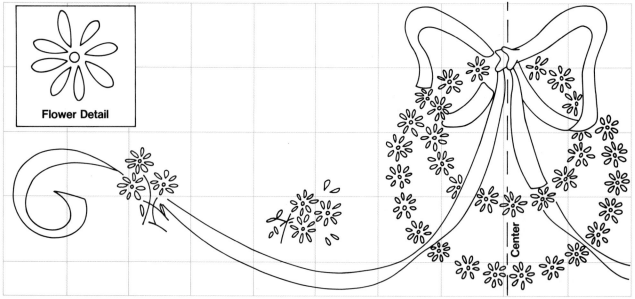

EMBROIDERED PILLOWCASE

1 Square = 1 Inch

of ch-5—picot made, 4 dc in the same sp; sk 4 dc, sc bet next 2 dc, sk 4 dc *, rep between * around; join with sl st to first sl st at beg of rnd. Fasten off.

EMBROIDERY: Referring to photograph for colors, satin-stitch ribbon using three strands of floss, and flower petals and leaves using two strands. Using two strands, embroi-der stems with outline stitches and work French knot flower centers.

Filet Crochet Bedspread

Shown on pages 160–161.
Size is 78x94 inches—sufficient for a single or double bed.

MATERIALS

J. & P. Coats Knit-Cro-Sheen cotton crochet thread (250-yard balls): 48 balls of white for the single/double spread shown. To make a larger spread, plan to allow 1 ball for each block; this will leave enough thread for the outside border.

Size 7 steel crochet hook

continued

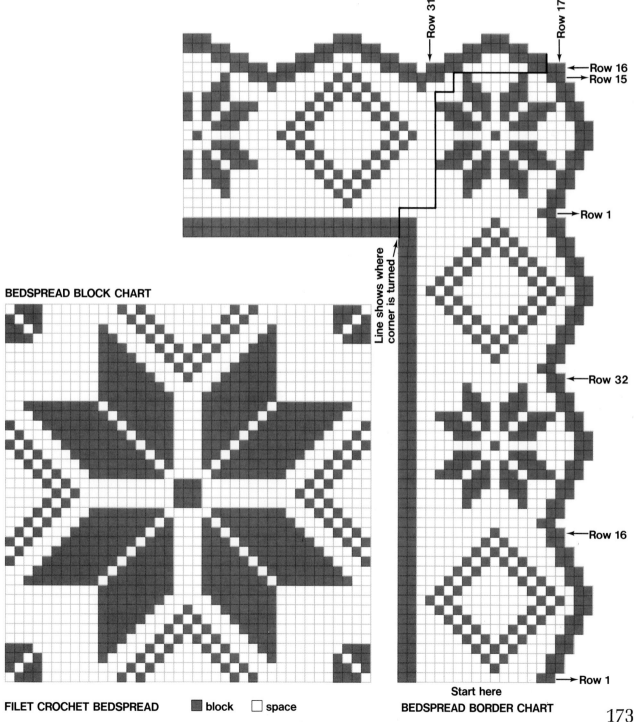

BEDSPREAD BLOCK CHART

FILET CROCHET BEDSPREAD ■ block □ space

BEDSPREAD BORDER CHART

173

continued from page 173
Elegant Treasures for Everyday Uses

Abbreviations: See page 92.
Gauge: 10 dc = 1 inch;
4 rows = 1 inch.

INSTRUCTIONS

The bedspread shown consists of six rows of eight blocks each, plus a border on three sides. You can make the bedspread any size because blocks and borders are worked separately and then sewn together. Blocks are approximately 11 inches square when pressed flat; the border is 6 inches wide at the points.

BLOCKS: Ch 12. *Row 1:* Dc in fourth ch from hook and in each of rem 8 sts. Ch 3, turn. *Row 2:* Dc in second dc, in each of rem 7 dc, and in top of turning ch. Ch 3, turn. Rep Row 2 twice more. At end of fourth row do not turn; ch 5 and work in rnds.

Rnd 1: Working along side of bl, dc in side of third row, ch 2, dc in side of second row, ch 2, make (dc, ch 5, dc) in corner, (ch 2, sk 2 sts, dc in next st) 2 times, ch 2, (dc, ch 5, dc) in next corner. Work across other 2 sides and third corner as before. End with dc in last corner, ch 2, dc in third st of initial ch-5—3 sps on each side of bl plus the 4 corner sps.

Rnd 2: Ch 3, 2 dc in sp, dc in third st of ch-5 of previous row. * (Ch 2, dc in next dc) 3 times, (3 dc, ch 5, 3 dc) in corner sp, dc in next dc. Rep from * around to last corner, end with 3 dc in last sp, ch 2, dc in top of beg ch-3. *Rnd 3:* Ch 3, 2 dc in sp. * Dc in each of 4 dc (count first ch-3 of previous rnd as a dc), (ch 2, dc in next dc) 3 times, dc in last 3 dc, (3 dc, ch 5, 3 dc) in corner sp. Rep from * around, end with last corner same as previous row.

Rnds 4–18: Continue working in bls and sps to make design as shown on chart, page 173. All sps consist of 2 dc with ch-2 between, and bls will have 2 dc in place of the 2 ch. On rnds 10–15, start row with (ch 5, dc) in first dc, then make other 3 corners by working (dc, ch 5, dc) in center st of corner ch. Finish rnd with dc in same place as starting ch,

then work (ch 2, dc) in third st of initial ch-5. Corners on rnds 16–18 are same as those of rnds 1–9. Fasten off at end of Rnd 18.

When blocks are complete, press squares flat. Sew together by hand with double strand of sewing thread in a matching color.

BORDER: *Row 1:* Ch 54, dc in fourth ch from hook and in each of next 5 ch, (ch 2, sk 2 ch, dc in next ch) 13 times, dc in each of last 6 sts. Ch 5, turn. *Row 2:* Dc in fourth and fifth chs from hook and in first 4 dc of previous row, ch 2, sk 2 dc, dc in next dc, (ch 2, dc in next dc) 4 times, 2 dc in next sp, (dc in next dc, ch 2) 8 times, dc in last 6 dc and in top of turning ch. Ch 3, turn.

Continue working in bls and sps to make design shown on chart. Make ch-5 to turn when a bl is increased on the edge; ch-3 to turn when work is even. Skip last 3 sts when a bl is decreased. Rep rows 1–32 several times, ending with Row 16, until work will fit along entire side edge of spread.

Border does not match row for row with edge of spread top. Ease border slightly during assembly.

CORNER: When border is the correct length (ending with Row 16), ch 5 to turn and start with Row 1 of corner. *Row 1:* Sk 2 dc, dc in next dc, ch 2, sk 2 dc, dc in next dc, make 13 more sps across and end with 2 bls.

Row 2: Work as shown, having only 12 sps on row. Heavy line on chart shows ends of rows. Follow chart through Row 15, ch 3, turn. *Row 16:* Make 2 bls as shown. Now follow instructions below and chart to make turned corner as shown.

Row 17: Ch 5, dc in fourth and fifth chs from hook, dc in corner of Row 16, 2 dc in side of last dc of that row, sl st in top of dc on Row 15.

Row 18: Ch 2, sl st in next available dc of Row 15, turn and dc in rem 4 dc and top of turning ch on Row 17 to make 2 bls. Ch 5, turn.

Row 19: Dc in fourth and fifth chs from hook and in first 4 dc of previous row, then make dc in top of dc at side of bl on Row 15. *Row 20:* Ch 2, dc in next dc on Row 15, turn and dc

in rem 5 dc and top of turning ch on Row 19 to make 2 bls. Ch 5, turn.

Rows 21–32: Continue following chart, attaching work at inner edge to Row 15 as before. Row 29 will be worked across side of corner section and attached to Row 1. *Row 33:* Work across as shown on chart, making the 2 bls at end of row over sides of 2 bls in previous section.

Continue with another straight section and turned corner as before, of sufficient length for end of spread. After second corner, work straight, making third side same length as first. Fasten off at end of third side.

TO ASSEMBLE: Press border flat; sew to bedspread by hand with double strand of sewing thread. After border has been sewn on, work 2 rows dc across top end of spread.

Crocheted Spiderweb Cloth
Shown on pages 162–163.
Finished size is 54 inches square.

MATERIALS
Clark's Big Ball 3-cord mercerized crochet cotton, Size 20 (300-yard balls): 13 balls
Sizes 9 and 10 steel crochet hooks

Abbreviations: See page 92.

INSTRUCTIONS
With Size 20 thread and Size 9 hook ch 8, sl st to form ring.

Rnd 1: Ch 4, 3 trc in ring, (ch 5, 4 trc in ring) 3 times, ch 3, dc in top of ch-4. (When starting following rows, consider beg ch-4 of previous row a trc.) *Rnd 2:* Ch 4, 2 trc over dc, * trc in first trc, ch 15, sk 2 sts, trc in last trc, make (3 trc, ch 5, 3 trc) in corner. Rep from * around, end with 3 trc in last corner sp, ch 3, dc in top of beg ch-4. (From now on, finish last corner on each rnd this way.)

Rnd 3: Ch 4, 2 trc over dc, * trc in first trc, ch 7, 2 sc over lp, ch 7, trc in fourth trc of next grp, (3 trc, ch 5, 3 trc) in corner. Rep from * around. *Rnd 4:* Ch 4, 2 trc over dc, * trc in first trc, ch 8, sc over lp, sc in each of 2 sc, sc over next lp, ch 8, trc in fourth trc of next grp, (3 trc, ch 5, 3 trc) in corner sp. Rep from * around.

Rnd 5: Ch 4, 2 trc over dc, * trc in first trc, ch 10, sc over lp, sc in each of 4 sc, sc over lp, ch 10, trc in fourth trc of next grp, make (3 trc, ch 5, 3 trc) in corner sp. Rep from * around.

Rnd 6: Ch 4, 2 trc over dc, * trc in first trc, ch 15, sk 2 sts, trc in last trc of same grp, 3 trc over lp, ch 9, sk first sc, sc in 4 center sc, ch 9, 3 trc over lp, trc in first trc, ch 15, sk 2 sts, trc in last trc of same grp, (3 trc, ch 5, 3 trc) in corner. Rep from * around.

Rnd 7: Ch 4, 2 trc over dc, * trc in first trc, ch 7, 2 sc over lp, ch 7, trc in fourth trc of next grp, 3 trc over lp, ch 10, sc in each of 2 center sc, ch 10, 3 trc over lp, trc in first trc, ch 7, 2 sc over lp, ch 7, trc in fourth trc of next grp, (3 trc, ch 5, 3 trc) in corner. Rep from * around.

Rnd 8: Ch 4, 2 trc over dc, * trc in first trc, ch 8, sc over lp, sc in 2 sc, sc over next lp, ch 8, trc in fourth trc of next grp, 3 trc over lp, ch 2, 3 trc over next lp, trc in first trc, ch 8, sc over lp, sc in 2 sc, sc over next lp, ch 8, trc in fourth trc of next grp, (3 trc, ch 5, 3 trc) in corner sp. Rep from * around.

Rnd 9: Ch 4, 2 trc over dc, * trc in first trc, ch 10, sc over lp, sc in 4 sc, sc over lp, ch 10, trc in fourth trc of next grp. Make 2 trc in sp and rep from * across side, with (3 trc, ch 5, 3 trc) in corner. Work rem sides to correspond. Rep rnds 6–9, inc the numbers of spiderwebs until cloth is about 4 inches shorter along side than desired finished measurement.

BORDER: *Rnd 10:* Work same as Rnd 6, but with ch 2 instead of ch 15 between trc grps. *Rnd 11:* Ch 4, 2 trc over dc, * (trc in first trc, ch 2, sk 2 trc, trc in fourth st of same grp, 2 trc in next sp) 2 times, make a third trc in last sp, ch 10, sc in 2 center sc, ch 10, 3 trc over lp. Rep from * across side with (3 trc, ch 5, 3 trc) in corner.

Rnd 12: Ch 4, 2 trc over dc, * (trc in first trc, ch 2, trc in fourth trc of same group, 2 trc in next sp) 3 times, make a third trc in last sp, ch 2, 3 trc in next sp. Rep from * across side, make corners as usual.

Rnd 13: Ch 4, 2 trc over dc, * trc in next trc, ch 2, trc in fourth trc of same grp, 2 trc in next sp. Rep from *

across side, make corners as usual. *Rnd 14:* Ch 4, trc over dc, * in next sp make 3 trc, ch 5, sl st in top of last trc made for picot, 3 trc in same sp. Rep from * across side, in corner make 5 trc, picot, 5 trc. Work around rest of cloth same way. In last corner make 5 trc and picot, sl st in top of beg ch-4. Fasten off. Starch; press.

Crocheted Wedding-Ring Cloth
Shown on pages 162–163.
Cloth is 59 inches in diameter.

MATERIALS
DMC Cébélia Size 30 crochet thread (50-gram balls): 9 balls of white
Size 7 steel crochet hook, or size to obtain gauge

Abbreviations: See page 92.
Gauge: 12 dc = 1 inch;
6 rows = 1 inch.

INSTRUCTIONS
Work pairs of entwined rings first; join pairs as they are worked. Then crochet center of cloth from inner edge of rings to center. Finally, work border along outer edge of rings.

RINGS (Make 48 pairs): **First Ring:** Ch 26, join with sl st to form ring.

Rnd 1: Ch 3, work 59 dc in ring, join with sl st to top of beg ch-3—60 dc, counting ch-3 as dc. *Rnd 2:* Ch 4, * sk next dc, dc in next dc, ch 1; rep from * ending sk last dc, join with sl st to third ch of beg ch-4—30 ch-1 sps. (Hereafter, when rnd is joined to third chain of beg ch-4, fourth chain of ch-4 may be referred to as ch-1 sp.) *Rnd 3:* * Sc in next ch-1 sp, ch 3; rep from * joining with sl st to first sc—30 ch-3 lps. Fasten off.

Second Ring: Ch 26. Lace beg of ch through center of First Ring, joining with sl st in first ch to form entwined rings. Complete same as First Ring—ring pair completed.

Third Ring: Work rnds 1–2 same as First Ring. Join to Second Ring as follows: *Rnd 3:* Work same as First

Ring until there are 11 ch-3 lps, ending with sc; ch 1, join with sc in tenth ch-3 lp from end of Rnd 3 of Second Ring, (ch 1, sc in next ch-1 sp of Rnd 2 of Third Ring, ch 1, sc in next lp of Second Ring) 2 times; ch 1, sc in next ch-1 sp of Third Ring; complete ch-3 lps around Third Ring, join with sl st to first sc. Fasten off.

Fourth Ring: Entwine with Third Ring same as Second Ring entwines with First Ring. Continue working ring pairs same as Third and Fourth rings, joining pairs to form one large band and joining last ring to First Ring in three ch-3 lps. Fasten off.

Overlap ch-3 lp at top of First and Second rings; overlap ch-3 lp at bottom of first and second rings, allowing 19 ch-3 lps on outer edge of ring at right between these 2 points and 17 ch-3 lps on outer edge of ring at left between these 2 points (see illustration, page 176).

CENTER: *Rnd 1:* Join thread in top overlapped lps of ring pair, **in same sp work (ch 3, dc, ch 2, 2 dc)—beg cluster (cl) made;** (ch 3; sk next ch-3 lp, **in next ch-3 lp work 2 dc and ch 2 and 2 dc—cl made)** 2 times; * ch 5, sk next 2 ch-3 lps of same ring and next 2 free ch-3 lps of next ring, (in next ch-3 lp work cl, ch 3, sk next lp) 2 times; ** in next overlapped lps work cl, (ch 3, sk next lp, cl in next ch-3 lp) 2 times; rep from * around ending at **, join with sl st to top of beg ch-3.

Rnd 2: Sl st to ch-2 sp of beg cl, ch 5, dc in next ch-3 lp, ch 2, dc in ch-2 sp of next cl, ch 2, dc in next ch-3 lp, ch 2; **cl in ch-2 sp of next cl—cl over cl made;** * ch 2, dc in center of ch-5 lp, ch 2, cl over next cl, ** (ch 2, dc in next ch-3 lp, ch 2, dc in ch-2 sp of next cl) 3 times; ch 2, dc in next ch-3 lp, ch 2, cl over next cl; rep from *, end at **, ch 2, dc in next ch-3 lp, ch 2, dc in next cl, ch 2, dc in next ch-3 lp, ch 2, join with sl st in third ch of beg ch-5. Join rnds 3–21 same as Rnd 2. (Where several consecutive rnds end the same way, instructions will be given first as above. Rnds 3–21 simply say "join.") *continued*

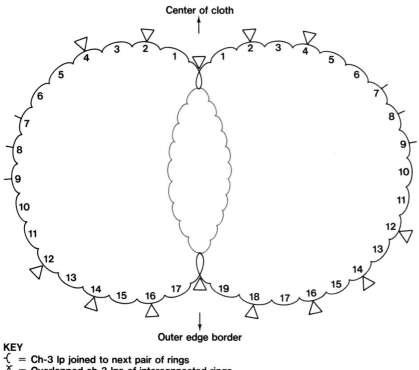

KEY
‏ ⸂ = Ch-3 lp joined to next pair of rings
⸫ = Overlapped ch-3 lps of interconnected rings
ⸯ = Cluster worked in ch-3 lp
⸮ = Cluster worked in interconnected rings

continued from page 175
Elegant Treasures for Everyday Uses

Unless otherwise indicated, for rnds hereafter, rep between *'s; omit instructions in [ ]'s until last rep. For last rep, beg at first *, work to [, follow instructions to]; omit directions (if any) from] to second *. Where [ ]'s begin with a number and "times," rep sts in ( )'s immediately preceding [the indicated number of times *on last rnd*. For example, "(ch 1, dc in next dc) 6 times [4 times, join]" means that on all reps except last one, (ch 1, dc in next dc) 6 times. On last rep of rnd, (ch 1, dc in next dc) 4 times, then join to end rnd. Where directions for last rep are "[join]," last rep ends at this point, with no more sts except for joining.

Unless otherwise indicated, work sts into same kind of sts; for example, "3 sc" means (sc in sc) 3 times.

Rnd 3: Ch 5, (dc in next dc, ch 2) 3 times; * dc in ch-2 sp of cl, ch 2, dc in next ch-2 sp, dc in next dc, dc in next ch-2 sp, ch 2, dc in ch-2 sp of

next cl, (ch 2, dc in next dc) 7 times [3 times, ch 2, join]; ch 2 *. *Rnd 4:* Ch 5, (dc in next dc, ch 2) 4 times; **2 dc in next dc—inc dc made;** dc in next dc, inc dc, (ch 2, dc in next dc) 9 times [4 times, ch 2, join]; ch 2 *.

Rnd 5: Ch 5, (dc in next dc, ch 2) 3 times; dc in next dc, * inc dc, 3 dc, inc dc, dc in next dc, (ch 2, dc in next dc) 8 times [3 times, ch 2, join] *.

Rnd 6: Ch 5, (dc in next dc, ch 2) 3 times; * sk next dc, inc dc, 5 dc, inc dc, ch 2, sk next dc, (dc in next dc, ch 2) 7 times [3 times, join] *. *Rnd 7:* Ch 5, (dc in dc, ch 2) 3 times; * inc dc, 7 dc, inc dc, ch 2, (dc in dc, ch 2) 7 times [3 times, join] *. *Rnd 8:* Ch 5, (dc in dc, ch 2) 2 times; dc in next dc, * inc dc, 9 dc, inc dc, dc in next dc, (ch 2, dc in dc) 6 times [2 times, ch 2, join]; *. *Rnd 9:* Ch 5, (dc in dc, ch 2) 2 times; * sk next dc, inc dc, 11 dc, inc dc, sk next dc, (ch 2, dc in dc) 5 times [2 times, ch 2, join]; ch 2 *.

Rnd 10: Ch 5, (dc in dc, ch 2) 2 times; * inc dc, 13 dc, inc dc, (ch 2, dc in dc) 5 times [2 times, ch 2, join]; ch 2 *. *Rnd 11:* Ch 5, (dc in dc, ch 2) 2 times; * inc dc, 15 dc, inc dc, (ch 2, dc

in dc) 5 times [2 times, ch 2, join]; ch 2 *. *Rnd 12:* Ch 5, dc in dc, ch 2, dc in next dc, * inc dc, 5 dc, ch 2, sk 2 dc, 3 dc, ch 2, sk 2 dc, 5 dc, inc dc, dc in next dc, (ch 2, dc in dc) 4 times [1 time, ch 2, join] *. *Rnd 13:* Ch 5, dc in next dc, * ch 2, sk next dc, inc dc, 4 dc, ch 2, sk 2 dc, (3 dc in next ch-2 sp, ch 2) 2 times; sk next 2 dc, 4 dc, inc dc, sk next dc, (ch 2, dc in dc) 3 times [1 time, ch 2, join] *.

Rnd 14: Ch 5, dc in next dc, * ch 2, inc dc, 3 dc, ch 2, 3 dc in next ch-2 sp, ch 3, trc in next ch-2 sp, ch 3, 3 dc in next ch-2 sp, ch 2, sk 2 dc, 3 dc, inc dc, (ch 2, dc in dc) 3 times [1 time, ch 2, join] *. *Rnd 15:* Ch 5, dc in next dc, * ch 2, inc dc, 2 dc, ch 2, 3 dc in next ch-2 sp, ch 3, sc in third ch of next ch-3 lp and trc and next ch, ch 3, 3 dc in next ch-2 sp, ch 2, sk 2 dc, 2 dc, inc dc, (ch 2, dc in dc) 3 times [1 time, ch 2, join] *.

Rnd 16: Ch 5, dc in next dc, * ch 2, inc dc, dc in next dc, ch 2, 3 dc in next ch-2 sp, ch 4, sc in last ch of next ch-3 lp, 3 sc, sc in next ch, ch 4, 3 dc in next ch-2 sp, ch 2, sk 2 dc, dc in next dc, inc dc, (ch 2, dc in dc) 3 times [1 time, ch 2, join] *. *Rnd 17:* Ch 5, dc in next dc, * ch 2, inc dc, ch 2, 3 dc in next ch-2 sp, ch 5, sc in last ch of ch-4 lp, 5 sc, sc in next ch, ch 5, 3 dc in next ch-2 sp, ch 2, sk next 2 dc, inc dc, (ch 2, dc in dc) 3 times [1 time, ch 2, join] *.

Rnd 18: Ch 5, dc in next dc, * inc dc, dc in next dc, 2 dc in next ch-2 sp, ch 2, sk next 3 dc, 3 dc in the next ch-5 lp, ch 4, sk next sc, 5 sc, ch 4, 3 dc in next ch-5 lp, ch 2, sk next 3 dc, 2 dc in next ch-2 sp, dc in next dc, inc dc, dc in next dc, (ch 2, join], (ch 2, dc in dc) 2 times *. *Rnd 19:* Ch 5, sk next dc, * inc dc, 4 dc, dc in next ch-2 sp, ch 2, 3 dc in next ch-4 lp, ch 3, sk next sc, 3 sc, ch 3, 3 dc in next ch-4 lp, ch 2, dc in next ch-2 sp, 4 dc, inc dc, ch 2, sk next dc, [join], dc in next dc, ch 2 *.

Rnd 20: Ch 5, * inc dc, 6 dc, dc in ch-2 sp, ch 2, 3 dc in next ch-3 lp, ch 2, trc in center sc, ch 2, 3 dc in next ch-3 lp, ch 2, dc in next ch-2 sp, 6 dc, inc dc, ch 2, [join], dc in next dc, ch 2 *. *Rnd 21:* Ch 5, * inc dc, 8 dc, dc in ch-2 sp, (ch 2, 3 dc in next ch-2 sp) 2 times; ch 2, dc in next ch-2 sp, 8 dc, inc dc, ch 2, [join], dc in dc, ch 2 *.

Rnd 22: Ch 3, * inc dc, 10 dc, dc in ch-2 sp, ch 2, 3 dc in next ch-2 sp, ch 2, dc in ch-2 sp, 10 dc, inc dc, ch 2, [join with sl st in top of beg ch-3], dc in dc *. Rnds 23–30 are joined as for Rnd 22. *Rnd 23:* Sl st to next dc, ch 3, dc in same dc, * dc in next dc, (ch 1, sk 1 dc, dc in next dc) 5 times; ch 1, sk 1 dc, 3 dc in ch-2 sp, ch 2, 3 dc in next ch-2 sp, (ch 1, sk 1 dc, dc in next dc) 6 times; inc dc, ch 2, [join], sk 1 dc, inc dc *. *Rnd 24:* Ch 3, dc in same sp as joining, * 2 dc, (ch 1, sk ch-1 sp, dc in dc) 4 times; ch 2, sk ch-1 sp, 3 dc in next ch-1 sp, ch 2, trc in next ch-2 sp, ch 2, 3 dc in next ch-1 sp, ch 2, sk 1 dc, (dc in dc, ch 1) 4 times; 2 dc, inc dc, ch 2, [join], inc dc *.

Rnd 25: Ch 3, 3 dc, * (ch 1, dc in dc) 3 times; ch 2, sk ch-1 sp, 3 dc in next ch-2 sp, ch 3, sc in last ch of next ch-2 sp and trc and next ch, ch 3, 3 dc in next ch-2 sp, ch 2, sk next dc, (dc in dc, ch 1) 3 times; 4 dc, ch 2, [join], 4 dc *. *Rnd 26:* Ch 3, 3 dc, * (ch 1, dc in dc) 2 times; ch 2, sk ch-1 sp, 3 dc in next ch-2 sp, ch 3, sc in last ch of ch-3 lp, 3 sc, sc in next ch, ch 3, 3 dc in next ch-2 sp, ch 2, sk ch-1 sp, (dc in dc, ch 1) 2 times; 4 dc, ch 1, [join], 4 dc *. *Rnd 27:* Ch 3, 3 dc, * ch 1, dc in dc, ch 1, sk ch-1 sp, 3 dc in next ch-2 sp, ch 4, sc in last ch of ch-3 lp, 5 sc, sc in next ch, ch 4, 3 dc in next ch-2 sp, ch 1, sk ch-1 sp, dc in dc, ch 1, 4 dc, ch 1, [join], 4 dc *.

Rnd 28: Sl st to next dc, ch 3, 2 dc, * ch 1, (dc in dc, ch 1) 2 times; 3 dc in next ch-4 lp, ch 4, sk 1 sc, 5 sc, ch 4, 3 dc in ch-4 lp, ch 1, sk 2 dc, (dc in dc, ch 1) 2 times; 3 dc, ch 2, sk dc and ch 1 and dc, [join], 3 dc *. *Rnd 29:* Ch 3, 2 dc, * (ch 1, dc in dc) 3 times; ch 1, 3 dc in next ch-4 lp, ch 3, sk 1 sc, 3 sc, ch 3, 3 dc in next ch-4 lp, ch 1, sk 2 dc, (dc in dc, ch 1) 3 times; 3 dc, ch 2, [join], 3 dc *. *Rnd 30:* Sl st to next dc, ch 3, 1 dc, * (ch 1, dc in dc) 4 times; ch 1, 3 dc in ch-3 lp, ch 2, trc in center sc, ch 2, 3 dc in ch-3 lp, ch 1, sk 2 dc, (dc in dc, ch 1) 4 times; 2 dc, ch 2, [join], sk dc and ch 2 and dc, 2 dc *.

Rnd 31: Sl st to the next dc, ch 4, (dc in dc, ch 1) 5 times; * sk 2 dc, 3 dc in ch-2 sp, ch 2, 3 dc in ch-2 sp, ch 1, sk 2 dc, (dc in dc, ch 1) 6 times; dc in ch-2 sp, ch 1, [join with sl st in third ch of beg ch-4], sk 1 dc, (dc in dc,

ch 1) 6 times *. *Rnd 32:* Ch 3, * (dc in ch-1 sp, dc in dc) 6 times; ch 2, 3 dc in ch-2 sp, ch 2, sk 2 dc, (dc in dc, dc in ch-1 sp) 6 times; (dc in dc, ch 1) 2 times; [join with sl st in top of beg ch-3], dc in dc *. When rnd beg to *right* of end of rnd just finished (for example, Rnd 33, *below*), ch-3 at beg of previous rnd is referred to as a dc when skipped or worked into.

Rnd 33: Turn, sl st to last dc worked, turn, ch 4, sk next dc, * 10 dc, (ch 1, 3 dc in ch-2 sp) 2 times; ch 1, sk 2 dc, 10 dc, ch 1, sk 1 dc, [join with sl st in third ch of beg ch-4], dc in dc, ch 1, sk 1 dc *. Join rnds 34–102 same as Rnd 33. *Rnd 34:* Ch 4, * sk 1 dc, 7 dc, ch 1, 3 dc in ch-1 sp, ch 2, trc in ch-1 sp, ch 2, 3 dc in ch-1 sp, ch 1, sk 2 dc, 7 dc, ch 1, sk 1 dc, [join], dc in dc, ch 1 *. *Rnd 35:* Ch 4, * sk 1 dc, 4 dc, ch 1, 3 dc in ch-1 sp, ch 3, sc in second ch of ch-2 sp and trc and next ch, ch 3, 3 dc in ch-1 sp, ch 1, sk 2 dc, 4 dc, ch 1, [join], sk 1 dc, dc in dc, ch 1 *.

Rnd 36: Ch 4, * sk 1 dc, 2 dc, ch 1, 3 dc in ch-1 sp, ch 3, sc in third ch of ch-3 lp, 3 sc, sc in next ch, ch 3, 3 dc in ch-1 sp, ch 1, sk 1 dc, 2 dc, ch 1, sk 1 dc, [join], dc in dc, ch 1 *. *Rnd 37:* Ch 4, dc in dc, ch 1, * 3 dc in ch-1 sp, ch 4, sc in third ch of ch-3 lp, 5 sc, sc in next ch, ch 4, 3 dc in next ch-1 sp, ch 1, sk 1 dc, (dc in dc, ch 1) 3 times [1 time, join] *. *Rnd 38:* Ch 4, (dc in dc, ch 1) 2 times; * sk 2 dc, 3 dc in ch-4 lp, ch 3, sk 1 sc, 5 sc, ch 3, 3 dc in ch-4 lp, ch 1, sk 2 dc, (dc in dc, ch 1) 5 times [2 times, join] *. *Rnd 39:* Ch 4, (dc in dc, ch 1) 3 times; * 3 dc in ch-3 lp, ch 3, sk 1 sc, 3 sc, ch 3, 3 dc in ch-3 lp, ch 1, sk 2 dc, (dc in dc, ch 1) 7 times [3 times, join] *.

Rnd 40: Ch 4, (dc in dc, ch 1) 3 times; * dc in dc, 3 dc in ch-3 lp, ch 2, trc in center sc, ch 2, 3 dc in ch-3 lp, sk 2 dc, (dc in dc, ch 1) 8 times [4 times, join] *. *Rnd 41:* Ch 4, dc in dc, ch 1, * (dc in dc) 2 times; dc in ch-1 sp, 4 dc, dc in ch-2 sp, ch 2, dc in ch-2 sp, 4 dc, dc in ch-1 sp, dc in dc, (dc in dc, ch 1) 4 times [2 times, join] *.

Rnd 42: Ch 4, dc in dc, ch 1, * 8 dc, 3 dc in ch-2 sp, 8 dc, (dc in dc, ch 1) 3 times [1 time, join] *. *Rnd 43:* Ch 4, dc in dc, ch 1, * sk 1 dc, 17 dc, ch 1, sk 1 dc, (dc in dc, ch 1) 3 times [1 time, join] *. *Rnd 44:* Ch 4, dc in dc, ch 1,

* sk 1 dc, 15 dc, ch 1, sk 1 dc, (dc in dc, ch 1) 3 times [1 time, join] *. *Rnd 45:* **Ch 4, dc in same sp as joining—beg inc sp made,** * ch 1, dc in dc, ch 1, sk 1 dc, 13 dc, ch 1, sk 1 dc, dc in dc, ch 1 [join], **in next dc work (dc, ch 1, dc)—inc sp made** *.

Rnd 46: Ch 4, (dc in dc, ch 1) 2 times; * sk 1 dc, 11 dc, ch 1, sk 1 dc, (dc in dc, ch 1) 4 times [1 time, join] *. *Rnd 47:* Sl st to next dc, beg inc sp, ch 1, dc in dc, * ch 1, sk 1 dc, 9 dc, ch 1, sk 1 dc, (dc in dc, ch 1) 2 times [1 time, dc in same sp as joining of previous rnd, ch 1, join]; inc sp in next dc, ch 1, dc in dc *. *Rnd 48:* Beg inc sp, * (ch 1, dc in dc) 2 times; ch 1, sk 1 dc, 7 dc, ch 1, sk 1 dc, (dc in dc, ch 1) 2 times; [join], inc sp in next dc *.

Rnd 49: Ch 4, (dc in dc, ch 1) 2 times; dc in dc, * ch 1, dc in ch-1 sp, ch 1, sk 1 dc, 5 dc, ch 1, sk 1 dc, dc in ch-1 sp, (ch 1, dc in dc) 6 times [2 times, ch 1, join] *. *Rnd 50:* Ch 4, (dc in dc, ch 1) 4 times; * dc in ch-1 sp, ch 1, sk 1 dc, 3 dc, ch 1, dc in ch-1 sp, ch 1, (dc in dc, ch 1) 8 times [3 times, join] *. *Rnd 51:* Ch 4, (dc in dc, ch 1) 5 times; * dc in center of 3 dc, ch 1, sk last dc of center 3 dc, (dc in dc, ch 1) 10 times [4 times, join] *.

Rnd 52: Ch 4, (dc in dc, ch 1) 4 times; * sk 1 dc, dc in ch-1 sp and dc and ch-1 sp, ch 1, sk 1 dc, (dc in dc, ch 1) 8 times [3 times, join] *. *Rnd 53:* Ch 4, (dc in dc, ch 1) 4 times; * inc dc, 1 dc, inc dc, ch 1, (dc in dc, ch 1) 8 times [3 times, join] *. *Rnd 54:* Ch 4, (dc in dc, ch 1) 3 times; * dc in dc, sk 1 ch, 5 dc, (dc in dc, ch 1) 7 times [3 times, join] *. *Rnd 55:* Ch 4, (dc in dc, ch 1) 3 times; * inc dc, 5 dc, inc dc, ch 1, (dc in dc, ch 1) 6 times [2 times, join] *. *Rnd 56:* Ch 4, (dc in dc, ch 1) 2 times; * dc in dc, sk 1 ch, 9 dc, (dc in dc, ch 1) 5 times [2 times, join] *.

Rnd 57: Ch 4, (dc in dc, ch 1) 2 times; * inc dc, 9 dc, inc dc, ch 1, (dc in dc, ch 1) 4 times [1 time, join] *. *Rnd 58:* Ch 4, dc in dc, ch 1, * dc in dc, sk 1 ch, 6 dc, ch 1, sk 1 dc, 6 dc, (dc in dc, ch 1) 3 times [1 time, join] *. *Rnd 59:* Ch 4, dc in dc, * ch 1, inc dc, 4 dc, ch 2, trc in ch-1 sp, ch 2, sk 2 dc, 4 dc, inc dc, [ch 1, join], (ch 1, dc in dc) 2 times *. *Rnd 60:* Ch 4, * dc in next 5 dc, ch 3, sc in second ch of ch-2 sp and trc and next ch, ch 3, sk 2

continued

continued from page 177
Elegant Treasures for Everyday Uses

dc, [dc in next 4 dc, join], dc in next 5 dc, ch 1 *. *Rnd 61:* Ch 4, (dc in dc) 3 times; * ch 4, sc in last ch of ch-3 lp, 3 sc, sc in next ch, ch 4, sk 2 dc, [2 dc, join], 3 dc, ch 1, 3 dc *. *Rnd 62:* Ch 4, * 3 dc, 2 dc in ch-4 lp, ch 3, sk 1 sc, 3 sc, ch 3, 2 sc in ch-4 lp, [2 dc, join], 3 dc, ch 1 *. *Rnd 63:* Sl st to ch-1 sp, ch 4, * sk 1 dc, 4 dc, 2 dc in ch-3 lp, ch 2, trc in center sc, ch 2, 2 dc in ch-3 lp, 4 dc, ch 1, [join], dc in ch-1 sp, ch 1 *.

Rnd 64: Turn, sl st into last ch-1 sp worked, turn, ch 4, dc in next ch-1 sp formed by last ch of beg ch-4 of Rnd 63 (on fol rnds that begin to *right* of join of previous rnd, this sp will be referred to simply as "next ch-1 sp"); * ch 1, sk 1 dc, 5 dc, 2 dc in ch-2 sp, ch 1, 2 dc in next ch-2 sp, 5 dc, [ch 1, join], (ch 1, dc in ch-1 sp) 2 times *.

Rnd 65: Ch 4, dc in dc; ch 1, * sk 1 dc, 6 dc, dc in ch-1 sp, 6 dc (*note:* these 13 consecutive dc's are "motif" in fol rnds), ch 1, [join], sk 1 dc, (dc in dc, ch 1) 2 times *. *Rnd 66:* Sl st to first ch-1 sp, ch 4, dc in next ch-1 sp, * ch 1, sk first dc of next motif, 11 dc, sk last dc of motif, (ch 1, dc in ch-1 sp) 3 times [1 time, ch 1, join] *.

Rnd 67: Turn, sl st into last ch-1 sp worked, turn, ch 4, (dc in next ch-1 sp, ch 1) 2 times; * sk first dc of next motif, 9 dc, sk last dc of motif, (ch 1, dc in ch-1 sp) 4 times [1 time, ch 1, join]; ch 1 *. *Rnd 68:* Ch 4, (dc in dc, ch 1) 2 times; * sk first dc of next motif, 7 dc, sk last dc of motif, (ch 1, dc in dc) 4 times [1 time, ch 1, join]; ch 1 *. *Rnd 69:* Sl st to first ch-1 sp, ch 4, (dc in next ch-1 sp, ch 1) 2 times; * sk first dc of next motif, 5 dc, sk last dc of motif, (ch 1, dc in ch-1 sp) 5 times [2 times, ch 1, join]; ch 1 *.

Rnd 70: Turn, sl st to last ch-1 sp worked, turn, ch 4, (dc in next ch-1 sp, ch 1) 3 times; * sk first dc of next motif, 3 dc, sk last dc of motif, (ch 1, dc in ch-1 sp) 6 times [2 times, ch 1, join]; ch 1 *. *Rnd 71:* Ch 4, (dc in dc, ch 1) 3 times; * dc in center dc of motif, ch 1, sk 1 dc, (dc in dc, ch 1) 6 times [2 times, join] *. *Rnd 72:* Sl st to first sp, ch 4, (dc in next ch-1 sp, ch 1) 2 times; * dc in ch-1 sp, dc in dc, dc in ch-1 sp (*note:* last 3 consecutive dc's are beg of motif), (ch 1, dc in ch-1 sp) 5 times [2 times, ch 1, join]; ch 1 *. *Rnd 73:* Ch 4, dc in dc, ch 1, * dc in dc, sk ch-1 sp, 3 dc, sk ch-1 sp, (dc in dc, ch 1) 4 times [2 times, join] *.

Rnd 74: Ch 4, dc in dc, * ch 1, inc dc, 3 dc, inc dc, (ch 1, dc in dc) 3 times [1 time, ch 1, join] *. *Rnd 75:* Turn, sl st to last ch-1 sp worked, turn, ch 4, dc in next ch-1 sp, ch 1, * dc in ch-1 sp, 7 dc, (dc in ch-1 sp, ch 1) 3 times [1 time, join] *. *Rnd 76:* Sl st to first ch-1 sp, ch 4, * sk next ch-1 sp, inc dc, 3 dc, ch 1, sk 1 dc, 3 dc, inc dc, ch 1, sk ch-1 sp, [join], dc in ch-1 sp, ch 1 *. *Rnd 77:* Ch 4, * inc dc, 2 dc, ch 2, trc in ch-1 sp, ch 2, sk 2 dc, 2 dc, inc dc, ch 1, [join], dc in dc, ch 1 *.

Rnd 78: Ch 4, * inc dc, 1 dc, ch 2, sc in second ch of ch-2 sp and trc and next ch, ch 2, sk 2 dc, 1 dc, inc dc, ch 1, [join], dc in dc, ch 1 *. *Rnd 79:* Ch 4, * inc dc, ch 3, 3 sc, ch 3, sk 2 dc, inc dc, ch 1, [join], dc in dc, ch 1 *.

Rnd 80: Ch 4, * sk 1 dc, 1 dc, 2 dc in ch-3 lp, ch 2, 3 sc, ch 2, 2 dc in ch-3 lp, dc in dc, ch 1, sk 1 dc, [join], dc in dc, ch 1 *. *Rnd 81:* Ch 4, * sk 1 dc, 2 dc, 2 dc in ch-2 sp, ch 2, trc in center sc, ch 2, 2 dc in ch-2 sp, 2 dc, ch 1, sk 1 dc, [join], dc in dc, ch 1 *.

Rnd 82: Turn, sl st to last ch-1 sp worked, turn, ch 4, dc in next ch-1 sp, * ch 1, sk 1 dc, 3 dc, 2 dc in ch-2 sp, ch 1, 2 dc in next ch-2 sp, 3 dc, [ch 1, join], (ch 1, dc in ch-1 sp) 2 times *. *Rnd 83:* Ch 4, dc in dc, ch 1, * sk 1 dc, 4 dc, dc in ch-1 sp, 4 dc, ch 1, sk 1 dc, [join], (dc in dc, ch 1) 2 times *.

Rnd 84: Ch 4, dc in dc, * ch 1, sk first dc of next motif, 7 dc, sk last dc of motif, [ch 1, join], (ch 1, dc in dc) 2 times *. *Rnd 85:* Ch 4, work decs and sps same as Rnd 84, but sk first and last dc of each motif, working 5 dc in motif, end ch 1, join. *Rnd 86:* Sl st to first ch-1 sp, ch 4, dc in next ch-1 sp, * ch 1, sk 1 dc, 3 dc, (ch 1, dc in ch-1 sp) 3 times [1 time, ch 1, join] *.

Rnd 87: Ch 4, dc in dc, ch 1, * sk 1 dc, dc in dc, ch 1, sk 1 dc, (dc in dc, ch 1) 3 times [1 time, join] *. *Rnd 88:* Turn, sl st to last ch-1 sp worked, turn, ch 4, dc in next ch-1 sp, * ch 1, dc in ch-1 sp and dc and ch-1 sp, [ch 1, join], (ch 1, dc in ch-1 sp) 2 times *. *Rnd 89:* Sl st to first ch-1 sp, ch 4, * dc in next ch-1 sp, 3 dc, (dc in ch-1 sp, ch 1) 2 times [1 time, join] *.

Rnd 90: Ch 4, * inc dc, 3 dc, inc dc, ch 1, [join], dc in dc, ch 1 *. *Rnd 91:* Turn, sl st to last ch-1 sp worked, turn, ch 4, * dc in next ch-1 sp, 7 dc, [join], dc in ch-1 sp, ch 1 *. *Rnd 92:* Sl st to first ch-1 sp, ch 4, * sk first dc of next motif, 7 dc, sk last dc of motif, ch 1, [join], dc in ch-1 sp, ch 1 *.

Rnd 93: Ch 4, * sk first dc of next motif, 5 dc, sk last dc of motif, ch 1, [join], dc in dc, ch 1 *. *Rnd 94:* Turn, sl st to last ch-1 sp worked, turn, ch 4, dc in next ch-1 sp, * ch 1, sk first dc of next motif, 3 dc, sk last dc of motif, [ch 1, join], (ch 1, dc in ch-1 sp) 2 times *. *Rnd 95:* Turn, sl st to last ch-1 sp worked, turn, ch 4, (dc in next ch-1 sp, ch 1) 2 times; * dc in center of 3 dc, ch 1, [join], (dc in next ch-1 sp, ch 1) 3 times *. *Rnd 96:* Sl st to first ch-1 sp, ch 4, dc in next ch-1 sp, * ch 1, dc in ch-1 sp and dc and ch-1 sp, [ch 1, join], (ch 1, dc in ch-1 sp) 2 times *.

Rnd 97: Sl st to first ch-1 sp, ch 4, * dc in ch-1 sp, 3 dc, (dc in ch-1 sp, ch 1) 2 times [1 time, join] *. *Rnd 98:* Ch 4, * inc dc, 4 dc, ch 1, [join], dc in dc, ch 1 *. *Rnd 99:* Ch 4, * sk 1 dc, 5 dc, ch 1, [join], dc in dc, ch 1 *. *Rnd 100:* Ch 4, * sk 1 dc, 3 dc, ch 1, sk 1 dc, [join], dc in dc, ch 1 *. *Rnd 101:* Work same as Rnd 95. *Rnd 102:* Sl st to first ch-1 sp, ch 4, * dc in ch-1 sp and dc and ch-1 sp, ch 1, [join], dc in ch-1 sp, ch 1 *. *Rnd 103:* Sl st to first ch-1 sp, ch 3, * 3 dc, dc in ch-1 sp, ch 1, [join with sl st in top of beg ch-3], dc in ch-1 sp *. *Rnd 104:* Sl st to next dc, ch 3, 2 dc, * ch 1, sk dc and ch-1 sp and dc, [join with sl st in top of beg ch 3], 3 dc *.

Rnd 105: Turn, sl st to last ch-1 sp worked, turn, ch 4, * dc in center dc of motif, ch 1, [join with sl st in third ch of beg ch-4], dc in ch-1 sp, ch 1 *. Rnds 106–118 are joined same as for Rnd 105. *Rnd 106:* Turn, sl st to last ch-1 sp worked, turn, ch 4, * dc in ch-1 sp and dc and ch-1 sp, (ch 1, dc in ch-1 sp) 2 times [1 time, ch 1, join]; ch 1 *. *Rnd 107:* Turn, sl st to last ch-1 sp worked, turn, ch 4, * dc in next ch-1 sp, 3 dc, dc in ch-1 sp, ch 1, [join], dc in ch-1 sp, ch 1 *.

Rnd 108: Ch 4, * inc dc, 4 dc, ch 1, [join], dc in dc, ch 1 *. *Rnd 109:* Turn, sl st to last dc worked, turn, ch 4, * sk next ch-1 sp and dc and ch-1 sp and dc, [4 dc, join], 5 dc, ch 1 *. *Rnd 110:* Sl st to first ch-1 sp, ch 4, * sk 1 dc, 3 dc, ch 1, sk 1 dc, [join], dc in ch-1 sp, ch 1 *. *Rnd 111:* Sl st to first ch-1 sp, ch 4, * dc in center dc of motif, ch 1, (dc in next ch-1 sp, ch 1) 2 times [1 time, join] *. *Rnd 112:* Sl st to first ch-1 sp, ch 4, (dc in next ch-1 sp, ch 1) 2 times; * dc in ch-1 sp and dc and ch-1 sp, (ch 1, dc in ch-1 sp) 4 times [1 time, ch 1, join]; ch 1 *.

Rnd 113: Ch 4, dc in dc, * ch 1, dc in dc, 3 dc, dc in dc, [ch 1, join], (ch 1, dc in dc) 2 times *. *Rnd 114:* Ch 4, * dc in dc, 5 dc, [join], dc in dc, ch 1 *. *Rnd 115:* Turn and sl st to last dc worked, turn, ch 4, * sk dc and ch-1 sp and dc, [4 dc, join], 5 dc, ch 1 *. *Rnd 116:* Turn and sl st to last dc worked, turn, ch 4, * sk dc and ch-1 sp and dc, [2 dc, join], 3 dc, ch 1 *. *Rnd 117:* Sl st to first ch-1 sp, ch 4 * dc in center of motif, ch 1, [join], dc in next ch-1 sp, ch 1 *. *Rnd 118:* Ch 4, * dc in dc, ch 1, [join] *.

Rnd 119: Ch 4, * sk 1 dc, trc in next dc, [join with sl st in top of beg ch-4] *. Fasten off; lace end through top of last rnd; pull to close. Secure.

BORDER: *Rnd 1:* Work along opposite (outer) edges of ring pairs; join thread in overlapped lps of a pair, beg cl in same lp, * (ch 3, sk next lp, cl in next lp) 4 times; ch 5, sk next 2 lps of same ring and next 2 free lps of next ring, (cl in lp, ch 3, sk 1 lp) 3 times; [join with sl st in top of beg ch-3], cl in next overlapped lps *.

Join rnds 2–4 same as Rnd 1. *Rnd 2:* Sl st to ch-2 sp of beg cl, beg cl in same sp, (ch 3, cl over cl) 4 times; * ch 4, (cl over cl, ch 3) 7 times [3 times, join]; cl over cl *. *Rnd 3:* Sl st to ch-2 sp of beg cl, beg cl, (ch 2, cl over cl) 4 times; * ch 3, (cl over cl, ch 2) 7 times [3 times, join]; cl over cl *. *Rnd 4:* (Work this rnd of cl using a ch-1 in center of cl instead of ch-2.) Sl st to ch-2 sp of beg cl, beg cl, * ch 2, cl over cl *, ch 2, join.

Note: To make border pattern fit, you must dec 24 sts, evenly spaced, while crocheting Rnd 5. To do so, mark 24 sts (1 st 24 times) around last rnd. Do not work into or count these sts when working Rnd 5.

Also note that because the rem of the border motif is worked 37 times

and there are 48 pairs of rings, any given part of the border motif will not fall twice in the same place in relation to the rings.

Rnd 5: Ch 5, sk 2 sts (each ch counts as a st); (dc in next st, ch 2, sk 2 sts) 8 times; * dc in 4 sts, (ch 2, sk 2 sts, dc in next st) 22 times; ch 2, sk 2 sts. * Rep bet *'s 35 times more, end dc in next 4 sts, ch 2, sk 2 sts, (dc in next st, ch 2, sk 2 sts) 13 times. Join with sl st in third ch of beg ch-5.

Join rnds 6–8 same as Rnd 5. *Rnd 6:* **Ch 5, dc in dc—beg sp over sp made, ch 2, dc in dc—sp over sp made;** 6 sps, * **2 dc in ch-2 sp, dc in dc—bl over sp made; ch 2, sk 2 dc, dc in next dc—sp over bl made;** bl over sp, 10 sps, 1 bl, [1 sp, ch 2, join], 10 sps *.

Hereafter, if bl is preceded by a ch-lp rather than a sp, begin bl with extra dc so all bls consist of 4 consecutive dc's. If rnd begins with bl, beginning ch-3 is counted as first dc of bl. For bls worked into ch-lps, work first or last dc of bl (whichever will not distort the design) into bl or sp below, so it does not slide along ch-lp.

Rnd 7: Beg sp, 6 sps, * 1 bl, ch 3, trc in next ch-2 sp, ch 3, bl over next sp, 8 sps, 1 bl, 1 sp, 1 bl, [ch 2, join], 8 sps *. *Rnd 8:* Beg sp, 5 sps, * 1 bl, ch 4, sc in last ch of ch-3 lp and trc and next ch, ch 4, 1 bl over next sp, 6 sps, 1 bl, ch 3, trc in ch-2 sp, ch 3, [dc in last st of bl to right on previous rnd, 2 dc in next sp, join], bl over next sp, 6 sps *. *Rnd 9:* Sl st to next dc, beg sp, 3 sps, * 1 bl, ch 5, sc in 3 sc, ch 5, sk ch-4 lp and bl, bl over next sp, 4 sps, 1 bl, ch 4, sc in last ch of ch-3 lp and trc and next ch, ch 4, [work last bl and join as for Rnd 8], 1 bl over next sp, 4 sps *.

Rnd 10: Sl st to next dc, beg sp, 1 sp, * 1 bl, 1 sp, bl in next ch-5 lp, ch 4, 3 sc, ch 4, bl in ch-5 lp, 1 sp over bl, 1 bl, 2 sps, 1 bl, ch 5, sc in 3 sc, ch 5, sk ch-4 lp, [work last bl and join same as for Rnd 8], bl over next sp, 2 sps *.

Rnd 11: Beg sp, * 1 bl, ch 3, trc in ch-2 sp, ch 3, bl in next ch-4 lp, ch 3, trc in center sc, ch 3, 1 bl in ch-4 lp, ch 3, trc in ch-2 sp, ch 3, bl over sp, 2 sps, 1 bl in ch-5 lp, ch 4, sc in 3 sc, ch 4, bl in ch-5 lp, [ch 2, join with sl st in third ch of beg ch-5], 2 sps *.

Rnd 12: Ch 3, 1 bl, * (ch 4, sc in last ch of ch-3 lp and trc and next ch, ch 4), bl in next ch-3 lp, ch 2, bl in next ch-3 lp, rep bet ( )'s, 1 bl, 2 sps, bl in ch-4 lp, ch 3, trc in center sc, ch 3, bl in ch-4 lp, [1 sp, ch 2, join with sl st in top of beg ch-3], 2 sps, 1 bl *.

Rnd 13: Ch 8, * sc in 3 sc, ch 5, bl over ch-2 sp, ch 5, sc in 3 sc, ch 5, bl over next sp, 2 sps, bl in next ch-3 lp, ch 2, bl in next ch-3 lp, 2 sps, [2 dc in sp, join with sl st to third ch of beg ch-8], 1 bl, ch 5 *. *Rnd 14:* Ch 3, * (bl in ch-5 lp, ch 4, sc in 3 sc, ch 4, bl in ch-5 lp, 1 sp) 2 times; (1 bl, 2 sps) 2 times; 1 bl, [ch 2, join with sl st in top of beg ch-3], 1 sp *.

Join rnds 15–23 same as Rnd 14. *Rnd 15:* Sl st to fourth dc of first bl, ch 3, * (bl in ch-4 lp, ch 3, trc in center sc, ch 3, bl in ch-4 lp, ch 3, trc in sp, ch 3) 2 times; bl in next sp, 3 sps, 1 bl, ch 3, trc in sp, ch 3, [join] *.

Rnd 16: Sl st to fourth dc of first bl, ch 3, * bl in ch-3 lp, (ch 2, bl in ch-3 lp, ch 4, sc in last ch of ch-3 lp and trc and next ch, ch 4), bl in next ch-3 lp, rep bet ( )'s, 1 bl, 1 sp, 1 bl, ch 4, sc in last ch of ch-3 lp and trc and next ch, ch 4, [join] *.

Rnd 17: Sl st to fourth dc of first bl, ch 3, bl in ch-2 sp, * ch 5, sc in 3 sc, ch 5, sk ch-4 lp, [join], bl over next sp *. *Rnd 18:* Sl st to fourth dc of first bl, ch 3, * bl in ch-5 lp, ch 4, sc in 3 sc, ch 4, bl in ch-5 lp, [ch 2, join], sp over bl *. *Rnd 19:* Sl st to fourth dc of first bl, ch 3, * bl in ch-4 lp, ch 3, trc in center sc, ch 3, bl in ch-4 lp, ch 3, trc in ch-2 sp, ch 3, bl in ch-4 lp, ch 3, trc in center sc, ch 3, bl in ch-4 lp, 3 sps, bl in ch-4 lp, ch 3, trc in center sc, ch 3, bl in ch-4 lp, ch 3, trc in sp, ch 3, [join] *.

Rnd 20: Sl st to first ch-3 lp, beg cl in same sp, (ch 2, cl in next ch-3 lp) 5 times; ch 2, cl in next sp, ch 2, * sk 1 sp, cl in next sp, ch 2, (cl in next ch-3 lp, ch 2) 10 times [4 times, join]; cl in next sp, ch 2 *. *Rnds 21–22:* Sl st to center sp of first cl, beg cl, * ch 1, cl over cl, [ch 1, join] *.

Rnd 23: Sl st to center sp of first cl, ch 3, dc in same sp, * **ch 3, sc in top of last dc—picot made,** 2 dc in same sp as last dc, ch 1, sc in next ch-1 sp, ch 1, ch 1, [join], 2 dc in center of next cl *. Fasten off.

BRUSSELS LACE

Even novice stitchers can quickly master the basic techniques of this time-honored, old-world craft and make exquisite lace doilies, coasters, place mats, and other elegant accessories for the home.

BRUSSELS LACE

Perhaps the most graceful of all the needle arts, lace making is also one of the oldest.

Brussels lace—also known as Battenberg, Belgian, or Renaissance lace—is an inventive blend of two ancient techniques: bobbin lace and needle lace.

Early forms of Brussels lace first appeared in Europe in the late 15th century. But the version of the technique explored here, which depends on readily available, machine-made lace tape for the speedy creation of designs, was at its most popular in the late 1800s.

By coiling narrow fabric tapes into intricate patterns, and then joining the loops with exquisite, hand-worked stitches (called infilling), this technique yields designs that are undeniably elegant, yet far easier and quicker to work than older, more tedious ways of making lace.

For step-by-step instructions on how to create the lovely doily pictured here, please turn the page.

BRUSSELS LACE

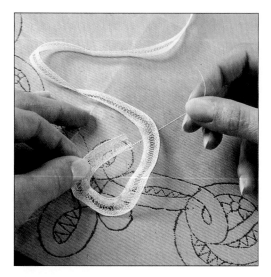

1 Brussels lace is made with a needle, some thread, and a special braided tape (available at crafts and needlework shops).

Draw threads are stitched into the lace tape along both edges. When either of the draw threads is pulled, the tape is gathered and can be curved to form looped designs, as shown *above*.

Brussels lace is worked on a paper pattern. To begin, draw the entire pattern to full size on a sheet of paper. Once the pattern is drawn, crush the paper lightly to make the paper more flexible.

2 Next, baste the lace tape to the pattern with thread of a contrasting color, *above right*.

Sew tapes first along the outer curves of the design. Then baste the inside curves to the paper.

As you work, gently pull the draw thread along the edge of the tape, so the tape curves to fit the design. When the tape is doubled over, or two lengths overlap, run an extra stitch through the layers, taking care that the tape lies flat.

3 After tape is basted over the entire design, work needle-weaving stitches, like the Russian stitch, *below right,* to fill open areas of the design. Work these infilling stitches with a tapestry or embroidery needle, using fine cotton crochet thread or pearl cotton embroidery floss.

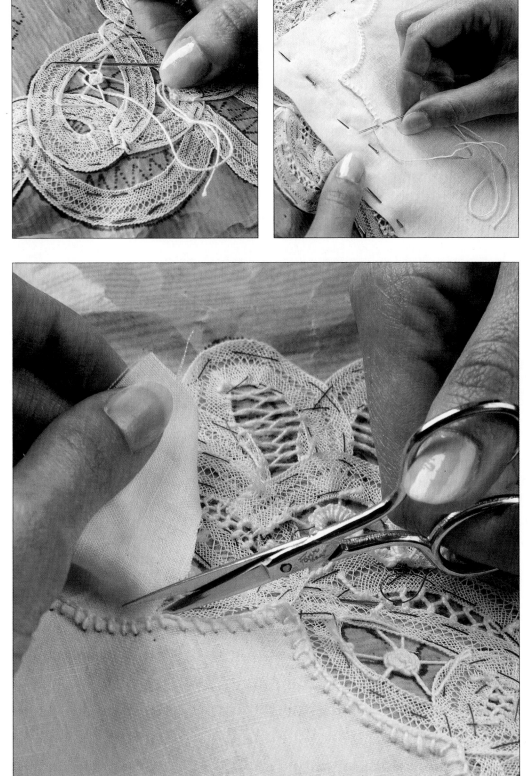

4 Following stitch indications on the paper pattern, weave the needle in and out of the threaded spokes to create a spiral effect in other open areas of the design, as shown *far left*. This is called the wheel stitch.

5 When all the infilling stitches are completed, pin and baste a piece of fine white linen to the wrong side of the design. (As you work the design, the side that faces up is the *wrong* side.)

Using small buttonhole stitches and the same thread used for the infilling stitches, attach the linen insert to the lace edging, as shown *near left, above*.

6 Finally, use embroidery scissors to carefully trim the excess linen, following the outline of the lace, *left*. Remove the basting threads, then lift the doily from the paper pattern and press on the wrong side.

INSTRUCTIONS FOR BRUSSELS LACE

General Instructions

Tapes for Brussels lace originally were made by hand, using bobbins, but ready-made tapes are now widely available. The tape is plain to enhance the filling stitches.

Drawstrings (or draw threads) are stitched into the Brussels tape along both edges. Pull gently on the drawstrings to gather and curve the edges of the tape, forming looped designs.

Battenberg lace is worked on a paper pattern; lace tape is basted to the paper and filling stitches are worked in pearl cotton thread. Use linen to fill the center of the design.

Brussels Lace Doily

Shown on pages 182–183.
Doily is 16 inches in diameter.

MATERIALS
11½ yards of ⅜-inch-wide white Brussels (or Battenberg) lace tape
Tracing paper or kraft paper
Permanent felt-tip marking pen
Black and white sewing thread
3 skeins white pearl cotton, Size 8
11¾x12-inch piece of white linen
Embroidery scissors
Sewing needle

INSTRUCTIONS
Trace the full-size pattern, *below,* onto tracing or kraft paper. Complete the circular design by flopping the pattern three times. Transfer all stitch markings to the paper pattern. You need not transfer the shading; instead, refer to the original pattern when basting the tape to the paper. Wrinkle paper pattern slightly for flexibility.

As you work the design, the side that faces up is the *wrong* side. You will baste the tape to the paper pattern in three pieces (tapes 1, 2, and 3); the tapes must be sewn in that order.

Cut the tape into three lengths: 5 yards for tape 1, 6 yards for tape 2, and ½ yard for tape 3.

Crimp the entire length of tape 1 slightly by gently pulling the drawstring along one side. Do not pull too tightly or tape will lose its shape.

To attach tape 1 to the pattern, start in the middle of one side. Curve a small portion of tape at a time, following pattern and basting tape in place as you go; use black sewing thread. Continue the basting, making sure tape lies flat and follows curves, until the entire length of tape 1 is attached.

Note: Sew in one direction only when basting tapes in place; keep edges of drawstring along the *same* side. For tight curves or folds, pull drawstring tighter. When beginning and ending tapes, leave ends loose so they can be whipstitched to tapes that already are sewn in place.

BRUSSELS LACE DOILY

Attach tapes 2 and 3 in the same way as tape 1, referring to the original pattern, *below,* for the position of the tapes. Press lightly between each basting. When all tapes are basted, sew together the tapes that touch or overlap, using white thread and tiny stitches. These stitches remain in the finished lace but do not show through.

Using pearl cotton and referring to diagrams, *right,* and markings on pattern, *below,* fill open areas with Russian and wheel stitches. Remember, the *wrong* side is facing up and stitches are worked atop (not through) the paper pattern.

The Russian stitch is worked by starting at the bottom of the opening and looping the pearl cotton from side to side. For wheel stitch, stretch an uneven number of foundation threads over the opening. To finish the wheel, alternately guide the needle under and over stretched threads four times. To end the stitch, guide thread through the center of the wheel and attach it to the last foundation thread. Press the lace.

Then press the linen fabric and pin the linen to the lace. (Linen will be larger than center, but it will be trimmed after it is attached.) Using pearl cotton, buttonhole-stitch along inner edge of lace to join lace tape and linen. Refer to stitch diagram, *right.* When completed, clip linen to within ⅛ inch of tape.

To remove lace from paper, cut basting stitches with embroidery scissors, leaving the paper pattern intact. Remove the clipped threads, then the paper. Press the piece.

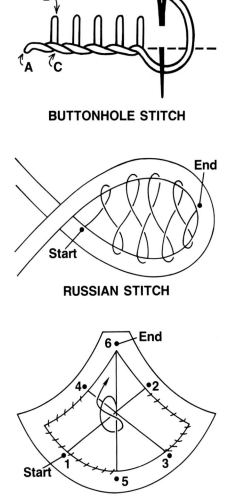

BUTTONHOLE STITCH

RUSSIAN STITCH

WHEEL STITCH

KEY

 Tape 1

Tape 2

Tape 3

Full-Size Pattern

187

WEEKEND CRAFTS

When do-it-yourself time is at a premium, you still can create a big impression. Quick-result projects like these make decorating a snap.

Gather up your paints and stencils and—presto!—you can transform garden-variety baskets into unique catchalls for everything from picnic treats and magazines to flowers for the table.

Here, we've whitewashed a collection of inexpensive baskets and stenciled on stylized blossoms in tribute to spring. Use these colors and patterns for inspiration, or choose shades and motifs that complement your decor, suit your storage needs, or celebrate your favorite season.

Directions begin on page 196.

WEEKEND CRAFTS

Add sizzle to summer furniture with these quick and easy decorating ideas.

Geometric quilting patterns, writ large and stitched in colored threads, enliven a canvas sling chair and companion pillow, *near right.*

Printed leaf patterns stamp an ordinary table, *center right,* as something special. Just brush acrylic paint onto the back of a leaf, position the leaf on the table, and roll lightly with a brayer, *above.*

For another simple seating fix-up, weave strips of fabric through a common wire-mesh chair, *far right.*

WEEKEND CRAFTS

A kid's nonstop imagination can inspire dozens of delightful projects to personalize his or her room—or the whole house. The silk-screened accessories shown here are just a sampling.

By repeating images of a single drawing, such as "Star-Faced Girl," you can print a quilt and matching curtains, decorate pillowcases and towels, or mass-produce a basketful of patchwork dolls.

Treasured "River Queen" and "City Bus" drawings translate into chunky pillows that will captivate grown-ups as much as kids.

In one weekend you can make reusable screens and print enough fabric to make any or all of these projects. Then stitch the designs as time permits.

The instructions include directions for reproducing your child's artwork using two silk-screening methods.

WEEKEND CRAFTS

You might call this spontaneous decorating, but there's nothing slapdash about these striking sponge and splatter projects.

Using brushes and sponges, a variety of paints, and a few simple techniques, you can transform everyday household items from ho-hum to high style in next to no time.

To brighten your surroundings, apply sponge and splatter flourishes to linens, dishes, even furniture. You'll discover that creative spirit, not artistic talent, is what really counts.

INSTRUCTIONS FOR WEEKEND CRAFTS

Stenciled Baskets

Shown on pages 188–189.

MATERIALS

Wicker baskets
Spray paint or latex semigloss
    paint in desired background
    color
Stencil paints or artist's acrylic
    paints; stencil brush
Small artist's brushes
Heavy, waxed butcher paper, clear
    acetate, or purchased stencils
Sharp crafts knife

INSTRUCTIONS

Sketch simple designs (refer to the photograph), or use purchased stencil designs.

Transfer each stencil motif onto heavy, waxed butcher paper, or trace onto a sheet of clear acetate. (*Note:* Working with clear acetate enables you to see portions of the design already worked so that the succeeding portions of the pattern can be aligned more easily.)

Make a separate stencil for each portion of the motif that is to be worked in a different color. Cut out stencils, using a crafts knife.

Spray or brush basket using the desired background color; let paint dry thoroughly. Using the photograph as a guide, plan the arrangement of motifs around the basket. The flower motifs may be grouped together for bouquets or scattered individually around the basket, as desired.

Tape the stencil in place on the basket. Using stencil paint or acrylics mixed to the consistency of light cream, dab paint through stencil onto basket with a stencil brush; use an up-and-down motion. Hold the edges of the stencil cutout firmly against the basket as you work, to prevent smudged edges.

When the design is complete, lift stencil straight up to avoid smearing paint. With small artist's brush, fill in any unpainted spots in the design resulting from the basket's rough texture. Let paint dry thoroughly before adding next motif or color. Add hand-painted highlights as desired.

Embroidered Sling Chair

Shown on page 190.

MATERIALS

Purchased chair with canvas sling;
    threads in assorted colors
Permanent marker
Dressmaker's carbon paper
Ruler and compass

INSTRUCTIONS

Referring to quilting patterns in books (or on quilts) and to the photograph for inspiration, create several geometric designs of your choice. Use a ruler for straight-edge designs and a compass for curved patterns. Remove the sling from the chair. Using dressmaker's carbon paper and a tracing wheel, trace patterns onto the front of the canvas.

Using closely spaced, wide zigzag stitches, machine-stitch twice over all design lines. Use a different color thread for each pattern. Trim all loose threads; replace sling on chair.

Embroidered Pillow Top

Shown on page 190.
Finished pillow is 14 inches square.

MATERIALS

½ yard of solid-colored fabric
Contrasting thread; compass
Contrasting cording (optional)
Pillow form or fiberfill

INSTRUCTIONS

Referring to the photograph, use a compass to create a similar pattern; or copy a design from a book of quilting patterns. Transfer design to an 18-inch square of fabric.

Using closely spaced, wide zigzag stitches, sew twice over all design lines. Tie off and trim loose threads. Trim fabric to 15 inches square. Cut backing fabric to correspond.

Baste cording in place, if desired. Stitch back to front, using ½-inch seams; leave an opening for turning. Trim seams, turn, and press. Stuff or insert pillow form; slip-stitch the opening closed.

Woven Grid Chair

Shown on page 191.

MATERIALS

Purchased lawn chair with plastic-
    coated metal grid seat and back
4-inch-wide strips of print and
    solid fabric in assorted colors

INSTRUCTIONS

Cut fabric into 4-inch-wide strips of manageable length (44-inch-long strips cut across the width of the fabric work well). Fold edges of each strip toward the center 1 inch; fold strip in half and press.

For Row 1, begin at the top left of the chair and weave strips through the chair grid from A to AA in the manner shown on the diagram, *below*. (Row 1 covers top of chair.)

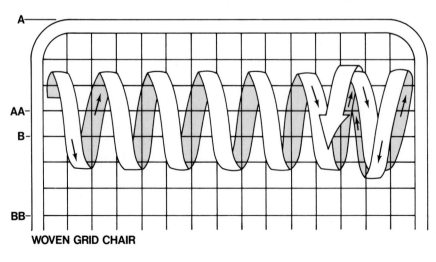

WOVEN GRID CHAIR

Change color for each successive row. Work Row 2 as shown in the diagram. Work Row 3 from B to BB. Continue weaving rows until chair is covered. Tack raw ends of strips in place. Fan out strips on Row 1 to cover top of chair.

Leaf Print Table
Shown on pages 190–191.

MATERIALS
Purchased wooden table
Assorted leaves (8 to 10 of each
  type); acrylic paint; soft brushes
Newspapers; paper towels
Brayer (available in art stores)
Polyurethane (optional)

INSTRUCTIONS
Use a different type of leaf for each row, as shown in photograph, or mix leaf types across table surface. Choose clean, supple leaves with well-defined shapes. Use a fresh leaf for each print.

Position a leaf on a pad of newspapers and paint leaf back with a thin, even layer of acrylic. Lift the leaf gently by the stem and position it on the tabletop. Lay a paper towel on top of the leaf and roll lightly with brayer. Remove towel and leaf. Repeat until top is completed. Protect with one or two coats of polyurethane, if desired.

Silk-Screened Designs
Shown on pages 192–193.

MATERIALS
White cotton organdy fabric
White latex enamel paint
Water-base textile paints or paper
  printing inks; squeegee
  (available at art stores)
Masking tape; rubber cement
Corrugated cardboard; mat knife
Heavy material for mat (such as a
  piece of old blanket)
½-inch-wide flat paintbrush
Several delicate artist's
  paintbrushes
Felt-tipped permanent pen

INSTRUCTIONS
Directions are for two silk-screening methods.

The first method uses paper cutouts for simple one-color printing. This is the easier method for beginners and is perfect for repeated designs. To change the design, just cut another motif from paper.

The second technique uses multiple screens, one for each printed color. This method is used to produce the "Star-Faced Girl" projects and the "River Queen" and "City Bus" pillows.

PAPER CUTOUT TECHNIQUE: To determine the dimensions of the cardboard screen, first decide on the size of the finished design. Add 1½ inches all around to figure the screen size, then add an additional 3 inches on all sides to determine the size of the cardboard frame. For example, a 6x6-inch finished design area needs a 9x9-inch inside screen area and a 15x15-inch cardboard frame.

Cut two squares of cardboard for the frame. With a mat knife, cut away interior, leaving a 3-inch-wide outer frame. Glue cardboard pieces together with rubber cement, placing corrugated ribs perpendicular to each other for maximum strength.

Press organdy, then cut it 1½ inches larger on all sides than the cardboard's dimensions. Place organdy over cardboard frame; tape one side of the fabric to frame back.

Move to the opposite frame side, stretching the fabric and taping it to the frame back. Continue in this manner with the third and fourth sides. The fabric should be taut, without wrinkles or creases. Using a wet sponge, thoroughly dampen the fabric and let dry. This will shrink the organdy, making it tauter.

Tape the interior frame edges to the organdy to prevent any paint from seeping between the frame and organdy. Apply a coat of latex enamel paint to the *frame and taped areas* on both sides; allow to dry. This makes the frame waterproof.

For a circular design, take a bowl (about 6 inches in diameter), turn it over on a piece of paper, and draw around it with a pencil. Enlarge the circle by about ¼ inch. Cut out the larger circle and, using a permanent marker, trace around the circle onto the organdy screen.

Using latex enamel, paint over all of the organdy *except* the interior of the circle. When dry, apply second coat. When completely dry, hold screen up to the light to make sure painted areas have no holes. If you find any, paint over them to prevent paint from seeping through later.

Trace several circles around the same bowl onto paper. The design to be silk-screened must fit within the circle; you must be able to cut it out, using scissors or a mat knife.

To experiment with an easy design, fold a circle into quarters and cut out a snowflake design. Or draw a simple design within the circle and cut it out carefully. Use as your design either the smaller pieces you've cut out, *or* the circle from which you've cut the shapes.

Prepare your work area before printing. Printing near a sink is a good idea. If you're printing a T-shirt, insert several layers of paper toweling between the shirt's front and back to prevent paint from seeping through to the other side. If you're printing fabric squares, press the cloth first; then cut it into pieces no smaller than 10 to 12 inches square.

Place the fabric to be printed atop a mat on a flat surface; smooth out wrinkles. Then place paper cutout atop fabric where design is desired. Carefully place the screen over the cutout, adjusting the screen so the design fits inside the circle.

Put a spoonful of textile paint on the screen *above* the circle, dribbling paint across the width of the screen. With a squeegee, gently pull paint across the circle. Repeat two or three times to make sure all open areas are well covered.

continued

continued from page 197
Weekend Crafts

Carefully raise screen and pull away fabric at the same time. The paper cutout, now adhered to the screen, will remain until washed off with water. The print may be repeated several times, if desired.

When finished, wash screen with sponge and dry with paper towels.

Drape printed fabric over a chair to dry for one to two hours. To set paint, iron wrong side of fabric for five minutes at wool setting.

MULTIPLE-SCREEN TECHNIQUE: Make cardboard screens, following the directions for the Paper Cutout Technique. Select a child's drawing. Place a clean, *unpainted* screen atop drawing. Trace drawing onto organdy using felt-tipped pen. Widen all lines to at least ⅛ inch.

Apply latex paint to all areas of screen *except* drawn lines; let dry. Coat screen again; let dry. Paint all areas you do not want to print. Only design lines should be totally free of paint. Dry for one hour.

If the design has two colors, prepare second screen in same manner.

Print design onto fabric following prodecure described above. Allow first pattern to dry; position second screen and print remaining portion of design in second color.

Use the printed design for quilt squares, pillow tops, curtains, or other projects of your choice.

Sponge-Painted Bowls, Baskets, and Wood Accessories
Shown on page 195.

MATERIALS
Assorted wooden, wicker, and clay items
Plastic picnic plates (for palettes); marine sponges in assorted sizes
Half pint of oil-base (or latex) semigloss paint in light color; half-pint of *each* contrasting color desired; primer
Solvent and varnish

INSTRUCTIONS
Prepare all surfaces before sponging. Seal all new surfaces with primer. Paint primed or old surfaces with *light-colored* semigloss or alkyd-base paint for best results. (Latex-painted surfaces are acceptable, but produce a softer sponged surface than oil-painted surfaces.)

FOR SPONGING WITH ONE COLOR OF OIL PAINT: Spoon a small amount of paint onto a plastic plate; pour a small amount of solvent onto another plate.

Dab sponge into paint, then into solvent. Practice sponging on newspaper. Thick, wet prints indicate too much paint on sponge; dab sponge on newspaper until effect is lightened. Sponge with light dabbing movements on smooth, dry, newly painted surfaces (baskets, woodenware, or walls). *To avoid muddy results, do not overwork sponging.*

FOR SPONGING WITH TWO COLORS OF OIL PAINT: Follow the instructions for one-color oil-paint sponging above. Allow first sponging application to dry before applying second color.

FOR ONE- AND TWO-COLOR LATEX-PAINT SPONGING: Follow instructions for oil-paint sponging, but substitute water for solvent to thin the paint. Varnish the sponged surfaces after they dry.

Splatter-Painted Tablecloth and Linens
Shown on pages 194–195.

MATERIALS
White cotton tablecloth
Purchased dish towels and napkins
Orange, yellow, and green permanent fabric dye
Small eyedropper
Plastic drop cloth; pans for paint

INSTRUCTIONS
Dilute dyes by mixing with equal parts of water. Spread tablecloth, towels, or napkins on floor over plastic drop cloth.

To make flower centers, drop yellow dye from eyedropper in each corner of fabric. Dye will spread nicely onto the fabric. For more spreading, apply drops of water to the fabric. (To apply water, dip fingertips into a bowl of water and flick onto fabric. Or, for finer detail, use eyedropper to add water. Flick your hand or the dropper in short, quick movements.)

For orange detail, apply small drops of orange dye onto the yellow flower centers. For leaves, fill the eyedropper with green dye and apply the dye to the fabric with a swinging motion. Add small droplets of green dye to the center of the fabric by flicking your wrist.

Let the fabric dry thoroughly in place atop the plastic drop cloth on the floor. Do not hang to dry or the colors may run. When dry, heat-set the colors with a warm steam iron.

Ceramic Dishes
Shown on page 194.

MATERIALS
Materials are available through ceramic supply stores.
Duncan cone 03 bisque dishes (saucers, cups, plates, or serving pieces)
Duncan underglazes in the following colors: RS 351 Poinsettia Red, RS 352 Poppy Orange, RS 353 Daffodil Yellow, RS 356 Parakeet Green, and RS 359 Kelly Green; Duncan RS 380 Red-Stroke Clear Gloss
Paintbrushes; natural sponges
Palette knife; glazed tile (for palette); paper cup; wooden stirring stick

INSTRUCTIONS
Remove any kiln dust and foreign particles from each bisque dish with a duster brush.

Working with one color at a time, use a palette knife to spread a small amount of underglaze over glazed tile palette. Lightly press a slightly dampened sponge into the color. Sponge glaze lightly onto the dishes, allowing some uncolored areas to show through.

Continue the procedure to color dishes as desired. We used red on plates and salt and pepper shakers, greens on cups and saucers, and yellow on bowls.

Glaze dishes before firing. Pour Red-Stroke Clear Gloss into a paper cup and use stir stick to mix the gloss with water until it is the consistency of milk. Working one piece at a time, pour the thinned glaze into each dish and roll it around until the inside of the dish is completely coated. Pour excess gloss back into the paper cup.

Fill a paintbrush with a generous amount of undiluted gloss and apply to the outside of each dish. Apply two coats of gloss, allowing the first coat to dry thoroughly before applying the next.

Glaze-fire pieces to cone 06. (If you do not have a kiln, ask for help at a local ceramics shop.)

Carved Chest
Shown on pages 10–11.

MATERIALS
15x26x28-inch unfinished wooden chest
Wood-carving tools (available at art, craft, and hobby shops)
Fine sandpaper; maple stain
Artist's oil paints in raw umber and crimson
Linseed oil; turpentine; varnish; wiping cloths
Grumbacher Tuffilm spray (available at art stores)
Medium-size round oil brush
Stain and varnish brushes
Graphite paper; carbon and white paper; ballpoint pen

INSTRUCTIONS
Enlarge patterns on page 200 onto white paper. With graphite paper and a ballpoint pen, trace patterns onto drawer fronts (flop patterns along dotted lines for right halves of designs). Draw letters for the name in the open space on the middle drawer. (*Note:* Adapt the design if chest is a different size.)

Using wood-carving tools, carve along the lines of the design. A small, curved gouge works well for single curved lines. For wider arcs, use a larger curved gouge. Carve out and away to achieve the varying widths. For straight lines, use a straight chisel. For large, straight grooves, use a V-gouge.

Note: If you're working with inexpensive wood, take special care when rounding curves to avoid excessive chipping.

When completed, sand and wipe all surfaces. Brush stain on the entire chest. Using a cloth, wipe away excess stain, leaving stain in the grooves. Let dry overnight.

Paint colors onto drawer fronts. Mix small amount of crimson oil paint with linseed oil to make a light, rose-colored stain. With a small paintbrush, stain the areas shown in gray on the pattern; let dry. With raw umber, paint the dark lines and other dark areas, as indicated on pattern. Let the paint dry for three days.

To set paint, spray with Tuffilm; when dry, varnish the chest. Clean brushes with turpentine.

Paper Collage
Shown on pages 12–13.

MATERIALS
Construction paper and various handmade or purchased papers in assorted weights and colors
15x19½-inch piece of mat board
Adhesive spray glue; white glue
Fine-point crafts knife
Scissors; pinking shears
Small piece of lace fabric
Brown kraft paper for pattern
Clear acrylic spray (optional)
Purchased frame

INSTRUCTIONS
To make the collage, choose from the many papers available from art supply, craft, stationery, and discount stores.

Combining papers and other materials of differing weights, colors, and textures will add interest to your design.

Choose from high-quality art papers as well as construction, manila, crepe, and tissue paper. Consider origami papers, which are available in light to medium weights in brilliant colors and occasionally in floral prints and foils. Gift wraps add charm and vitality to paper projects and are available in a range of surfaces from glossy to matte to velour.

You also can achieve interesting effects by adding snippets of greeting cards and postcards, seals, threads, laces, and fabric scraps.

When selecting colors, refer to the photograph or experiment.

Enlarge the pattern on page 201 onto paper to make a master pattern. If desired, trace and cut apart a second pattern; use pieces as guides for cutting colored papers and trims. Begin cutting pattern pieces from assorted papers. Use shears to cut straight edges and a crafts knife (or small, curved manicure scissors) for tiny, intricate pieces.

Arrange the pattern pieces on the rectangle of mat board, referring to the master pattern for placement. The pieces should cover the entire surface of the mat board. Position the pieces carefully so they are layered or overlapped as necessary, building from the background of the design to the foreground. Some of the pieces should fit together like a jigsaw puzzle, with the edges abutting, but not overlapping.

To secure large pieces, apply spray glue to the back of each piece. Let the piece dry several seconds (until tacky), then press it into place. Use small dabs of white glue to secure small pieces.   *continued*

TOP DRAWER

MIDDLE DRAWER

(Put name here)

BOTTOM DRAWER

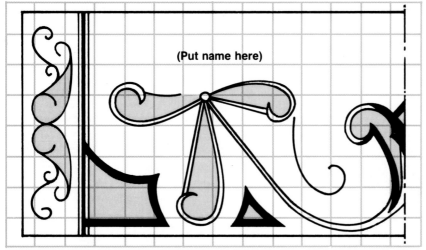

CARVED CHEST   **1 Square = 1 Inch**

continued from page 199
Weekend Crafts

Use a crafts knife to cut out open areas in the trellis, railing, chairs, shutters, windowpanes, mail basket, and potted plants.

Cut horizontal strips of medium-weight paper for house siding. Refer to the photograph and glue strips in place; leave a small space between each strip. Construct the porch floor in the same manner, cutting planks from gray paper and gluing them to a brown paper background.

Fill the remaining mat board surface with pieces for sky, trees, and grass. For grass, add a strip of green paper with a pinking-sheared edge across the bottom of the picture.

Layer the pattern pieces atop the house and porch, referring to the master pattern for placement. Cut small, irregular rectangles for the roof shingles. Add the shutters and windowpanes, placing them atop black paper to simulate the interior of the house. Use scraps of lace for the curtains.

Add the door, front steps, and mail basket. Weave small, brown-paper strips together to make the doormat. To make the door, glue white pieces onto gray background. Position the chairs in place on the porch. Glue small, multicolored paper triangles together to make the seat cushion.

Cut the trellis and the railing from white paper and glue the pieces in place. (The trellis has a symmetrical design, as indicated on the pattern.) Weave strips of green paper in and out of the trellis for the vine, adding small blossoms of colored paper.

Using pinking shears, cut the two plants and position them inside clay pots cut from rust-colored paper.

Let the collage dry thoroughly, keeping a weight on it overnight. Finish it with a coat of clear acrylic spray, if desired. Frame as desired.

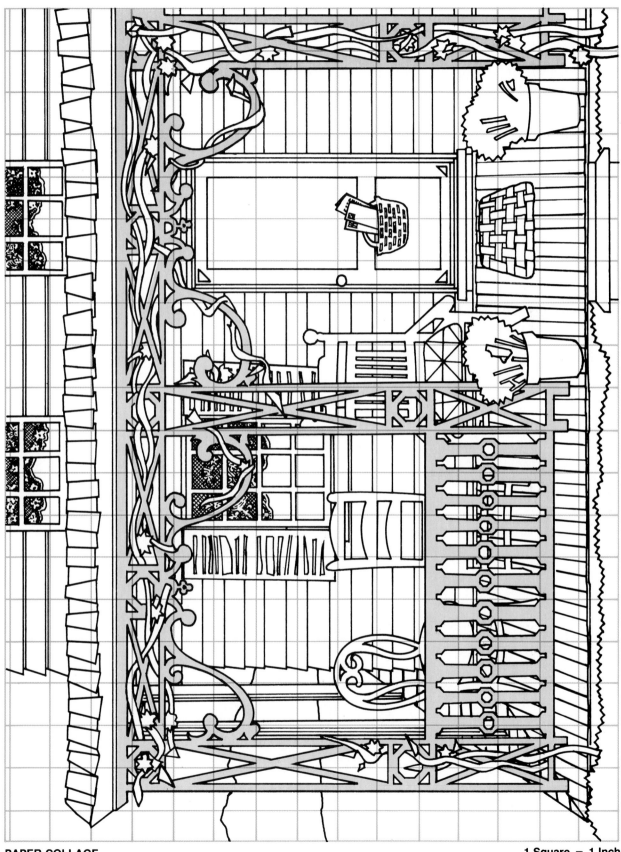

PAPER COLLAGE

1 Square = 1 Inch

NATURAL MATERIALS

On backyard strolls and hikes in the country, make the most of nature's bounty. Look for interesting seasonal materials to add spice and texture to a floral arrangement, centerpiece, or table setting.

NATURAL MATERIALS

Late summer and early fall are the perfect seasons for collecting leaves, berries, seedpods, grasses, and dried weeds to stockpile for a winter's worth of crafting.

Except for the corn husks, all the materials used to create the graceful wreath and the pumpkin centerpiece pictured here can be gathered on an autumn stroll in the country.

As for the corn husks, which are also used here for the decorative flowers and the Indian doll, you can salvage an ample supply when you serve corn on the cob to the family; or you can purchase prepackaged, dried husks from your local crafts supplier.

To create a handsome harvest wreath like this one, *far left,* use an assortment of pressed leaves, dried grasses, reeds, and dried stalks of goldenrod.

Attach these dried wild things to a 16-inch wire hoop with florist's wire and masking tape. Fill out the design with an assortment of pale and pretty corn-husk flowers.

The pumpkin and gourd centerpiece, *near left,* is a perfect complement to cozy dinners or casual buffets on a cold, crisp evening. Enhance the arrangement with sprigs of berries and seedpods artfully wired together with dried leaves, grasses, and a few corn-husk flowers.

Any doll collector would cherish the lovely corn-husk Indian maiden in the foreground of the picture.

Crafted of subtly dyed, natural corn husks, the doll has hair of unspun wool. She is wrapped in a graceful blanket of woven raffia.

For more details on crafting with natural materials, please turn the page.

NATURAL MATERIALS

While it's possible to find an ample supply of natural materials in crafts stores these days, gathering your own enables you to come up with a greater variety, and often yields some unexpected treasures. It's cheaper, too.

Throughout the summer months, keep your eyes open for promising clumps of grasses and weeds in the neighborhood. Check these sites regularly as autumn approaches so you can harvest the plants as soon as they've matured, and before they become bedraggled.

Pick grasses, weeds, and wildflowers, such as goldenrod, at their peaks and bring them home to dry. After you've gathered the flowers, strip excess foliage, turn the plants upside down, and tie the stems together in small bunches.

To dry the plants, hang them upside down in a dark, dry place for two or three weeks.

When collecting thistles and pods, like the milkweed pods *at left,* wait until most of the seeds have been released. Depending on how you plan to use the material, leave the pods attached to their branches, or remove them to be washed, dried, and stored in airtight plastic bags.

Cones from fir, pine, spruce, and cedar trees also are commonly available and uncommonly useful in natural arrangements.

Clean the cones with a stiff brush to remove dirt. Then place any cones that are sticky in a 200° oven to dry them and to open up the scales. After the cones have cooled, rinse them in water and dry thoroughly.

To collect leaves for your projects, select those that have already turned color, but are not yet brittle. Press individual leaves between the pages of a book for a week or so to dry, then iron them between sheets of waxed paper, using a medium-hot iron.

Use floral tape to attach leaf stems to wire for use in arrangements.

1 Dried corn husks are among the most versatile of natural materials. Cut into loopy slivers and clustered around a dried thistle, *top right,* they make wonderfully fanciful flowers.

2 Or you can create more structured blossoms with softly shaped petals, like the one being wired into the wreath, *center right.*

3 The charming Indian doll, *below right,* is a corn-husk tour de force. Construct the upper body on a wire armature, using a small plastic-foam ball for the head. Then pad the base and clothe it with husks to resemble a human form.

Create the doll's skirt with dyed husks layered atop a cardboard cone. (A hole cut in the top allows for insertion of the doll's torso.)

After the parts are assembled, add a wig of wool yarn, arrange the doll's arms in a graceful pose, and drape the figure in a blanket of woven raffia.

For complete instructions on these projects, please turn the page.

INSTRUCTIONS FOR NATURAL MATERIALS

Dried-Flower Wreath

Shown on page 204.

MATERIALS

16-inch wire hoop
Pressed leaves; dried grasses,
    reeds, and goldenrod
Corn husks
Floral tape
Florist's wire
Scissors
Thread
Waxed paper
Masking tape
Straight pin
Fabric dyes (for colored husks)

INSTRUCTIONS

CORN-HUSK FLOWERS: You can make these flowers in the husks' natural color, or you can dye them pretty, soft-pastel colors. In either case, before beginning, wash the husks in soapy water to remove all dirt and any insecticide residue. Even if you use bleached husks purchased from a crafts store, you still must wash them; otherwise, dyes may not take.

Next, dye the husks, using the fabric dyes according to the manufacturer's directions. Experiment with dyes to obtain colors you desire. Allow dyed husks to dry completely.

Soften the corn husks with *warm* water; work with the husks while they are still damp.

For the center of the flower, roll one strip of husk into a tight ball, with the grain going up and down. Fasten wire at the center and wrap the ball tightly with thread near the wire. With a pin, shred the husk into narrow pieces.

To make the flower petals, cut 4-inch-long U-shaped petals from the husks. Attach four to five petals to each flower center and tie them securely with thread. Wrap the wire coming from the flower center with floral tape.

FLOWER BUDS: Using thread, attach seedpods from dried grasses or other natural materials to an 8- to 10-inch length of wire.

For each bud, cut two 2-inch pointed petals from husks. Wrap petals onto the wire at the base of the bud center. Wrap wire with floral tape for a short distance, continuing to add buds and petals as you go down the wire.

LEAVES: Press colored leaves in a book to dry. Then place the leaves between sheets of waxed paper and press with a medium-hot iron. Remove leaves from waxed paper and attach the stems to a strip of wire with floral tape, adding leaves as you wrap tape around the rest of the wire. For easiest assembly, it is best to make several 8- to 12-inch lengths of wire.

OTHER EMBELLISHMENTS: Wrap small bunches of dried grasses, reeds, and goldenrod onto wire with thread and floral tape. Work with these as separate units that will be attached singly to the wire hoop.

WREATH ASSEMBLY: Wrap the wire hoop with masking tape to make it less slippery.

To complete the wreath, place the flowers, leaves, and bunches of grasses in a pleasing arrangement around the hoop. Then attach the units to the tape-covered wire hoop with florist's wire. Secure the wires with masking tape if necessary to prevent slippage.

Pumpkin Centerpiece

Shown on pages 204–205.

MATERIALS

Gathered flowers, leaves,
    seedpods, and weeds, such as
    small dried sunflower centers,
    rose hips, and Queen Anne's
    lace
Corn husks
Pumpkin
Florist's wire
Floral tape
Thread
Sharp needle

INSTRUCTIONS

FLOWERS: To make the corn-husk flowers for the pumpkin, secure the center of a small dried sunflower or a dried thistle onto wire with thread.

Wash the husks in soapy water to remove all dirt and any insecticide residue. (Bleached husks from a crafts store also must be washed.)

Soften the husks by soaking them in *warm* water; work with the husks while they are still damp.

Fold five or six corn husks in half *widthwise* to make 3- to 4-inch-wide loops. With thread, attach each loop to the flower-center wire. Cut the husk loops into ½-inch-wide sections. Wrap wire with floral tape to secure in place and conceal threads.

OTHER EMBELLISHMENTS: Wrap leaves, seedpods, dried weeds, and rose hips onto various lengths of wire with floral tape, leaving 1½ inches of bare wire at one end of each length. Add corn-husk flowers as desired. The number of wire lengths will depend on the size of your pumpkin and the size of the arrangement you desire.

ASSEMBLY: To arrange dried materials on pumpkin, pierce shell near stem with sharp needle. Insert wires into pumpkin. Bend wires toward pumpkin into desired arrangement.

Corn-Husk Indian Doll

Shown on page 204.

MATERIALS

For doll
Dried corn husks
Florist's wire; thread
Masking tape; scissors
Cardboard for skirt base
Plastic-foam ball for head
Cotton balls
Glue; pins
Fabric dye in light blue, pink, and
    light brown
Natural roving or yarn for hair
Small feathers
Indian beads

For woven blanket
Raffia
Scraps of cotton fabric
Fabric dyes; pins
Two *each* of 14-inch and 26-inch
    artist's stretcher strips
Nails; hammer; glue
Tapestry needle

INSTRUCTIONS
Wash the husks in soapy water to remove all dirt and any insecticide residue. (Bleached husks from a crafts store also must be washed.)

Then dye the corn husks for the skirt and skin with fabric dye following the manufacturer's directions. Dye several husks light brown for the head and arms. Dye six to eight husks *each* with light blue and light pink for two layers of the doll's skirt.

To make the doll
Soften the husks by soaking them in *warm* water; work with the husks while they are still damp.

For the head, place a small foam ball in the center of a light-brown-dyed corn husk and cover completely. Tightly wrap husk with thread around bottom of ball to form neck. Insert a 6-inch length of wire into bottom of foam ball.

For the arms, cut an 11-inch length of wire; bend ends into small loops. Wrap light brown husks around the loops, continuing to middle of wire; secure by wrapping with thread. Attach the wire coming from the head to center of arms about ½ inch below neck; wrap tightly with thread to secure.

For the bust and waist, place two cotton balls side by side in the center of a corn husk and fold long sides toward the center; fold the husk in half across the width and slip onto lower part of head wire, sliding it up to meet arms. Wrap a piece of thread around the bottom of the husk securely to form the waist.

Wrap thread back and forth over shoulders and around waist to join the pieces. Center a 3-inch-wide piece of husk on each shoulder for the dress bodice. Cross the husks over the bust in front and back, gathering at the waist. Secure tightly with thread.

For the skirt, cut a 15-inch-diameter half circle from cardboard and roll into a cone, leaving a 5-inch opening at the bottom and a 1-inch opening at the top.

Layer the cone with husks, overlapping pieces lightly and pinning them at the bottom. Make the first layer of blue-dyed husks, the second of natural husks, and the third of pink-dyed husks. Start the second and third skirt layers about 1 inch above the previous layer. Glue each layer in place before proceeding to the next.

Insert the bodice through the top of the skirt and glue in place. Remove pins and thread after the corn husks are completely dry.

Cut natural roving (unspun wool, available in weaving-supply stores) or hand-spun yarn into 8-inch lengths for hair. Gather loosely in center with thread and attach to top of head with glue. Wrap each side with a small piece of raffia for braids; glue at base of neck. Tie feathers to a length of thread; secure with glue. Thread beads as desired and attach to top of head.

To make the blanket
Note: The doll blanket may be fashioned from an inexpensive purchased place mat of woven raffia, if desired. Trim place mat to 7x17 inches; soak in warm water to soften and form to body with pins; let dry and glue in place.

To weave raffia blanket, put artist's stretcher strips or 1x2-inch pine boards together to form a framework to act as a loom. Hammer small finishing nails ¼ inch apart on both 14-inch sides of the loom, beginning in center and working toward edges until nail section measures 7 inches wide. Tie lengths of raffia to the nails as warp (vertical) threads.

To dye the raffia for weft (horizontal) threads, follow manufacturer's directions for dyeing fabric.

Weave narrow *fabric* strips under, then over, under, then over the raffia warp, continuing for 3 inches to create selvage for knotting warp threads and decorative fringe.

Thread raffia through a tapestry needle; weave in same manner as rags, securing ends and beginning new pieces as needed. Work with a variety of dyed shades of raffia to create stripes of a subtle, multicolored effect. When piece measures 17 inches, cut from loom; tie warp threads together to secure; trim the fringe at each end. Soak blanket in water and drape it around the doll's shoulders. Pin in place until completely dry; attach with glue.

continued

continued from page 209
Homework
Natural Materials

Preserving Fresh-Cut Flowers

Drying fresh garden flowers requires somewhat different methods from those described on the preceding pages for weeds, grasses, and other wild materials.

To begin with, fresh flowers can be dried all year round, whenever they are available.

Start by picking or buying a bouquet of your favorite blossoms. Zinnias, carnations, black-eyed susans, roses, daffodils, yarrows, pansies, and daisies can all be dried successfully. A mixed bouquet may be more to your taste than one made of a single variety. Keep in mind the drying process tends to darken and intensify natural colors, so it's best to start with whites, brights, or pastels.

Drying with silica gel

A sandlike material available in garden and hobby shops, silica gel can be used to absorb the moisture from flowers. The gel is a compound of sand-size crystals mixed with larger blue crystals. When the crystals are dry, the gel is blue; when they are damp, the gel turns pink. As long as the gel retains its blue color, it can be used again and again. When it turns pink, simply heat it in a warm oven until the pink crystals turn blue again.

To dry your flowers, you'll need a number of containers with airtight lids. Make sure the containers are deep enough to hold the largest blooms. Trim the stem of each flower to about 1 inch.

Sprinkle or sift a layer of silica gel into each container and position the flowers (blossoms up) in rows so that about ½ inch of each stem is buried in the gel.

Gently add more crystals in and around the blossoms until they are completely covered. Be careful not to distort the natural shapes of the flowers.

DRYING TIME: Cover the containers and tape the edges around the lids. Leave the containers in a dry, dark place for at least 10 days, perhaps longer, depending on the size of the flowers. (Large blossoms usually require 12 to 14 days.)

After 10 days, check the flowers; the petals should be dry but not brittle. If the petals still feel fresh and supple, leave the flowers in the containers and continue to check them every two or three days.

When the flowers are dry, carefully remove them from the silica gel; then gently shake the crystals from the flower petals.

If you are interested in saving time and can afford to pay a bit more money, buy nontoxic flower preservers in crafts and hobby stores. These powders are made especially for flowers and foliage and will dry most flowers in three to seven days.

PREPARING DRIED BLOSSOMS: When you are ready to arrange the flowers, attach florist's wire to the stems with twists of floral tape and cut the wire to the desired length. (Florist's wire and floral tape are available at crafts and hobby shops, and at most florist's shops and greenhouses.) Arrange the flowers as desired, using a suitable container or vase.

CARING FOR FLOWERS: While these flowers are preserved to last for months, even years, they are still susceptible to changes in the atmosphere. Dried flowers keep best during winter months, and survive summer when in air-conditioned surroundings. To help them withstand the changes in weather, spray your flowers with vinyl sealant. This spray helps the flowers resist moisture once they are dry. To freshen and restore their colors, periodically spray the flowers with a light coating of the sealant.

Drying in a microwave

A microwave oven can dry flowers and leaves even more quickly and easily than silica gel or powders. It also preserves the color and shape of the blooms much better than conventional drying methods do.

You will need the following materials and supplies:
Several choice buds or flowers at the peak of their bloom, and a selection of nicely shaped leaves
Silica gel *or* a mixture of two parts cornmeal to one part borax
Plastic, glass, paper, or ceramic bowl or cup to contain the gel and a bloom
A fine-mesh sieve or strainer
A heat-resistant glass or ceramic container for water
Toothpicks, artist's brush, florist's wire, and floral tape

Microwave drying differs slightly from the other drying methods described above, so follow these directions carefully.

Select flowers that are firm in shape, and cut stems to within 1 inch of the blossoms. Bright, light-colored blooms can be better preserved than darker flowers, and thick-petaled blossoms are better than more delicate varieties.

First pour about 1½ inches of silica gel or of the cornmeal and borax mixture into a bowl. The container should be large enough to allow 2 inches between the top layer of the gel and the top of the bowl; this allows for expansion of the gel during heating.

Place a single flower in the bowl, blossom up. Don't let the bloom touch the sides of the bowl. Using a sieve, gently sift the gel granules over the top of the flower. Use a toothpick to spread the gel under the petals and around and inside the center of the flower; the bloom should be *completely* covered.

Pour 8 ounces of water into a glass or ceramic container (a measuring cup works fine). Place the water in one corner of the microwave oven. It remains there for the entire drying process.

Put the gel-covered flower in the oven. *Do not cover the container.* Dry one flower at a time to find proper timing. Drying times will vary depending on the number of flowers in the oven.

Set your oven timer. The color of the gel will change from blue to pink as moisture is absorbed and the flower dries. Drying times range from several seconds to three minutes, depending on the bloom's size and texture, on whether you use gel or the cornmeal and borax mixture, and on your oven's heating capacity. Don't be afraid to experiment with different times.

For future reference, keep a record of drying time and size and type of each flower. Use the listings below as a guide for each bloom:

Zinnia—2 minutes
Carnation—2 minutes
Black-eyed susan—2 minutes
Rose—2 minutes
Daffodil—1½ minutes
Daisy—1 minute
Pansy—45 seconds
Leaves—2 minutes

When the timer stops, remove the flower container from the oven and set the bowl on newspaper. *Don't touch the gel;* allow it to cool for 20 minutes.

Pour off the top layer of the gel. Gently lift out the flower, which will be limp, and place it on top of the remaining gel in the bowl. Let the flower rest until it is firm enough to handle (5 to 20 minutes). Save the remaining gel. Once cold, it can be reused to dry other materials.

When the flower is firm, *gently* remove the remaining gel granules from the blossom with an artist's brush. These flowers are still quite fragile. Avoid tearing the petals.

Place the dried bloom atop a container of cool gel. Allow it to rest overnight uncovered until it is firm and easy to handle.

You can now insert a length of florist's wire through the flower stem and into the head; or simply attach the stem to a length of wire with a twist of floral tape. Add a few dried leaves, if desired. *Note:* Do not add wire to the flowers until they are dried and ready for assembly. Using metal in a microwave oven can void the oven's warranty and eventually cause the oven to malfunction.

Pressing flowers
If you prefer to use your flowers in a picture or wall hanging rather than in a bouquet or arrangement, try pressing them.

For pressed flowers, it is best to pick the blossoms at midday, when the petals are completely open and the morning dew has dried. Select flowers that are flat, such as daisies, violets, and pansies.

Clip the stems and place each flower between two sheets of blotting paper. To do this, gently roll the top sheet of blotting paper onto the flower, making sure that all the petals are open and flat.

Place blotting paper between two pages of a book and weight the book with several bricks or any other small, heavy items. Place the book in a well-ventilated, well-lit room away from direct heat or dampness for 4 to 6 weeks, depending on the size of the blooms. It is a good idea to put slips of paper or tags between the pages to remind you where the flowers are located.

A faster way to press flowers, but one that requires more materials, is outlined below.

After cutting away the stems, place one sheet of blotting paper on a large board and cover it with a thin layer of silica gel. Lay the flowers atop the gel, making sure that all the petals are open and flat, and that the petals do not touch each other. Then sprinkle gel over the flowers.

Cover this layer with tissue paper, another sprinkling of silica gel, and a second piece of blotting paper.

Gently place the covered board in a plastic bag and tie to seal. Weight the board with books or bricks and place it in a well-ventilated room away from direct heat or dampness for a week.

When the flowers are pressed, carefully remove them from the blotting paper and shake them gently to remove the gel. The flowers are now ready to arrange on a background of your choice.

Use a cement-type glue to adhere the flowers to the background; gently press the petals in place. If desired, apply clear acrylic spray for added protection. Or frame the finished arrangement under glass for a handsome wall decoration.

Drying everlastings
These flowers can be cut and hung to dry. They will remain lovely for months in bouquets.

Cut these flowers before they are in full bloom, remove their leaves, and hang them, heads down, in a dark, airy place for several weeks.

Strawflowers, statices, lunarias, and thistles are examples of colorful everlastings. They are easy to find in flower shops or to grow in your own garden.

Making potpourris
Fragrant flower petals, combined with spices, herbs, and even evergreens, add delightful odors to any room or closet.

Dry potpourris are quite easy to make. Simply dry the petals of scented flowers, such as roses, lavenders, and verbenas, in a cool, dry, shady place for about two weeks until they are crackly. Then combine them with spices (ground cloves, cinnamon, orange or lemon peel) and mix well. As a fixative, add orrisroot to the mixture. Place the mixture in an airtight container for three to five weeks, shaking the mixture frequently. For lovely gifts, place the potpourris in decorative containers.

A HOUSE WITH CHRISTMAS SPIRIT

Christmas comes but once a year, yet the warmth and coziness of that lovely season linger all year round in the home of Judith and Richard Oken.

Although the yule-tide color scheme—used throughout the house—evokes memories of Christmases past, the Okens' imaginative mix of fabrics and accessories is season-spanning, delightfully personal, and warmly inviting at any time of the year.

During the holidays, Judith adds seasonal touches with greenery, ribbon bows, and a marvelous mix of toys, handicrafts, and folk art treasures that she has collected over the years.

213

A House with Christmas Spirit

At Christmastime, every nook and cranny of the Oken home sparkles with holiday spirit.

Parading across the fireplace mantel, *above,* are Noah's ark and a full complement of colorful animals. To integrate this fanciful collection into the setting, Judith stenciled trees onto the wall, creating a permanent display.

Come Christmas, she adds tiny packages wrapped in plaid papers, in honor of the season.

To give the family room a seasonal flavor, Judith replaces most of the books in the corner bookcase with a few artfully wrapped packages and the family's collection of traditional nutcrackers, *opposite.*

Imaginative display ideas such as these—using personal collections of crafts and folk art in unexpected settings—make for original decorating in any season.

A House with Christmas Spirit

Judith's collections focus on two favorite themes—heart designs and variations on the Little Red Schoolhouse quilt pattern. Both themes appear on dozens of handcrafted items in the house.

An antique quilt and the painted scene on the piano pick up the house motif and establish a country mood, *left.* Atop the piano, a rotating display of favorite toys and folk art figures changes with the seasons.

In December, Judith replaces a backdrop of potted plants with fresh pine boughs. Gaily wrapped packages on the piano bench cheerfully herald the holidays.

Stenciled hearts and graceful vines make a permanent statement on the newel, *right,* but the pattern takes on added punch at Christmas, framed by holiday garlands and plush satin bows.

For tips on how to spread Christmas spirit throughout *your* house, please turn the page.

217

SUGGESTIONS FOR A HOUSE WITH CHRISTMAS SPIRIT

Decked out in the festive reds and greens traditionally associated with Christmas, the Oken home (pictured on the preceding pages) sparkles with holiday spirit from January right through December. When Christmas comes around, Judith just adds a touch of greenery here, a few bows and packages there, and the house is dressed for the holidays.

For most of us, though, getting the house ready for Christmas is a once-every-year affair, often requiring a substantial investment of time, energy, imagination, and money. By taking a few tips from Judith's bag of decorating tricks, you can make the most of the year-round materials you have on hand to create holiday decorations that are simple, personal, and guaranteed to leave you more time to spend with your friends and family.

The colors of Christmas—
choose your own palette
Red and green may be the traditional colors of Christmas, but there's no hard-and-fast rule that says you must use them. If country calicos dominate your decorating scheme—or pale pastels, muted naturals, or a modernist blend of chrome and glass—play up these colors, moods, and textures at holiday time.

Fresh greens, where available, sound an appropriately festive note in any decor. An abundance of greenery, done up in wreaths and garlands, is one way to salute the season. But a few judiciously placed sprigs of holly and a carefully ar-

ranged spray of pine boughs tied with ribbon and hung on the front door bespeak Christmas just as surely.

And if you choose Christmas accents—gaily wrapped packages, decorative bows, balls and baubles—in colors and textures that complement your year-round decorating scheme, you'll find that you need fewer displays to establish an overall holiday mood.

Showcase your special collections
This is the time of year to pull out all the stops and put some of your favorite things to work. Even if at first glance your treasured collections don't seem to have much to do with Christmas, remember that when you add a sprig of greenery and a festive bow or two to *any* grouping of objects—presto! Suddenly it looks a lot like Christmas.

For example, group an assortment of children's stuffed animals, a few wooden pull toys, or your collection of antique dolls on a bed of greens to make a one-of-a-kind table centerpiece or mantel decoration. Pay tribute to the season by tying ribbon bows around the animals' necks, scattering glass Christmas balls

among the wooden toys, or tucking a tiny, beribboned package into the arms of each doll.

An artful grouping of bottles, baskets, candlesticks, and porcelain figures, or even a collection of antique tools or a crock filled with old-fashioned kitchen utensils, can be the focal point of an interesting and delightfully personal Christmas still life. Decorate with whatever items best reflect your individual tastes and interests. It's a wonderful way to participate in the sharing, festive spirit of the season.

Imaginative tree trims
You can save money and personalize your tree by extending the use-what-you-have philosophy to the Christmas tree itself.

For example, you may find a gold mine for your tree among the things you use every day. From the kids' toy chest, select small stuffed animals, model cars, toy soldiers or astronauts, along with other miniature items and colorful, lightweight trims. Tie these "ornaments" to the branches with loops of tinsel cord, twine, or satin ribbon.

The kitchen cupboard offers an equally abundant supply of unusual tree trims. Suspend silver spoons and demitasse cups, napkin rings and shiny tin cookie cutters, candy molds, sample tins of tea, and so forth, from loops of ribbon or cord.

Needlecraft and sewing accessories also merit a place on the tree. String plump pincushions, a pair of ornate embroidery scissors, artfully knotted skeins of needlepoint yarn,

218

or balls of embroidery floss. Tie on a tiny starched doily and a few crocheted medallions if you have them.

Best of all are family mementos, odds and ends that have been stashed away over the years just waiting to be put to use. Seek out old family photos and favorite recent snapshots to tuck into lightweight, golden, dime store frames. Or glue the photos onto colorful squares of cardboard and trim them with bits of glued-on lace and ribbon.

Any of the following items will also make a most original contribution to your family Christmas tree: An antique pocket watch or some costume jewelry, old valentines and postcards, a pair of baby bootees, baby stockings and an antique christening cap, old-fashioned bow ties (tied of course), pretty handkerchiefs, and scraps of antique fabric or lace knotted around plastic-foam balls. In short, anything and everything that's pretty, humorous, not too heavy, and of sentimental value to you and your family makes a charming addition to your tree.

If your stock of knickknacks and family mementos is low, decorate the tree with colorful bows of ribbon. Or make your bows from 3-inch-wide strips of stiffly starched calico fabric, cut and trimmed into shape with pinking shears. (After the holidays, untie the bows and use them for scrap-craft projects or as sashing strips for your next patchwork-quilt design.)

Accent the bows with strings of tiny lights or glass tree ornaments that are all the same color but of different shapes and sizes.

Alternative trees

Your Christmas tree needn't be an evergreen. If you're looking for a change, stack a bunch of sturdy boxes in a pyramid, drape them with a colorful cloth, and pile on a collection of inexpensive greenhouse plants (ivy and philodendrons are good choices). Trim this living tree with small glass balls nestled among the leaves.

If you don't have a green thumb, try a graceful grouping of bare branches instead. Arrange branches in a large vase or tall basket and trim them with tiny lights, fabric bows, pieces of gaily wrapped candy, or family treasures hung from strands of gold thread or narrow satin ribbon.

Christmas all through the house

Ambience is as much a part of decorating for Christmas as the traditional tree, wreath, and ball of mistletoe.

Candlelight is one of the easiest ways to add a holiday glow to any room in the house. Quantity is the key here: Use dozens of inexpensive white votive candles massed in clear glass containers. Almost any piece of clear glassware will do, including drinking glasses and jelly jars. The glass reflects, repeats, and magnifies the candle flames, casting a flickering glow that is both festive and flattering.

For a special candle centerpiece, assemble a collection of fat white candles of different heights and sizes on the center of a handsome silver tray or mirror, or atop a glass

or ceramic cake stand. Trim with bits of greenery, clusters of glass balls, or strings of tinsel.

The seductive smell of freshly baked cookies and candies wafting from the kitchen is another certain sign of Christmas. For the days when holiday cooking is not on your schedule, simmer a seasonal mix of herbs and spices on the back of the stove. Or prepare a bowl of pomanders (oranges and lemons studded with cloves and dusted with a mixture of cinnamon and nutmeg) to keep on the hall table and scent the air with holiday aromas.

And don't forget to extend your Christmas decorating to every room in the house. For example, you might surprise holiday guests with a small bouquet of greens and holly atop the bureau or bedside table in the guest room. Or, in the guest bath, set out a decorated basket of sample soaps and toiletries, along with a stack of holiday towels reserved for Christmas company.

Finally, the soft strains of carols and other seasonal music are sure to set a festive holiday mood throughout the house, whatever your decor.

CREDITS

We would like to express our gratitude and appreciation to the many people who helped with this book.

Our heartfelt thanks go to each of the artists and designers who so enthusiastically contributed ideas, designs, and projects.

Thanks also to the photographers whose creative talents and technical skills added much to the book.

We are happy as well to acknowledge our indebtedness to the many companies, collectors, needlecrafters, and others who generously shared their pieces with us, stitched projects, or in some other way contributed to the production of this book.

Designers

Linda Bender—robin, 18
Charlotte Biro—afghan, 82; tablecloth, 114–115; doily, 156; wedding-ring tablecloth, 163
Susan Douglas—pillows, 156–157
Phyllis Dunstan—pierced paper, 134–137
Mary Engelbreit—child's furniture, 14–15
Sara Gutierrez—rug, 61
Julia Haas—stamp printing, 54–57
Janet Harrington—collage, 12–13; redwork, 142–147
Diane Hayes—towels, 154–155
Jan Hollebrands—crafts from natural materials, 204–207
Laura Holtorf-Collins—sampler, 62–63; perforated-paper embroidery, 81; filet crochet panels, 116–117
Rebecca Jerdee—checkerboard, 88; paint and paper patchwork, 104–107; curtain, 118; splatter designs, 194–195
Gail Kinkead—pillows, 82; bedspread, 160–161; spiderweb tablecloth, 162
Susan Knight—patchwork projects, 6–7
Joyce Kuhar—quilt, 16–17

Ann Levine—pillows, 60–61
Mickey Lorber and Gene Rosenberg—rug and pillow, 120
Susan Maher—quilt and rug, 37–39, 42–43
Janet McCaffery—toys, pillows, and accessories, 20–25
Charles and Alice Proctor and Merr Shearn—silk-screen projects, 192–193
Bev Rivers—tabletop, 190–191
Gene Rosenberg and Mickey Lorber—rug and pillow, 120
Merr Shearn and Charles and Alice Proctor—silk-screen projects, 192–193
Mimi Shimmin and Evelyn Whitcomb—rug, 86–87
Rhoda Sneller—place mats, 85
Leslie Stiles—chest, 10–11
Suzy Taylor, ASID—floor, 10–11; moose, 36–37; furniture and room adaptations, 36–43
Sara Jane Treinen—afghan, 6–7
Evelyn Whitcomb and Mimi Shimmin—rug, 86–87
Jim Williams—table, 19; rug, 89; chairs and pillow, 190–191
DeElda Wittmack—sampler, 66

Photographers

Ernest Braun—212–217
Mike Dieter—10–11, 20–25, 82–83, 114–115, 118, 156
Jim Hedrich for Hedrich-Blessing—14; 15, top; 18–19, 88–89, 121
Thomas Hooper—8
Bill Hopkins—36–39, 80, 85
William N. Hopkins—52–53, 60–63, 81, 86–87, 102–103, 110–111, 120, 132–133, 180–181, 184–185, 192–193
Mike Jensen—142–147
Jim Kascoutas—66–67, 116–117, 119, 156, 160–161
Scott Little—15, bottom; 17, 40–43, 54–57, 104–107, 134–137, 190–191, 204–205, 207
Van Jones Martin—9
Bradley Olman—12–13, 112–113, 188–189
Perry Struse—3, 6–7, 16, 64–65, 84, 154–155, 157, 158–159, 162–163, 194–195, 202–203, 206

Acknowledgments

David Ashe for the Design Concern

The Brunnier Gallery and Museum Farmhouse
Scheman Building
Iowa State University
Ames, IA 50011

C.M. Offray and Sons, Inc.
261 Madison Ave.
New York, NY 10016

Cotswold Cottage at Greenfield Village
P.O. Box 1970
Dearborn, MI 48121

DMC
107 Trumbull St.
Elizabeth, NJ 07206

Dot's Frame Shop
1910 Army Post Rd.
Des Moines, IA 50315

Duncan Enterprises
P.O. Box 7827, Dept. PR
Fresno, CA 93747

Linda Emmerson

Dixie Falls

Donna Glas

Heirlooms, Inc.
Engelbert House Antiques
1910 Army Post Rd.
Des Moines, IA 50315

Joan Toggitt, Ltd.
35 Fairfield Pl.
West Caldwell, NJ 07006

Little House
Elkader, IA 52043

Meadow Brook Hall
Rochester, MI 48063

Judith and Richard Oken

Pella Historical Society
P.O. Box 145
Pella, IA 50219

Margaret Sindelar

Diane Upah

Sue Veigulis

The Whole Kit and Kaboodle
8 W. 19th St.
New York, NY 10010

Julie Wiemann

Woodlawn Plantation
P.O. Box 37
Mount Vernon, VA 22121

Younkers Store for Homes
100 Merle Hay Mall
Des Moines, IA 50322

INDEX

For photographs, see pages noted in **bold** type; remaining numbers refer to instruction pages.

222